T0087742

Texas Wildflowers

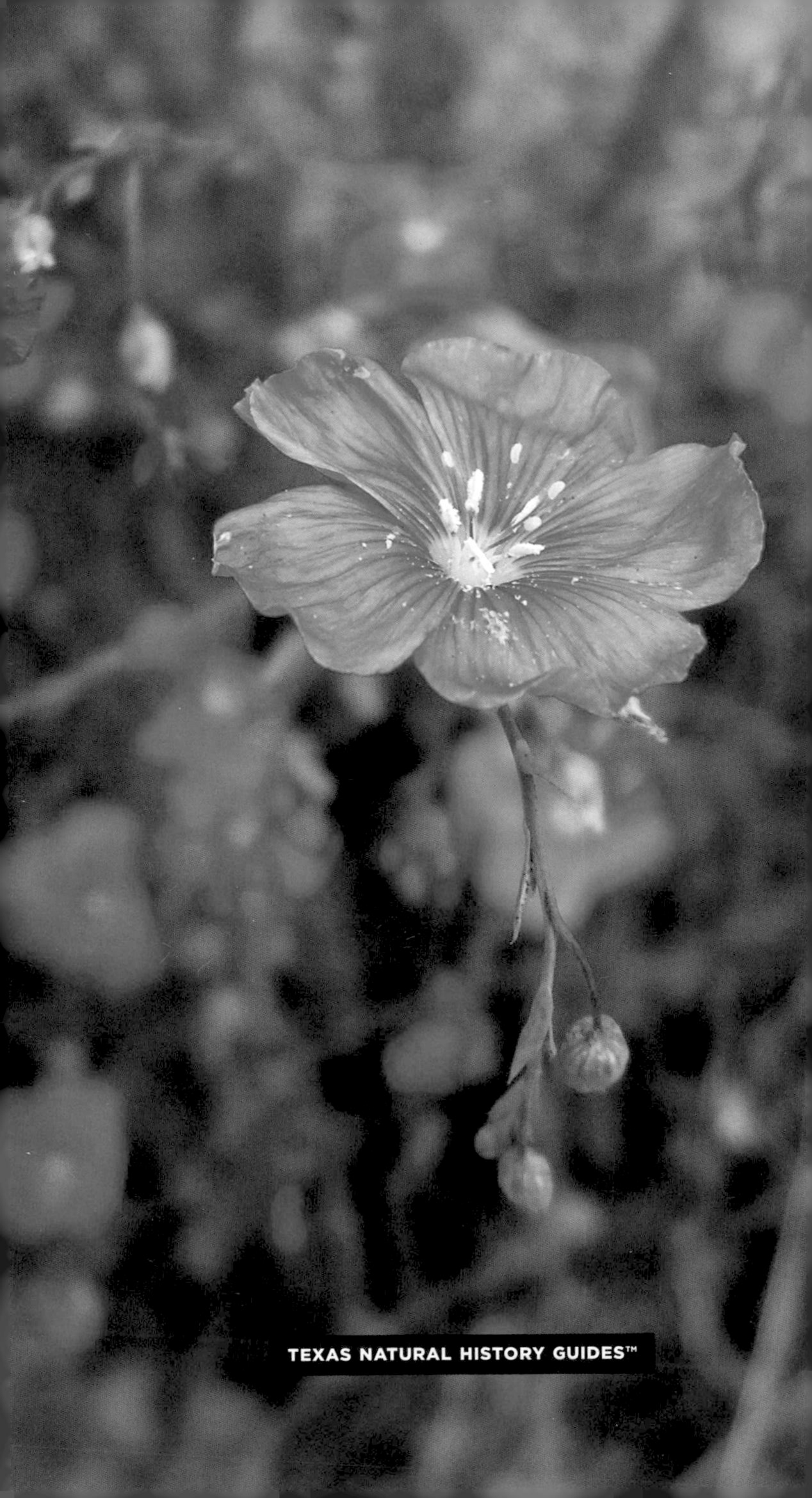
TEXAS NATURAL HISTORY GUIDES™

Texas Wildflowers

A FIELD GUIDE

NEW EDITION

Campbell and Lynn Loughmiller

UPDATED BY
Joe Marcus, Lady Bird Johnson Wildflower Center

FOREWORD TO THE FIRST EDITION BY
Lady Bird Johnson

UNIVERSITY OF TEXAS PRESS ◆ AUSTIN

Requests for permission to reproduce material from this
work should be sent to:
  Permissions
  University of Texas Press
  P.O. Box 7819
  Austin, TX 78713-7819
  utpress.utexas.edu/rp-form

♾ The paper used in this book meets the minimum requirements of ANSI/NISO Z39.48-1992 (R1997) (Permanence of Paper).

Library of Congress Cataloging-in-Publication Data
Names: Loughmiller, Campbell, author. | Loughmiller, Lynn,
    author. | Marcus, Joe, editor.
Title: Texas wildflowers : a field guide / Campbell and Lynn
    Loughmiller ; foreword to the first edition by Lady Bird
    Johnson.
Description: New edition / updated by Joe Marcus, Lady Bird
    Johnson Wildflower Center. | Austin : University of Texas
    Press, 2018. | Includes bibliographical references and index.
Identifiers: LCCN 2017008984
    ISBN 978-1-4773-1476-0 (pbk. : alk. paper)
    ISBN 978-1-4773-1477-7 (library e-book)
    ISBN 978-1-4773-1478-4 (non-library e-book)
Subjects: LCSH: Wild flowers—Texas—Identification.
Classification: LCC QK188 .L68 2018 | DDC 582.1309764—dc23
LC record available at https://lccn.loc.gov/2017008984

doi:10.7560/314760

Contents

Notes on the New Edition

When Campbell and Lynn Loughmiller published the first edition of *Texas Wildflowers: A Field Guide* in 1984, they gave a wonderful gift to anyone who traveled the highways and byways of Texas and admired the great diversity of natural beauty found along the way. The Loughmillers' clear love of Texas's flora shone forth both through their stunning photographs and through their homey, conversational descriptions of the species included in the pages of that first edition. My dog-eared copy of that edition is just as valuable to me today as it was then.

Sadly, in the years following the introduction of their field guide to Texas's wildflowers, we lost both Campbell and Lynn. But time moves forward, and by 2005 much had changed in our understanding of Texas's flora, especially in the area of nomenclature. In short, botanists had changed the names of many Texas wildflowers. Most of those changes were a result of our better understanding of the relationships between species.

Because of the Loughmillers' close connection to Lady Bird Johnson—her foreword was published in the first edition and has been included in each edition since—and to the Lady Bird Johnson Wildflower Center, to whom they donated their botanical image collection, the University of Texas Press turned to the Wildflower Center to edit a new edition. My former boss and mentor, Dr. Damon Waitt, took up the challenge and with skill and the lightest hand possible, brought the book up to date in 2008.

And still, time marches on.

By 2015, botanical nomenclature continued to be in its perpetual state of flux, but also nature lovers were looking for different characteristics in their field guides. So the press asked me to take a swing at revising the book, this time with some structural changes. Somewhat naively perhaps, I accepted.

For those readers familiar with the earlier editions of this field guide, the changes you will find in these pages are not inconsequential. The biggest change is the overall organization of the book. The first two editions were organized by family, then by genus and species—the way most botanists would want a book organized. This edition is organized first by flower color, then by flowering time, and finally by genus and species. Our hope is that this new organizational scheme will make the book more useful to novice wildflower enthusiasts by making the identity of their mystery flower easier to find. For those who prefer to search for plants by family name, a family name index is provided in the back of the book.

In moving away from the family-based organization, by necessity we lost the excellent family discussions written by the Loughmillers. I have tried to incorporate as much of that information as possible into the species descriptions in the pages of this book.

This edition also introduces a more formal organizational style for the species descriptions. Each page includes sections for "Plant and Leaves," "Flowers and Fruit," "Flowering," "Range and Habitat," and finally, "Comments." Many of the comments are excerpted from the Loughmillers' original work. Our hope is that this new format will make the information the reader is seeking easier to find.

When travelers find an unknown wildflower on a roadside or along a trail, they typically ask themselves two questions: "What plant is that?" and "What is its story?" Early in their travels, the Loughmillers surely asked themselves those very questions, and ultimately the results of their investigations were shared with the world in the pages of that first edition of this field guide.

It is my fondest hope that within the pages of this edition you will find the answer to that first question for some of your unknown Texas wildflowers and will find enough of those plants' stories to lead to a deeper and richer understanding and appreciation of Texas's remarkable native flora.

I would like to thank the Lady Bird Johnson Wildflower Center for allowing me to work on this project. Also, I am indebted to the many wonderful wildflower photographers who have graciously contributed their work to the Wildflower Center's Native Plant Information Network Image Gallery and have allowed us to also publish them in this field guide. Finally, I wish to give the most heartfelt thank you to Annelia Williams, whose numerous suggestions and excellent organizational skills provided much invaluable assistance in the development of this new edition.

JOE MARCUS
Lady Bird Johnson Wildflower Center

Foreword to the First Edition

I welcome this new field guide for Texas wildflower enthusiasts.

Just reading the text and seeing the beautiful color photographs—all 300 of them—makes me want to reach for my sunhat, put on my walking shoes, take this knowledge-filled book, and fare forth to seek and discover!

That is exactly what the authors—Campbell and Lynn Loughmiller—have been doing for forty years. I had the fun of hearing about their wildflower adventures firsthand.

"We load our trailer with typewriter, cameras, sunburn lotion, and insect repellent, and we just set out. We don't know where we are heading, and we don't care where we spend the night," the Loughmillers explained.

How wonderful to own your own time and let instinct lead you to the flowerscapes that abide in Texas, from the phlox of South Texas to the wonderful world of cactus in West Texas!

The authors have traveled and photographed hundreds of beautiful field scenes and then knelt down for close-ups of the "inhabitants." Selecting the ones for this book from a vast array of color slides was a "terrible task, like choosing among your grandchildren," they told me.

Their trails brought them to the University of Texas Press and into publication with this stunning and useful field guide, which has been ably reviewed for technical accuracy by Dr. Lynn Sherrod, botanist at the University of Texas at Tyler.

We share a sense of poetry among the wildflowers. To borrow from Wordsworth, I gasp and "my heart with rapture fills" when I come upon a pasture filled with bluebonnets set among the feathery pale green of mesquite trees in spring, and beyond, the gnarled and twisted live oaks—the scene punctuated by exclamation points of brilliant coral Indian paintbrush and white Mexican poppies!

One of the favorite pastimes of my childhood was to walk in the woods of East Texas exploring, particularly in the springtime. I knew where the first wild violets bloomed and looked for the dogwood—those white blossoms, like stars spangling the bare woods. And I hunted for the delicate wild roses that grew along the fences in the rural farm country where I grew up. Ever since, I have had a love affair with nature I have never ceased to savor. It has enriched my life and provided me with beautiful, serene memories. For me, wildflowers have been part of the joy of living.

We all have our favorite highway strips and fields to explore in springtime, but with this book, we discover wildflower hunting—*somewhere* in Texas—is an activity for extended seasons. For instance, in July, I came upon graceful wands of gleaming red Standing Cypress—now mostly along steep embankments and fence rows where the June mowing had not obliterated them before their flowering season. Will they disappear forever from the Texas scene?

Last September, I walked on a meadow near the LBJ Ranch and saw the embroidery of Snow-on-the-mountain among the waving grasses, and in the distance the Blue Mistflower of the river valley and the purple spikes of Gayfeathers brightening the roadsides. What poetry! There are so many delicious surprises that come when we are rich with rain. I yearn to see, identify, and cultivate more of the flowers for late summer and fall.

It is a truism that the more you learn, the more you want to learn. This book leads one on and on. I gradually find myself reaching for the botanical name and translating the ones I do not know. My mail tells me there are thousands of people who share my enthusiasm for wildflowers and hunger to know more. Take this book in hand and experience the delight of coming upon a scarlet bloom along a stream bank and tracking it through the book to its identity: the Cardinal Flower!

My world of wildflowers is expanding each day with the National Wildflower Research Center, which we founded in December 1982 on a farm-to-market road near Austin. There, I hope we will learn about germination, growth habits, and where and how to plant the treasure trove of wildflowers both for their aesthetic and conservation potential. As a practical person, I want to know more of the simple "how-to's"—and, yes, the "how-not-to's." I hope very much we can make such information available to the expanding constituency of those who care.

I am so grateful for the unflagging pursuit of the Loughmillers, and to the University of Texas Press for its timely publication and for its generosity in sharing the sales of this book with the Wildflower Center.

LADY BIRD JOHNSON (1912–2007)
Honorary Co-Chair
National Wildflower Research Center

Introduction to the First Edition

This book has grown out of our long-standing interest in wildflowers and our increasing appreciation of the extraordinary diversity we have found as we photographed them in all parts of the state. The varied topography, soil types, rainfall, and temperature combine to give Texas more than 5,000 species. They are found from elevations of 8,000 feet in the Guadalupe Mountains of west Texas to the subtropical Rio Grande Valley near sea level, and from the Chihuahuan Desert to southeast Texas, where the annual rainfall is 56 inches.

We were tempted to include as many as possible of the larger, showier, more colorful species, as well as those harbingers of spring, the violets, bluets, and others, which have, since our childhood, promised the end of winter and the beginning of longer, brighter, warmer days. While the reader will find here many of these favorites, we have also tried to include in our selection representative specimens from all parts of the state.

We were impressed by the fact that the inconspicuous flowers often grow where nothing else is to be found. It is an arresting sight when, on the rocky slopes of the sunbaked Chihuahuan Desert, for example, one comes across the delicately beautiful Four-nerved Daisy or the Prickleleaf Gilia. Somehow their appeal is magnified by the stark setting.

People the world over draw satisfaction from studying, classifying, collecting, sketching, photographing, or simply observing wildflowers. When circumstances deprive us of this pleasure we begin to understand how much a part of our lives flowers are—as integral and rewarding as bird songs, blue skies, rain showers, the smell of rich earth, or the crispness of a change of seasons.

We have attempted to organize this book for a broad audience, for what we might describe as the interested layperson. As with all scientific disciplines, botany has of necessity developed its own professional language. For the professional that scheme is necessary and valuable, but too many laypersons get lost in terminology when they must wade through it in order to make the simplest identification. A lapful of dictionaries, textbooks, and glossaries is neither essential nor especially conducive to the enjoyment of flowers. We have included a short glossary of terms that are regularly used to make descriptions of flowers more meaningful and precise. These terms should not distract one from the purpose of the book, which is to promote the recognition and enjoyment of wildflowers. It is our hope that the organization will prove satisfactory both for readers seeking no more than a quick confirmation of a plant's identity and for those embarking upon a more sophisticated study.

Identification of flowers down through family and genus is rarely very difficult, but determining the species can be tedious and often frustrating. This is true for the scientist as well as the knowledgeable amateur. In the preparation of this book we have sometimes found disagreement between eminent scientists as to the classification of flowers. It has extended not only to the species but also sometimes to the genus, and occasionally even to the family. For example, there are many species of *Verbena* in Texas. Some of them differ so slightly that no amateur could detect any difference whatever, nor could the scientist, either, without a microscope. Based on these minute variations, a flower is assigned to one species or another. Over a period of time, however, botanists finally come to a common agreement about most plants. In the process, old classifications sometimes disappear and are replaced by new ones. This should not discourage the amateur, however, who may find the genus to be sufficiently definitive. Should one's interest carry one further, a 10X hand lens will be helpful in all cases, essential in some.

Though books such as this one typically devote much space to matters of plant classification, it is not necessary to know the name of a flower in order to appreciate it. People drive hundreds of miles in favorable years to see the desert floor in bloom, or to enjoy a high mountain meadow ablaze with the brief, intense colors of summer, without knowing the name of a single flower they see—and they are amply rewarded. A personal experience one spring made this point convincingly as we stopped to see a man and his wife in a lonely location surrounded by forty miles of desert. The husband was not there, and his wife told us, "Bill rode up the canyon this morning to see if the wildflowers are blooming." He returned shortly with a small bouquet he had gathered. These people knew the flowers—knew them more completely and appreciated them more fully than most persons we have known; where they grew, when they bloomed, their size, shape, color, markings, and other details. We realized again that it is better to know the nature of a flower than its name.

Still, most people want to know the names of flowers, as this facilitates communication and seems to bring the flowers closer to us. If they do not know the name they will give it one; hence, the many common names. Since common names vary from one place to another, they are not useful to denote particular plants. We have included common names but have also used the Latin names, which are definitive and do not vary from place to place.

The distribution of flowers over the state is constantly changing because their seeds are dispersed by wind, water, birds, animals, automobiles, and other agents. We can describe the general areas where different species grow, but a flower is often found well beyond its generally accepted range. Simply put, a flower grows where you find it. The Texas Department of Transportation has done a fine job of seeding the wide rights-of-way along our highways with native flowers and does not mow the vegetation until after the flowers have gone to seed. This has resulted in a remarkable floral display in many areas of the state. Even in areas never touched by human efforts at reseeding, numbers of species can be found along every road. They may not be obvious to people who are hurrying from here to there, but those who take a break and step out of their automobiles will be surprised, if not refreshed, at the display almost at their feet. We have often stopped in the most unlikely places—what some would call "waste places"—and have rarely gone unrewarded.

Blooming periods also vary, and many times a species that blooms in the spring will bloom again in the fall if the moisture and temperature are favorable. This is especially true in southwest Texas, where the blooming period is often related as much to moisture as it is to the season of the year. Sometimes a species will disappear from the landscape and not be seen for several years, but under favorable conditions it will reappear in impressive numbers.

Pollination of flowers is an important process, both to the flower and to the insect that accomplishes it. Insects are attracted to flowers by their color, fragrance, or nectar. It is interesting that colorful, conspicuous flowers are seldom fragrant, as fragrance is not necessary for them to attract insects. The honeybee is perhaps the best-known insect in the pollinating process, assisting the plant and making honey at the same time. Farmers are glad to pay beekeepers to put bees in their crops as it increases the yield substantially. To us, however, butterflies are more interesting, as they are sometimes as beautiful as the flowers. In photographing the flowers of some species, we often ended up spending more time photographing the butterflies that were attracted to them.

One of the most specific relationships in the pollinating process is that of the *Yucca* and the *Pronuba* moth, which have become so interdependent that neither can survive without the other. The moth does not visit the flowers of any other species but makes sure it pollinates this one well. It gathers a ball of pollen from one flower and deposits it on the pistil of another, even rubbing it in with its head after laying its eggs half an inch below. When the larvae develop they feed on the seed. Of the thirty or so species of *Yucca*, of which Texas has several, all except one depend on a species of the *Pronuba* moth for pollination, a different moth species for each plant species. The moth does not eat the pollen or the nectar, but the larvae live in the plant's ovary, thus perpetuating their own species and that of the *Yucca*. No moth, no *Yucca*, and vice versa.

Many flowers close at night, some by day. We had an interesting experience with one of them—*Hibiscus lasiocarpos*, or False

Cotton—late one afternoon when we stopped to photograph it, several of the blossoms had already closed so tightly that it seemed as if they had never opened. Carefully we pulled the petals apart on one of them to see how they overlapped each other, and when we lifted the last petal we found a bumblebee right in the center. We opened seven others and found bumblebees in five of them. We did not know whether they had chosen the flowers as a good place to spend the night or whether they had inadvertently stayed past closing time and were trapped.

All of our photographs were taken in the field where the flowers grew in their natural environment. We like to show their natural habitat, to put them "in their place." Usually we take two pictures—one of the whole plant and a close-up of the flower. This has presented some difficult choices in selecting pictures for this book, as we could not include both.

Photography is always rewarding but can sometimes be tedious. When, for instance, one is photographing a west Texas flower in March, and a strong wind whips the long-stemmed flower 180 degrees in a fitful dance for five minutes without letup, and you wait for that one fleeting instant when it comes to a dead stop, with the merciless sun burning your face as you wait—well, it takes all of one's patience and half one's religion to maintain equanimity. At that point, there is a good argument for removing the flower to a protected area and composing the picture in leisurely comfort.

In east Texas it is much the same. You set up for a picture only to find you are knee-deep in grassburs, that you have aroused a mound of fire ants or brushed against a nettle, or that you have become host to chiggers, ticks, or mosquitoes. But then, what satisfaction would there be in walking up to a flower on a calm, clear day, setting up the tripod, and "pulling the trigger"?

Many wildflowers are suitable for gardens, and we have mentioned some of these in the text. Persons interested in using them in home landscaping will find many seed companies that specialize in wildflower seeds. The Lady Bird Johnson Wildflower Center's website (www.wildflower.org) serves as a clearinghouse for information on native plants, seed collection, commercial sources, and wildflower propagation.

ACKNOWLEDGMENTS

We express our appreciation to Lynn Sherrod, Barton H. Warnock, and Marshall Johnston for their help in identifying many of the flowers we photographed, and to Del Weniger and Harry Barwick for their help in identifying some of the cacti. We should also like to acknowledge the help the late Lance Rosier gave us in locating and identifying many flowers of the Big Thicket.

CAMPBELL LOUGHMILLER (1906–1992)

Species Descriptions

White
Flowers

Erythronium albidum

White Dogtooth-violet, White Troutlily, White Fawnlily

LILIACEAE (LILY FAMILY)

PLANT AND LEAVES: White Dogtooth-violet is an herbaceous perennial growing from a bulb to about 1 inch in diameter. The bulb produces a scape that rises 2 to 6 inches tall above the soil and arches near the end. In nonflowering years the plant often produces stolons or droppers by which it vegetatively reproduces. The bulb produces one leaf in nonflowering years and two leaves in years when the plant has a flowering scape. The leaves, 1¼ to 1½ inches wide and 4 to 8 inches tall, are smooth and shiny, with each side curved toward the center. They are mottled with whitish or russet spots or blotches, giving rise to the Troutlily and Fawnlily appellations.

FLOWERS AND FRUIT: Each scape is topped with a single, usually nodding, flower having six white, pinkish, or lavender tepals with a bright yellow zone in the flower's throat. The tepals of mature flowers curve strongly backward toward the stem and are ¾ to 1½ inches long. Its six stamens have yellow anthers. This species' fruit is a three-sided capsule resembling a partially deflated football.

FLOWERING: White Dogtooth-violet appears in Texas in the latter part of February and is often finished flowering by mid-March. It flowers as late as May in the northern parts of its range.

RANGE AND HABITAT: Found on rich soils in hardwood forests in both bottomland and uplands, this species can be found in northeast and north-central Texas. It also can be found from the Great Plains over most of the eastern half of the United States, excluding New England, the Carolinas, and Florida.

COMMENTS: Dogtooth-violet, Troutlily, and Fawnlily are all descriptive names used pretty much interchangeably in common names for members of the genus *Erythronium*.

Anemone berlandieri

Tenpetal Anemone, Tenpetal Windflower

RANUNCULACEAE (BUTTERCUP FAMILY)
Synonym: *Anemone decapetala*

PLANT AND LEAVES: Tenpetal Anemone is a deciduous perennial herb arising late each winter from a tuber and growing 4 to 10 inches in height. The few, somewhat fleshy leaves are often three parted, but sometimes two or one parted, and are borne well below the flower, often near the ground. Each rounded leaf part is typically partially cleft into two or more lobes.

FLOWERS AND FRUIT: Above the foliage, a single peduncle rises to bear one flower, 1 to 2 inches across when open. The common name of this species is a bit misleading. The flower parts appearing to be petals are actually sepals, and though there are sometimes 10 of them on a flower, the number can range from 8 to 20. The pistils form a thimble-shaped structure, up to about 1 inch long. Above the sepals, a ring of approximately 60 stamens surround the central head of pistils. The head develops into a fruiting body containing numerous achenes.

FLOWERING: Flowering may begin as early as late January, though it usually starts in late February or early March and continues to April or sometimes early May.

RANGE AND HABITAT: Widespread throughout most of the state, especially in the limestone soils of the Hill Country, Tenpetal Anemone's range extends along the coastal states to Virginia. It is also at home in Oklahoma, Arkansas, and Kansas.

COMMENTS: Tenpetal Anemone is the most common windflower in Texas and one of the earliest native plants to flower each spring. The genus name, *Anemone*, is taken from the ancient Greek word meaning "daughter of the wind."

Halesia diptera

Two-winged Silverbell

STYRACACEAE (SNOWBELL FAMILY)
Synonym: *Halesia diptera* var. *magniflora*

PLANT AND LEAVES: Two-winged Silverbell is a large, slow-growing, woody, deciduous shrub or small tree that can attain a height of 35 feet in extreme cases but usually tops out around 15 feet tall. Leaves are borne on short stems. They are arranged alternately and are more or less elliptical in shape, 3 to 6 inches long and 2 to 4½ inches wide, and with finely toothed margins and distinctly raised veins.

FLOWERS AND FRUIT: The tree's pendulous bell-shaped flowers, which appear before the leaves or just as they are developing, grow in small clusters of two to six flowers along the stem, each flower on a separate, short pedicel. The calyx is cup shaped with four sepals. The corolla has four, or sometimes five, snow-white lobes, each about 1 inch long and ½ inch wide, separate nearly to the base. There are 10 stamens with white filaments and yellow anthers tightly clustered in the flower's center and one white pistil extending through the cluster of stamens and beyond by about ¼ inch. The fruit is nut-like and elliptical, with two or four winged appendages. If there are four wings, two are noticeably larger than the others.

FLOWERING: Flowering usually begins in late February or early March and continues for a week or two. Flowering may take place as late as April.

RANGE AND HABITAT: Two-winged Silverbell can be found in mature forests on moist, sandy soils from southeast Texas along the coastal states to South Carolina.

COMMENTS: This lovely understory tree is one of our first woody species to flower each spring. When flowering, it really does appear to be adorned with silvery bells.

Yucca treculeana

Spanish Bayonet,
Don Quixote's Lace

AGAVACEAE (CENTURY-PLANT FAMILY)

PLANT AND LEAVES: Spanish Bayonet is a woody, arborescent perennial often growing in colonial clumps with stems about 6 inches in diameter and reaching up to 20 feet in height. Leaves are fleshy and stiff, with a sharp spine at the tip, and up to 4 feet long and 3 inches wide. When first emerged, the leaves are nearly vertical. Over time, as other leaves are produced, the older leaves gradually decline toward horizontal and eventually may hang nearly vertical, pointing toward the earth. This arrangement of the plant's foliage gives it a somewhat messy but spherical outline.

FLOWERS AND FRUIT: This species' inflorescence is a many-flowered panicle rising 4 to 6 feet above the foliage at maturity. The flowers are borne on short pedicels and hang down when open. There are six cream-white tepals—the sepals are sometimes tinged purple—and six cream-colored stamens with bright yellow pollen at the anthers' tips. The flowers usually do not open wide and typically maintain a more or less spherical shape. The fruit is pendulous and fleshy, shaped like a small cucumber and averaging about 3 inches in length and 1 inch in diameter. Each fruit contains many disk-shaped, black seeds stacked one upon the other.

FLOWERING: Flowering begins in February and is usually finished by April.

RANGE AND HABITAT: Spanish Bayonets are common in south-central Texas and northern Mexico brushlands, where their inflorescences can be seen rising above the surrounding chaparral like bright, white signal beacons.

COMMENTS: Indigenous peoples have many uses for *Yucca* species. Rope, sandals, mats, and baskets are made from the leaf fibers. The buds and flowers are eaten raw or boiled, and the fleshy fruits can be dried and eaten.

Dimorphocarpa wislizeni
Spectacle Pod, Tourist Plant
BRASSICACEAE (MUSTARD FAMILY)
Synonyms: *Dithyrea griffithsii*, *Dithyrea wislizeni*

PLANT AND LEAVES: Spectacle Pod is a branched or unbranched herbaceous winter annual or annual growing 8 to 30 inches tall, often toward the lower end of that range. Its basal leaves—to about 2 inches long—are generally lance shaped and deeply pinnately lobed. Stem leaves are similar in size and overall shape to the basal leaves, but their edges are mostly smooth or occasionally slightly toothed.

FLOWERS AND FRUIT: Each stem is usually terminated by a showy raceme of white or lavender four-petaled flowers. The uniquely shaped fruit—technically a silicle—looks for all the world like a tiny pair of green goggles, thus the common name, Spectacle Pod. Each half of the two-lobed fruit contains a single seed.

FLOWERING: Flowering begins as early as February for winter annuals, and specimens with flowers may be found as late as October.

RANGE AND HABITAT: Spectacle Pod is common on sandy soils and

is found on desert flats, washes, dunes, and along roadsides. It occurs in the Trans-Pecos and across the Desert Southwest to Nevada and south to the Mexican states of Chihuahua and Coahuila.

COMMENTS: This small but eye-catching species can be encountered along just about any roadside within its native range where sandy flats occur.

Chionanthus virginicus

White Fringe-tree, Grancy Graybeard

OLEACEAE (OLIVE FAMILY)

PLANT AND LEAVES: White Fringe-tree is a shrub or occasionally a small tree with more or less rounded form. Most plants top out at about 15 feet tall and 10 feet in breadth, but specimens can reach 35 feet in height. Leaves are deciduous, opposite, lance shaped, and 4 to 8 inches long and 2 to 4 inches wide; the leaf petiole is about 1 inch long.

FLOWERS AND FRUIT: The numerous delicate, fragrant, white to greenish-white flowers are composed of four to six strap-shaped petals 1 inch long and about ¹⁄₁₆ inch wide. They hang in showy, branched clusters 4 to 6 inches long. Flowers open before or with the first leaves. The blue fruit (drupe), which matures in great quantities in the fall, has a waxy bloom and looks like a miniature plum. The drupes are about ½ inch long.

FLOWERING: Flowering occurs in March and April in Texas and as late as May or June in more northern regions.

RANGE AND HABITAT: White Fringe-tree is found in southeast Texas along forest edges, on fencelines, and in other locations where birds often perch. Its native range extends across the South to as far north as New Jersey.

COMMENTS: Male and female flowers are borne on separate plants, the male-flowered plants being a bit showier. Specimens of either sex are among the loveliest of our native shrubs. We have photographed this lacy-looking tree in March and April from Jefferson to Beaumont and west of Palestine.

Cornus florida

Flowering Dogwood, Dogwood

CORNACEAE (DOGWOOD FAMILY)

PLANT AND LEAVES: Flowering Dogwood is a small, deciduous, widely branched tree, usually with a single trunk but sometimes multitrunked. Commonly reaching 20 feet in height, trees 30 to 40 feet tall are not rare. The tree's spread is typically as broad as its height and often significantly exceeds its height. The bark is notably attractive, broken into small squarish blocks. Like the leaves of all members of Cornaceae, those of this species are opposite. They are 3 to 5 inches long and 1½ to 2½ inches wide, on ¾ inch petioles, shiny green above, paler below, heavily veined, and lightly toothed. The tree is beautiful in the fall also, its leaves turning to all shades of red, orange, and bronze.

FLOWERS AND FRUIT: All dogwoods flower, so a better common name for this species might be Showy-bracted Dogwood. The beauty of the dogwood is not in the flowers, as one might expect, but in the four broad, creamy white or sometimes pink,

petal-like bracts. The floral bracts are 1¼ to 2½ inches across and surround the floral cluster. The true flowers are minute, greenish white, and with four tiny petals. The fruits are clusters of persistent, scarlet, oblong drupes about ½ inch long.

FLOWERING: This species flowers during March and April; its fruits mature in November.

RANGE AND HABITAT: Needing rich, acidic soils to thrive, its Texas range is mostly restricted to the Pineywoods. Its native range covers most of the eastern United States.

COMMENTS: There is much to appreciate about Flowering Dogwood. It adds color to woodland areas virtually year-round, the layered effect of its branches is sublimely beautiful, and it is a forgiving and easy-to-grow landscape plant that works well in shade or in full sun.

Hymenocallis liriosme

Texas Spiderlily, Spring Spiderlily

LILIACEAE (LILY FAMILY)

PLANT AND LEAVES: Texas Spiderlily is a perennial herb growing from a nearly spherical bulb about 2 inches in diameter. The bulb produces a flowering scape growing 1 to nearly 3 feet tall. The plant's glossy, dark green leaves all emerge from the bulb and are 6 to 30 inches long and about 1 inch wide.

FLOWERS AND FRUIT: The plant's scape is topped by an umbellate inflorescence bearing 3 to 10 or more flowers. Each stellate flower has six tepals that unite to form a green tube 2 to 4 inches long and narrow but suddenly flaring and curving backward slightly as it ages. The flowers are pure white with a greenish throat and green ribs in the back side of the tepals. The flowers are pleasingly fragrant.

FLOWERING: Flowering begins in March and continues until May.

RANGE AND HABITAT: Found in large colonies—sometimes very large colonies—along roadside ditches and around the edges of swamps or ponds; particularly abundant along the coast and in the Big Thicket. This species is also native to Louisiana, Mississippi, Alabama, Arkansas, and Oklahoma.

COMMENTS: Texas Spiderlily and the 15 other North American

members of its genus are elegant species with showy but unusual, and thus memorable, flowers. This species and the similar Northern Spiderlily (*Hymenocallis occidentalis*) are Texas's only two native members of the genus.

Podophyllum peltatum

Mayapple, American Mandrake, Ground Lemon

BERBERIDACEAE (BARBERRY FAMILY)

PLANT AND LEAVES: The erect, single-stemmed Mayapple plant is an herbaceous perennial that grows from a rhizome to about 20 inches tall. Each plant's stem is topped by two large, umbrella-shaped leaves, which are 6 to 8 inches across and with the leaf petioles attached to the lower surface, near the center. The leaf blades are thin, light green, and deeply lobed. Leaf margins may be smooth or toothed.

FLOWERS AND FRUIT: A single, fragrant, nodding flower emerges from the axil of the plant's two leaves. Its posture and the leaves arching over it tend to obscure the flower unless it is viewed from the side, near ground level. The flower has six to nine waxy petals, usually white but occasionally pink. Twelve

yellow stamens highlight the center of the flower. A single berry, about the shape, size, and color of a lemon, ripens in summer and is the source for the common name Ground Lemon.

FLOWERING: Most flowering occurs March to April with few Texas plants flowering as late as May.

RANGE AND HABITAT: Mayapple is abundant on damp, rich soils in mature, mixed deciduous forests of the east Texas Pineywoods. Beyond Texas, its range covers all of the eastern United States as far west as eastern Nebraska and stretches north into Ontario, Quebec, and the Maritime provinces of Canada.

COMMENTS: Mayapple is toxic and should not be eaten. It tends to form large colonies from creeping, underground stems and thick, fibrous roots. The common name American Mandrake owes its origin to the similarity of its roots to two unrelated Old World species known as mandrakes.

Argemone albiflora ssp. *texana*

Texas Prickly-poppy, White Prickly-poppy

PAPAVERACEAE (POPPY FAMILY)

PLANT AND LEAVES: Texas Prickly-poppy is a winter annual or biennial herb. During winter months, a rosette of leaves grows very close to the ground. In early spring, the plant bolts; that is, it produces a rapidly growing stem that soon branches widely and reaches 1 to 4½ feet in height, averaging 2 to 3 feet tall. The stems, leaves, fruits, and all other aboveground plant parts other than flowers are well armed with sharp prickles. The leaves have multiple jagged and deeply cut lobes, are green

to blue in color, and usually have prominently white-colored primary and secondary veins.

FLOWERS AND FRUIT: The large flowers, up to 4 inches across, are cup shaped to nearly flat and are borne at the top of the stems. The flower's three sepals end with a spine. The six petals are nearly circular with irregular outer margins. They have a crepe-like appearance due to the way they are folded in the bud. The flower's numerous stamens are yellow, and its stigma is purple. The fruit is a spiny, elliptical capsule about 1½ inches long and with three horns at its apex.

FLOWERING: Flowering occurs between March and June.

RANGE AND HABITAT: Texas Prickly-poppy can be found on roadsides and on disturbed soils. It grows in most of Texas, but the heaviest concentrations we have seen were in the south-central part of the state, where we saw snow-white fields of 30 acres or more. Outside Texas, it ranges north and east, appearing in most of the eastern half of the United States.

COMMENTS: Wounds of the stem or leaves exude yellow sap, which is helpful in identifying the species.

Minuartia drummondii

Drummond's Sandwort, Drummond's Stitchwort

CARYOPHYLLACEAE (PINK FAMILY)
Synonyms: *Arenaria drummondii*, *Stellaria nuttallii*

PLANT AND LEAVES: Drummond's Sandwort is an herbaceous annual often found in large, showy colonies. It grows 2 to 8 inches high. Leaves are opposite and narrow, about 1 inch long and ¼ inch wide.

FLOWERS AND FRUIT: The flowers, which appear almost to be too large for the plant supporting them, are white and about 1 inch across. They have five deeply notched, broad petals. The sepals are visible at the base of the flower's petals, making the throat of the flower green. There are also greenish streaks on the petals. The pistil and stamens are yellow.

FLOWERING: Flowering may begin in March and continue until June, though most flowering occurs in April and May.

RANGE AND HABITAT: As its common name implies, Drummond's Sandwort prefers sandy soil on moist prairies and open woodlands. It is most at home in the sandy hills of the Post Oak Savannah ecoregion of east-central Texas, but some populations can be found in suitable habitat in Oklahoma and Arkansas.

COMMENTS: Some flowering plants of Drummond's Sandwort can be found each spring, but it is a species that depends on ideal conditions to flourish. When conditions are right, it can carpet the ground with white in an eye-popping, unforgettable display.

Yucca constricta

Buckley's Yucca

AGAVACEAE (CENTURY-PLANT FAMILY)

PLANT AND LEAVES: Buckley's Yucca is an herbaceous shrub. Usually growing as an acaulescent plant, it sometimes forms a trunk. Making a rounded mound from a rosette, its leaves are typically bluish green and narrow and about 2 feet long with attractive curling, whitish filaments along their margins.

FLOWERS AND FRUIT: Inflorescences are showy, 3 to 10 feet in height, and bear panicles of greenish-white pendant flowers. The fruit is a cylindrical capsule containing thin, glossy black seeds.

FLOWERING: The flowering season for Buckley's Yucca begins in March and may continue to as late as June.

RANGE AND HABITAT: Mostly a native of Texas, its range extends into northern Mexico. In Texas, it is found on the Edwards Plateau, where it grows in open woodlands, meadows, and savannahs.

COMMENTS: Buckley's Yucca is a particularly attractive member of its genus and is very useful as a landscape plant.

Yucca faxoniana

Faxon's Yucca, Spanish Dagger, Eve's Needle

AGAVACEAE (CENTURY-PLANT FAMILY)
Synonym: *Yucca carnerosana*

PLANT AND LEAVES: Faxon's Yucca is an arborescent plant that can reach 20 feet in height. Though usually single stemmed, some plants may form two to four branches. Leaves are light green, stiff, 1 to 2 inches wide, up to 4 feet long, and armed with needle-sharp tips that make them as lethal as daggers.

FLOWERS AND FRUIT: Inflorescences rise to about 3 feet above the leaves and bear many creamy white flowers.

FLOWERING: The flowering period for Faxon's Yucca starts in March and ends in June.

RANGE AND HABITAT: This species is native to Texas and New Mexico and also to the Mexican states of Chihuahua and Coahuila. In Texas, it is found in the Big Bend in the Guadalupe Mountains.

COMMENTS: The greatest floral display we have seen produced by this yucca was at Dagger Flat in Big Bend National Park, between Persimmon Gap and Panther Junction in early April. One stalk weighed 70 pounds and had more than 1,000 flowers. The species was named in honor of Charles E. Faxon, a noted plant illustrator.

Aphanostephus skirrhobasis

Arkansas Lazy Daisy, Arkansas Doze Daisy

ASTERACEAE (ASTER FAMILY)

PLANT AND LEAVES: Arkansas Lazy Daisy is an annual, herbaceous species with multiple stems and a mounding habit. It looks much like a small version of the nonnative, invasive species Ox-eye Daisy (*Leucanthemum vulgare*). Leaves are arranged alternately and are ½ to 2½ inches long, the lower ones sharply toothed, the upper ones smooth. Stems and leaves have soft hairs.

FLOWERS AND FRUIT: At the end of each stem, the plant produces classic daisy-type flower heads with yellow disc flowers in the rounded, button-shaped center and bright white ray flowers around the edges. For romantics of an earlier era it was very difficult to see this species without stopping to take a few moments to find out whether "he" or "she" loved them or loved them not.

FLOWERING: Mostly March to July, but flowering plants may be found year-round in some locales.

RANGE AND HABITAT: One or more of the three botanical varieties of this species (*Aphanostephus skirrhobasis* var. *skirrhobasis*, *A. s.* var. *kidder*, and *A. s.* var. *thalassius*) can be found in Arkansas, Oklahoma, Kansas, New Mexico, Texas, Florida, or northeastern Mexico. All three varieties occur in Texas. *Aphanostephus s.* var. *skirrhobasis* is widespread in Texas. The range of *A. s.* var. *kidder* is restricted to the Rio Grande Valley, and *A. s.* var. *thalassius* lives in sand dunes along the Gulf Coast.

COMMENTS: Members of this genus are commonly called Lazy Daisy or Doze Daisy for their flower heads' habit of closing and nodding at night and not opening until around midday.

Cnidoscolus texanus

Texas Bull Nettle, Tread-softly, Spurge Nettle
EUPHORBIACEAE (SPURGE FAMILY)

PLANT AND LEAVES: Texas Bull Nettle is a perennial herb growing from a large, potato-like root. The fleshy tuber enables the plant to thrive even in the hottest, driest years. The plant has one to several stems emerging from the root and branching

near the ground. It reaches 8 to 32 inches tall, and its spread is often wider than its height. Leaves are alternate, 2 to 4 inches long, divided into five irregularly shaped lobes with rather jagged edges.

FLOWERS AND FRUIT: Flowers are either male or female, but both are borne in the same inflorescence. Each flower has five (sometimes seven) white, petal-like sepals, united below; there are no petals. The fruit, an oblong capsule about ¾ inch long, has three or sometimes four lobes, each containing a seed. When the seeds mature, the outside "fleshy" part of the capsule shrinks and exposes the durable shell that encloses them.

FLOWERING: Flowering occurs March to July.

RANGE AND HABITAT: Texas Bull Nettle is found statewide, especially in eastern Texas, preferring sandy fields and pastures. It is also native to Oklahoma, Arkansas, Louisiana, and Northern Mexico.

COMMENTS: There is an old adage that goes, "Everything in Texas bites, pricks, sticks, or stings!" That, of course, is not true, but if your bare leg should brush against any part of this plant, it will do a very credible job of imparting a very painful sting. All exposed parts of Texas Bull Nettle, with the exception of its sepals, are armed with glass-like stinging hairs that insert an acidic allergen into the skin on contact. Further, if any part of the stem is broken, a milky sap appears; some people are allergic to this as well as the "sting" of the hairs.

Erigeron philadelphicus

Philadelphia Fleabane, Fleabane Daisy

ASTERACEAE (ASTER FAMILY)

PLANT AND LEAVES: Philadelphia Fleabane is an herbaceous plant that, depending on where it is growing, may act as an annual, a biennial, or a perennial. In most places, it completes its life cycle in two years. It grows 12 to 30 inches in height.

FLOWERS AND FRUIT: There are many flower heads arranged in corymbs on each much-branched stem. Flower heads are ½ to

¾ inch across. Each head bears more than 150 white (or sometimes pinkish) ray flowers. The laminae of these ray flowers are
finer than those of other daisies or asters. Its disc flowers are
five-toothed and yellow. The yellow center, along with the large
number of very fine ray flowers, are this species' best recognition features.

FLOWERING: Flowering occurs from March to August.

RANGE AND HABITAT: Philadelphia Fleabane grows along roadsides and in fields and woodlands across virtually all of North
America. Further, it has been introduced and has escaped from
cultivation in much of the rest of the world, often becoming a
nuisance weed. In Texas, it occurs in the eastern half of the state.

COMMENTS: Another species, *Erigeron tenuis*, is very similar except
that the leaves are narrower. These two species are often found
growing together in east Texas, though *E. philadelphicus* is
more abundant in the calcareous clay of north-central Texas
and *E. tenuis* is more common in the sandy soils of east Texas.

White Rocklettuce

ASTERACEAE (ASTER FAMILY)

PLANT AND LEAVES: White Rocklettuce is an herbaceous perennial that reaches about 16 inches in height when in flower. Leaves are mostly at ground level, narrow, and often lobed halfway to the midrib. Both the stems and the leaves contain a milky sap.

FLOWERS AND FRUIT: The showy flower heads are ligulate and about 2 inches across. Individual florets decrease in size toward the center of the head. Flowers of most plants are white with yellowish or yellow-green centers when viewed from above, though some plants have pink or purple flowers. When viewed from below, most flowers have at least some pink or lavender color. The end of each floret is noticeably squared and has five fine teeth as if trimmed with a pair of pinking shears. The heads close by midmorning on sunny days.

FLOWERING: White Rocklettuce is mostly early spring flowering, but specimens in flower may be seen any time from March to August.

RANGE AND HABITAT: The native range of White Rocklettuce is centered in Mexico. It finds its northern limits in Texas and Oklahoma and in southern New Mexico and Arizona. It also ranges south into Central America. In Texas, it is common on arid, grassy prairie with limestone soils.

COMMENTS: Sometimes called White Dandelion, this species does resemble the yellow-flowered *Taraxacum* spp. to which it is fairly closely related.

Clematis drummondii

Old Man's Beard, Texas Virgin's Bower, Goat's Beard

RANUNCULACEAE (BUTTERCUP FAMILY)

PLANT AND LEAVES: Old Man's Beard is a rampant perennial climbing vine growing to as much as 15 feet in height. Like other clematises, it climbs by means of unusual tendril-like, clasping leaf petioles and leaf rachises. Leaves are opposite and compound, with five to seven leaflets ½ to 1 inch long, coarsely cut, and sometimes toothed.

FLOWERS AND FRUIT: Flowers are usually clustered in loose inflorescences of 5 to 12 flowers. Male and female flowers grow on separate plants. The male flowers are ½ to 1 inch across. Their four petal-like sepals are light greenish yellow, almost white, sometimes tinged pink, narrow, and with margins slightly crinkled. There are no petals. The stamens of male flowers are quite conspicuous. The central column of 40 to 80 or more pistils on female flowers is surrounded by a number of sterile staminodes. When the seeds mature, the vine is covered with great masses of silky, feathery plumes, 2 to 4 inches long, that are attached to the plant's seeds.

FLOWERING: Old Man's Beard may flower any time between March and September.

RANGE AND HABITAT: Often found covering pasture fences and

shrubs in old fields, Old Man's Beard is at home on disturbed soil and on scrublands from central Texas westward through the Trans-Pecos. Its native range extends as far west as California and into northern Mexico.

COMMENTS: Old Man's Beard, sometimes called Drummond's Clematis, is named in honor of Scottish botanist Thomas Drummond, an early plant explorer in Texas.

Asclepias asperula

Antelope-horns Milkweed

ASCLEPIADACEAE (MILKWEED FAMILY)

PLANT AND LEAVES: Antelope-horns Milkweed grows 1 to 2 feet tall with sprawling stems that form large, dense clumps up to 3 feet across. The leaves are 4 to 8 inches long, narrow, and irregularly grouped. Stems are densely covered with minute hairs.

FLOWERS AND FRUIT: The flowers are crowded into a ball-shaped inflorescence, 3 to 4 inches across, at the end of the flower stem and are intricately arranged. Above the partially divided greenish petals is a crown, out of which extend five white and maroon appendages with large, ball-like, white ends, all symmetrically arranged. The stamens and pistils are somewhat hidden within the flower's bizarre architecture but are perfectly designed to facilitate pollination by visiting bees. The fruit is a capsule that splits open when mature, releasing many seeds, each with a bit of fluff attached that allows them to be carried away by passing breezes.

FLOWERING: Flowering may occur any time conditions allow but mostly takes place from March to October.

RANGE AND HABITAT: This species grows in dry, sandy, or rocky places throughout most of the western two-thirds of Texas. Its native range extends north to Kansas and west to Nevada and California.

COMMENTS: Antelope-horns Milkweed is probably the most common member of its genus in Texas. As such, it is critical for the development of the first new generation of Monarch butterfly larvae during each year's amazing migration cycle. Its common name is a nod to the species' fruiting capsule, which resembles an antelope's horn . . . sort of.

Melampodium leucanthum

Blackfoot Daisy

ASTERACEAE (ASTER FAMILY)

PLANT AND LEAVES: Blackfoot Daisy is a mounding herbaceous perennial or subshrub. Plants are seldom over 12 inches high and spread 1 to 2 feet across. Leaves are dark green and narrow, about 1½ inch long and ¼ inch wide.

FLOWERS AND FRUIT: When flowering, the rounded, mounding habit of this species resembles a large bouquet. Each flower head is 1 inch across or less and has 8 to 11 ray flowers, with

two or three broad teeth at the tip. Flower heads are borne at the tip of short branches that grow from the axils of the upper leaves. The yellow-orange disc flowers contrast sharply with the white or sometimes creamy-white ray flowers.

FLOWERING: This species begins flowering about March and may still be found flowering as late as October.

RANGE AND HABITAT: Blackfoot Daisy is a native of the southwestern Great Plains and the Chihuahuan and Sonoran Deserts of the US Southwest and northern Mexico. It prefers bare rocky soils or open grasslands where there is a lack of competition. In Texas, its range covers all west Texas and extends to the eastern edge of the Edwards Plateau.

COMMENTS: The low mounding habit, love of heat and drought, floriferousness, and long flowering period of Blackfoot Daisy make it an excellent choice for borders in xeric gardens or sweeps of white between boulders in rock gardens.

Nymphaea odorata ssp. *odorata*
American White Water-lily, Fragrant Water-lily
NYMPHAEACEAE (WATER-LILY FAMILY)

PLANT AND LEAVES: American White Water-lily is a rooted aquatic herbaceous perennial. The species' large rhizomes are rampant and quickly form large colonies in favorable conditions. The leaves have long petioles and are bright green above, reddish or purplish underneath, and almost round. They are narrowly and deeply cut almost to the center, where the stem is attached. They are 4 to 16 inches across, floating on the surface of the water or just beneath.

FLOWERS AND FRUIT: The peduncle ascending from the root bears a single flower, white or occasionally pinkish, sweetly fragrant, 2 to 7 inches across, and floating on the water. Flowers open in the early morning and close about noon. There are four sepals and many rows of white petals, often more than 25, which are ¾ to 4 inches long, thick, and pointed at the tip. There are more than 70 stamens. The outer stamens are large and petal-like, becoming smaller toward the flower's center.

FLOWERING: Flowering begins in March and may continue to October.

RANGE AND HABITAT: Although American White Water-lily is native or introduced across North America and occurs in nearly every US state and most Canadian provinces, in Texas its range is limited to the eastern third of the state. However, it easily naturalizes anywhere with suitable habitat.

COMMENTS: Another subspecies, *Nymphaea odorata* ssp. *tuberosa*, is native to northeastern North America, and its range does not reach Texas. In Texas, *N. o.* ssp. *odorata* is the only white-flowered water-lily you're likely to encounter in natural settings.

Aloysia gratissima

Whitebrush, Beebrush

VERBENACEAE (VERBENA FAMILY)
Synonyms: *Lippia ligustrina*, *Aloysia ligustrina*

PLANT AND LEAVES: Whitebrush is a thicket-forming, deciduous shrub, 3 to 10 feet tall, and with many branches. The branches are slender but stiff, gray pubescent, and often terminated with a spine. The wood is yellow and brittle. The leaves are about 1 inch long and ¼ inch wide and are borne in clusters.

FLOWERS AND FRUIT: Inflorescences of vanilla-scented flowers extend as spikes, 1 to 3 inches long, above the plant's foliage. Its flowers are very fragrant, pure white, about ¼ inch across, and funnel shaped with four rounded petals. The flowers occur in such profusion they nearly conceal the plant beneath. Whitebrush flowers shortly after a rain, and the flowers last for several days. The fruit is a small, dry drupe that contains two seeds.

FLOWERING: Flowering can occur any time from March to November.

RANGE AND HABITAT: The shrubs grow most commonly along the arroyos and overflow areas west of the Pecos River in west Texas and in south and central Texas. Whitebrush is also native to southern Arizona and parts of South America.

COMMENTS: The Big Bend country is noted for an excellent, light-colored honey made from the flowers of Whitebrush, or maybe more appropriately, Beebrush.

Hydrocotyle bonariensis

Salt Pennywort, Largeleaf Pennywort

APIACEAE (CARROT FAMILY)

PLANT AND LEAVES: Salt Pennywort is a fleshy, perennial herb, 6 to 10 inches tall and forming large colonies. It spreads by rhizomes and by creeping stems that root at each node. It has round, undivided leaves, 2 to 4 inches across, that are attached to the stem in the center of the leaf. The leaf edge is scalloped.

FLOWERS AND FRUIT: The flower head is an umbel 2 to 3 inches across. Individual flowers are tiny, with five greenish or white petals.

FLOWERING: Flowering occurs when there is sufficient soil moisture, between March and November.

RANGE AND HABITAT: Abundant along the Gulf in sandy soils extending from high-tide level inland; adapted to salty, brackish marshes. Salt Pennywort can be found anywhere along the Gulf of Mexico and the Atlantic coastlines from the southern tip of Texas to southern Virginia. Outside the United States,

the distribution of this species is interesting. It is considered native throughout the Americas and also much of coastal Africa.

COMMENTS: This species is sometimes called Dollarweed, though the species most often invading lawns is a close relative, *Hydrocotyle umbellata*. Some taxonomists now classify the genus, *Hydrocotyle*, in the family Araliaceae.

Nothoscordum bivalve

Crow Poison, False Garlic

LILIACEAE (LILY FAMILY)

PLANT AND LEAVES: Crow Poison is a perennial herb that grows from a bulb about ½ inch in diameter. Most plants produce a single scape 8 to 16 inches tall. One to four leaves emerge from the bulb. They are about ⅛ inch wide but often quite long, 4 to 12 inches.

FLOWERS AND FRUIT: Flowers are borne in loose umbels atop the scape. The pure white or creamy-white flowers are about ½ inch across, have six tepals with a green to brown stripe on the back side, and have six stamens with yellow anthers. The fruit is a more or less spherical capsule about ⅜ inch in diameter.

FLOWERING: Most flowering occurs from March to May, but as conditions permit, this species may flower at almost any time and is often the only plant found flowering in late December.

RANGE AND HABITAT: Crow poison can be found across Texas but sparingly west to the Trans-Pecos and in the Panhandle. Its native range extends north to Nebraska and east to North Carolina and includes the entire South.

COMMENTS: Looking very much like members of the related genus *Allium*, Crow Poison easily can be distinguished because neither its flowers nor its crushed stem emit any odor. One must wonder at the common name of this species, but no evidence points to it being at all poisonous to crows.

Allium canadense var. *canadense*

Canada Onion, Meadow Garlic, Wild Onion

LILIACEAE (LILY FAMILY)

PLANT AND LEAVES: Canada Onion is a perennial herb, growing from a bulb about 1 inch in diameter and reaching 8 to 20 inches tall. Unlike most other alliums, its bulbs do not produce bulbels at their bases. It has three to five smooth, narrow, grass-like leaves that are shorter than the flower stem.

FLOWERS AND FRUIT: The umbel of Canada Onion is unusual. Replacing most—often all—flowers on the plant's 1 to 1½ inch diameter inflorescence are bulbils, tiny white, yellow-green, or pinkish bulblets that eventually fall to the ground and produce new plants. While still on the plant, the individual bulbils often produce flowers or even flowering umbels. The flowers are white to lavender with six tepals about ¼ inch long. The flowers rarely produce seeds, the plant reproducing primarily asexually by means of its many bulbils.

FLOWERING: Flowering may occur any time from April until July. In Texas, the flowering season is mostly limited to April and May.

RANGE AND HABITAT: Canada Onion is common throughout east Texas in meadows and fields, along roadsides, and in lawns. Its native range covers most of the eastern half of North America.

COMMENTS: Canada Onion is a common sight in the spring. Crow Poison (*Nothoscordum bivalve*) is similar and shares the same habitat, but the Canada Onion can be identified by its strong, pungent scent. The plant's bulb is edible and tastes very much like the nonnative, cultivated Onion (*Allium cepa*).

Cooperia pedunculata

Hill Country Rain Lily, Prairie Rain Lily

LILIACEAE (LILY FAMILY)
Synonym: *Zephyranthes drummondii*

PLANT AND LEAVES: Hill Country Rain Lily is a perennial herb 6 to 12 inches tall, growing from a bulb that can be 1½ to 2 inches in diameter. Its fleshy, arching, glossy, gray-green leaves are about ¼ inch wide and 8 to 12 inches long.

FLOWERS AND FRUIT: Flowers are trumpet shaped for a few hours after opening, but the flowers' six tepals, all white, spread widely to 2 inches across as they mature; they last only a day or two. The flowers, fragrant at night, top a single scape, usually 7 to 9 inches high. Soon after flowering, a three-lobed capsule develops where the flower had been. When mature, the capsule splits open along three seams and releases dozens of glossy, jet-black, wafer-like seeds having the texture of crepe.

FLOWERING: Flowering occurs primarily in April and May, usually about two days after a rain. Flowering may occur sporadically through the summer and fall, and also after rains. In years with long periods of drought in winter and early spring, heavy rains can trigger a spectacular flush of flowers, often blanketing fields and meadows in snowy white drifts of flowers.

RANGE AND HABITAT: Hill Country Rain Lily is common in east, central, and south Texas and in northern Mexico.

COMMENTS: Hill Country Rain Lily is one of several species of rain lilies native to Texas. A similar white-flowered species, Drummond's Rain Lily (*Cooperia drummondii*), has smaller flowers and does not appear until summer and fall in most years. We have seen hundreds of thousands of Hill Country Rain Lilies flowering between Luling and Goliad in late April.

Lonicera albiflora

White Honeysuckle, Texas Honeysuckle

CAPRIFOLIACEAE (HONEYSUCKLE FAMILY)

PLANT AND LEAVES: White Honeysuckle is a perennial shrub or trailing vine usually growing to about 4 to 6 feet tall and 4 to 5 feet broad. If there is handy vegetation nearby, the plant can climb by twining to 10 feet in height. It has oppositely arranged, glossy, egg-shaped leaves about 1½ to 2½ inches long and 1 to 1½ inches wide. The two leaves at the end of each stem and just below the plant's inflorescence are perfoliate; that is, they are fused to one another and surround the stem like a broad collar. Plants in west Texas—which some authorities classify as *Lonicera a.* var. *dumosa*—have leaves with pubescence along their margins and on their lower surfaces.

FLOWERS AND FRUIT: White Honeysuckle bears showy clusters of sweetly fragrant white or yellowish-white flowers at the ends of its stems. It bears bright red or orange-red berries in clusters, which ripen in autumn.

FLOWERING: This species flowers during April and May. Berries mature in October and November.

RANGE AND HABITAT: White Honeysuckle is native to canyons, bluffs, and rocky slopes on caliche and sandy soils in central, north-central, and west Texas, often in associations with junipers. It is also native to southern Oklahoma, New Mexico, and Arizona.

COMMENTS: Its bright red fruit makes the plant aesthetically attractive to people and attractive to birds as culinary delights, assuring its wide distribution. Though this species is a good selection as a garden accent in areas with some afternoon shade and not-too-rich soil, it should be located in an area not visited by deer, which savor its tender stems.

Marshallia caespitosa

Barbara's Buttons, Puffballs

ASTERACEAE (ASTER FAMILY)

PLANT AND LEAVES: Barbara's Buttons is an herbaceous plant with several unbranched stems arising each spring from a perennial rootstock. The stems may be 4 to 24 inches, with most stems' height in the 8- to 16-inch range. The stems grow from a crown along with a rosette of narrow, grass-like leaves. The leaves are about 3 inches long and ⅜ inch wide. There are sometimes no leaves on the stems. More often, a few narrow leaves—most

concentrated on the lower half—are borne alternately on the stem. The stem leaves are similar to the leaves of the rosette and may reach 6 inches in length.

FLOWERS AND FRUIT: Each stem is terminated by a single capitulum with numerous showy white or occasionally pale lavender disc flowers. The tube of each disc flower has several long, curly lobes. Barbara's Buttons has no ray flowers. A pistil with two stigma lobes that curl into circles extend from the center of each flower. The flowers open from the outside of the head inward.

FLOWERING: Barbara's Buttons flowers in April and May.

RANGE AND HABITAT: Two botanical varieties of this species are native to Texas. *Marshallia c.* var. *caespitosa* has no stem leaves and is found on rich soils mostly in the Sabine River drainage in east Texas and western Louisiana. *Marshallia c.* var. *signata* does bear stem leaves and is common on limestone soils in central and north Texas, where it is often found growing on road cuts.

COMMENTS: Barbara's Buttons bears a passing resemblance to a nonnative species with a similar name, Bachelor's Buttons (*Centaurea cyanus*). Our native is easy to cultivate and is very popular with native plant gardeners.

Penstemon cobaea

False Foxglove,
Foxglove Beardtongue

SCROPHULARIACEAE (FIGWORT FAMILY)

PLANT AND LEAVES: False Foxglove produces multiple herbaceous, unbranched, downy stems, 12 to 20 inches tall, from a perennial crown. Its leaves are opposite, broadly lance shaped, and with toothed margins and attach directly to the stem.

FLOWERS AND FRUIT: Flowers are 1½ to 2 inches long and may be

whitish, violet, or pink, usually with purple lines in the throat. They grow on the upper part of the stem, in loose clusters on very short stems in the axils of the small upper leaves or bracts.

FLOWERING: Flowering occurs during April and May.

RANGE AND HABITAT: False Foxglove is common on dry or well-drained limestone, sandy, or gypsum soils in pastures and on roadsides in east-central and central Texas. It is native to the southern and central Great Plains and may be found as far north as Nebraska.

COMMENTS: *Penstemon* species grow all across Texas, and any part of the state can lay claim to at least one of them. Nearly all members of the figwort family have four stamens, but those in the genus *Penstemon* have five. The fifth one, technically a staminode, does not have an anther and is often bearded; thus, the name "beardtongue." This species is known as False Foxglove because of its physical similarity to the Eurasian genus *Digitalis*, known colloquially as Foxglove.

Sambucus nigra ssp. *canadensis*

Common Elderberry, American Black Elderberry

CAPRIFOLIACEAE (HONEYSUCKLE FAMILY)
Synonym: *Sambucus canadensis*

PLANT AND LEAVES: Common Elderberry is a large, deciduous, multistemmed shrub that normally grows 6 to 12 feet tall but may reach 30 feet. The plant spreads by stolons, and where habitat conditions allow, it often forms thickets. The wood of the stem is soft, with a large central core of white pith. The leaves are opposite, odd-pinnately compound, 4 to 12 inches long and about a third as wide, and each has 5 to 11 leaflets, usually 7. The leaves' lower one or two pairs of leaflets are often themselves compound with three leaflets. The leaflets are lance shaped, 2 to 6 inches long, with tiny pointed teeth.

FLOWERS AND FRUIT: Flowers are fragrant and are arranged in large convex or flattened heads 4 to 10 inches across. Each creamy-white flower (greenish at first) is about ¼ inch across

and trumpet-shaped, ending in five petal-like lobes. The fruit is a purplish-black berry, ⅕ inch in diameter, that is used widely for making wine and jelly.

FLOWERING: Flowering usually occurs in April or May, but some plants occasionally flower in summer.

RANGE AND HABITAT: Common Elderberry grows in consistently damp places with rich soil, commonly along streams, ditches, or roadsides. It can be found in east and central Texas. Its range extends across most of North America except for the Great Basin region and the Pacific Northwest.

COMMENTS: In days gone by, children would often remove the pith from sections of stems and make whistles or blowguns from them. The plant's berries are eaten and their seeds distributed by wild mammals and birds.

Yucca thompsoniana

Thompson's Yucca, Beaked Yucca

AGAVACEAE (CENTURY-PLANT FAMILY)

Synonym: *Yucca rostrata*

PLANT AND LEAVES: Thompson's Yucca grows 6 to 12 feet high, tree-like, and with a trunk 5 to 8 inches in diameter. The trunk is usually unbranched. The leaves are narrow and stiff and grow in a radiating mass near the top; they are 8 to 24 inches long and about ½ inch wide in the middle. They gradually widen from the base to the middle then narrow to a needle-like

spine at the tip. The margins are horny, pale yellow, and more or less fine toothed.

FLOWERS AND FRUIT: The stout, 2- to 3-foot flowering stalk holds a dense panicle of white flowers slightly above the foliage. Another common name for this species, Beaked Yucca, refers to a beak-shaped appendage of its fruit.

FLOWERING: Thompson's Yucca flowers during April and May.

RANGE AND HABITAT: Native to Texas in the United States and to Chihuahua and Coahuila in Mexico. In Texas, its range is limited to the Trans-Pecos ecoregion.

COMMENTS: Many yuccas become unkempt in time, with shaggy, brown leaves hanging down. Thompson's Yucca's dead leaves hug the plant's trunk and help it maintain a neat appearance.

Zigadenus nuttallii

Nuttall's Death Camas

LILIACEAE (LILY FAMILY)

Synonyms: *Toxicoscordion nuttallii*, *Zigadenus texensis*

PLANT AND LEAVES: Nuttall's Death Camas is an herbaceous perennial growing from a more or less spherical bulb about 1½ inches in diameter and with a black, papery covering. Its leaves

all emerge from the bulb and are about ⅜ inch wide and up to 18 inches long.

FLOWERS AND FRUIT: A stout scape emerges in early spring from the bulb and grows to about 2 feet in height. Topping the scape is a very symmetrical, rounded to pyramidal inflorescence of as many as 60 creamy-white flowers, each about ⅝ inch in diameter. Like other members of its family, its flowers have six tepals. The stamens have large yellow anthers.

FLOWERING: Flowering begins in early April and may continue well into May.

RANGE AND HABITAT: Nuttall's Death Camas is a native of rocky, limestone meadows, prairies, and slopes. In Texas, it can be found from northeast Texas west to the Edwards Plateau. Its range also includes Louisiana, Arkansas, Oklahoma, and Kansas.

COMMENTS: Several other species of *Zigadenus* can be found in Texas. Unlike Crow Poison (*Nothoscordum bivalve*), which is not actually known to be poisonous, death camus species are all poisonous and should not be eaten. Sheep are often poisoned by members of this genus.

Arisaema dracontium

Green Dragon, Dragonroot

ARACEAE (ARUM FAMILY)
Synonym: *Muricauda dracontium*

PLANT AND LEAVES: Green Dragon is an herbaceous perennial growing each year from a corm. It produces one leaf on a tall petiole early each spring that grows to 12 to 18 inches at the time of flowering and ultimately to as much as 3 feet in height before dying to the ground in late fall. The odd arrangement of the U-shaped, palmately lobed leaf makes it appear to be two leaves.

FLOWERS AND FRUIT: A slender spathe, which encloses the plant's flower-bearing spadix, soon emerges from near the middle of the leaf petiole. After flowering, the spathe withers and leaves the berries—usually more than 100—exposed and developing on the spadix. Green Dragon is self-infertile and must receive

pollen from another plant to produce viable fruit. Pollination is by flies. The fruits are bright red when mature.

FLOWERING: Flowering occurs from April to June. Fruits are mature in the fall.

RANGE AND HABITAT: This close relative of Jack-in-the-pulpit (*Arisaema triphyllum*) can be found in moist hardwood forests, often near springs and streams. It is native to virtually all of eastern North America as far west as the southern Great Plains. In Texas, Green Dragon grows in rich, moist woodlands over most of the eastern half of the state and as far west as the southeastern Hill Country.

COMMENTS: Calcium oxalate crystals in its tissues make all parts of Green Dragon inedible to humans, though its berries are readily eaten by wild turkeys. The presence of this species in the wild is an indicator of a healthy ecosystem.

Magnolia grandiflora
Southern Magnolia, Evergreen Magnolia
MAGNOLIACEAE (MAGNOLIA FAMILY)

PLANT AND LEAVES: Southern Magnolia is a broadleaf evergreen tree that in the extreme can reach 90 feet in height, with a trunk more than 6 feet in girth, and may live to 200 years or more. But any way you measure them, these trees are simply magnificent. A typical tree has stout limbs from near ground level to the top. They have a dense growth of smooth, leathery, evergreen leaves, elliptical in shape, 5 to 10 inches long, shiny on top, felted and rusty below.

FLOWERS AND FRUIT: Creamy-white flowers have a lemon fragrance and discolor easily if bruised. They appear on the ends of thick, tough stems all over the tree. The flowers are cup shaped, about 8 to 12 inches across, with several thick tepals that are wider near the tip, where they are cupped. The flowers open in the morning and close at night for two or three days; then all the stamens are shed and the flower reopens, turns brown, and disintegrates. The flowers produce cone-like seedpods that contain large red seeds. When the pods open,

the seeds often fall from their place and hang by silky threads. Children often use the seeds for beads.

FLOWERING: Flowering begins in April, peaks in mid-May, and continues to June.

RANGE AND HABITAT: Southern Magnolia is native from southeast Texas and along the coastal plain to Virginia. It prefers deep, rich river bottoms and moderately moist woodlands.

COMMENTS: The tree is often planted in yards, but the leaves fall gradually throughout the year so that frequent raking is required. Grass will not grow well, if at all, under the tree.

Magnolia virginiana
Sweetbay Magnolia
MAGNOLIACEAE (MAGNOLIA FAMILY)

PLANT AND LEAVES: Sweetbay Magnolia is a shrub or tree that grows 30 to 60 feet high on average. Specimens often have multiple trunks, but those growing as single-trunked trees will reach greater heights. Bark is relatively smooth, with only small ridges. Leaves are leathery, simple, green above and

whitish below, 3 to 6 inches long and 1 to 2½ inches wide. This magnolia holds its leaves over winter and sheds them just as new leaves form.

FLOWERS AND FRUIT: Flowers are creamy white and about 3 inches in diameter. They open in the morning and close at night for two or three days. They have 8 to 14 petals and emit a wonderful fragrance evocative of vanilla. The fruit—technically a follicetum—is a cone-shaped aggregate of follicles bearing bright red seeds that are eaten and distributed by American Robins, Northern Mockingbirds, Gray Catbirds, and others.

FLOWERING: Flowering occurs from April to June.

RANGE AND HABITAT: This swamp-loving native tree can be found anywhere in the coastal plain with adequate soil moisture from southeast Texas to Massachusetts.

COMMENTS: The leaves of Sweetbay Magnolia are a favored food for deer and cattle and are browsed heavily in the winter when other food is scarce. *Magnolia* species are among the oldest trees on earth—at least 90 million years—and arose possibly before the arrival of bees but after beetles had come on the scene. Even today, magnolias are often pollinated by beetles, though honeybees are attracted, too.

Stewartia malacodendron

Silky Camellia

THEACEAE (TEA FAMILY)

PLANT AND LEAVES: Silky Camellia is a large, open-branched, rounded, deciduous shrub growing up to 25 feet tall but usually in the 10- to 12-foot range. Its bark is thin and brown or cinnamon colored. Like other members of its family, Silky Camellia leaves are alternate. They are 2 to 4 inches long and half as wide with finely toothed margins, silky below, and with distinct veins.

FLOWERS AND FRUIT: This species' saucer-shaped flowers are showy and range from 2 to 4 inches in diameter. The flowers have five nearly round, creamy-white petals with wrinkled margins. The large cluster of stamens in the flower's center has purple filaments and bluish-gray anthers. Its stigma has five finger-like lobes. The fruit is a rounded, beaked capsule usually containing only two seeds.

FLOWERING: In Texas, flowering occurs sometime during April, May, or June.

RANGE AND HABITAT: Silky Camellia plants grow in rich woods. Its historic range stretched from east Texas through coastal states to Virginia and also included Arkansas. Today, it still inhabits those same states, but its populations are generally small and widely scattered.

COMMENTS: Theaceae is a family with showy flowers, the most familiar of which are the well-known camellia and the important tea plant. The great majority of species in this family are native to Asia. Silky Camellia is uncommon throughout its native range and rare in Texas. Osa Hall, who worked for years with the Texas Forest Service, showed us an area where a number of them grew. It was his custom, except with persons he knew well, to blindfold people he took to this location lest they return to get specimens for transplanting.

Polygala alba
White Milkwort
POLYGALACEAE (MILKWORT FAMILY)

PLANT AND LEAVES: White Milkwort is a perennial herb producing a cluster of unbranched stems each spring from the crown of a perennial rootstock. The stems are narrow, 8 to 14 inches tall. There may be one or two circles of leaves near the ground, but most leaves grow singly and alternately along the stem. They are very narrow and up to 1 inch long.

FLOWERS AND FRUIT: The flowers are very small—not even ¼ inch long—but are arranged in dense racemes. They are white with a green center and sometimes purple highlights. Flowering begins at the base of the inflorescence and proceeds upward.

FLOWERING: Flowering begins in April and may continue until July.

RANGE AND HABITAT: White Milkwort is common on dry, rocky soils, caliche, and sandy ground in east, south-central, and southwest Texas. It is especially common around juniper woodlands and on road cuts. Its native range extends west to Arizona and north through the western Great Plains to Saskatchewan, Canada.

COMMENTS: White-flowered plants—especially ones with flowers

as tiny as those of this species—rarely grab our attention. But there is something about those little white spiky clusters waving in the breeze that make us stop and look. This is the most widely distributed species of *Polygala* in Texas.

Arbutus xalapensis

Texas Madrone

ERICACEAE (HEATH FAMILY)
Synonym: *Arbutus texana*

PLANT AND LEAVES: Texas Madrone is a tree usually growing to
about 12 feet in height, though it can reach 30 feet or more.
Its most striking feature is the thin, pinkish, smooth bark,
which peels off in thin sheets. New growth is covered with
velvet-like hairs. The leaves are 2 to 4 inches long and about
1 inch wide. They are shiny, stiff, and rather thick and have
smooth margins.

FLOWERS AND FRUIT: The racemes of urn-shaped flowers resemble
those of its distant relative blueberry. The flowers are ½ inch
long or less, white to slightly pink. Blackish-red berries ripen
from September to December, and mature fruit frequently can
be found on trees that are still flowering.

FLOWERING: Flowering occurs primarily in spring, beginning in
April, but may continue until September.

RANGE AND HABITAT: There are two geographically well-separated
groups of *Arbutus xalapensis* in Texas. The easternmost popu-

lation can be found on rocky limestone hillsides and bluffs throughout most of the Edwards Plateau. Specimens of a disjunct western population are fairly rare but can be found in the Chisos, Davis, and Guadalupe Mountains of west Texas. Its native range also extends into New Mexico and through Mexico into Central America.

COMMENTS: Growing Texas Madrone in the garden is not for the faint of heart, but the best success is usually had by directly sowing seed in suitable, well-drained soil. Texas Madrone is especially unforgiving of root disturbance and transplanted specimens rarely thrive.

Sagittaria lancifolia ssp. *media*

Duck Potato, Arrowhead, Bulltongue Arrowhead

ALISMATACEAE (WATER-PLANTAIN FAMILY)
Synonym: *Sagittaria falcata*

PLANT AND LEAVES: A perennial, herbaceous wetland plant to as much as 6 feet tall when flowering and with lance-shaped leaves.

FLOWERS AND FRUIT: The flowers are quite distinctive, with three green sepals and three white petals, ¼ to ½ inch long. The pistils often are flattened and form a tight, round green center.

FLOWERING: The flowering period for Duck Potato begins in April and continues to September.

RANGE AND HABITAT: Duck Potato can be found in swamps and permanently wet places in US coastal areas in all states on the Gulf of Mexico and all states on the Atlantic Seaboard from

Florida to Delaware. It also occurs in Central America, South America, and the West Indies. In Texas, its native range is mostly limited to the counties on the upper Gulf Coast, though it has been spread by cultivation to other parts of the state.

COMMENTS: The genus *Sagittaria* gets its name from the arrow-shaped leaves of some species, though the leaves of *Sagittaria lancifolia* ssp. *media* are long and narrow. One or more species of *Sagittaria* can be found in any section of Texas that has ponds, swamps, muddy shallows, lazy streams, or even roadside ditches. The tubers and young shoots that grow in the mud are said to have been a staple food of Native Americans. Early settlers called them Duck Potatoes because they are a favorite food of ducks and other waterfowl. Another plant in the same family, with flowers resembling those of Duck Potato and growing in similar conditions, is Lanceleaf Burhead (*Echinodorus cordifolius*). It grows to 4 feet high and flowers April to June.

Fallugia paradoxa

Apache Plume

ROSACEAE (ROSE FAMILY)

PLANT AND LEAVES: Apache Plume is a perennial, woody shrub growing 4 to 6 or even up to 8 feet tall with many widely spreading and ascending branches. The evergreen species' leaves, which are lobed and curled under along the edges, are up to ¾ inches long, are arranged alternately, and grow in small clusters.

FLOWERS AND FRUIT: The flower is attractive, about 1 inch across, with five white petals and many stamens and pistils borne on long, naked stems; it resembles a rose flower. The plant gets its common name from the numerous reddish, feather-like appendages, 1 to 2 inches long, that are part of the plant's fruit.

FLOWERING: Flowering occurs any time between April and October.

RANGE AND HABITAT: Apache Plume's Texas range begins on the southwestern reaches of the Edwards Plateau and proceeds west across the Trans-Pecos ecoregion. Beyond Texas's western border, it can be found across most of the Four Corners

states and in Nevada and California. It grows in a variety of desert, xeric grassland, and mountain habitats.

COMMENTS: Apache Plume adapts well to desert conditions and is abundant in the Big Bend at elevations of 3,000 to 8,000 feet. It is browsed by cattle and goats. It grows rapidly with sufficient moisture and is often used as an ornamental. *Fallugia* is monotypic; that is, it contains the single species *Fallugia paradoxa*, and no others.

Gaillardia aestivalis
Lanceleaf Blanketflower
ASTERACEAE (ASTER FAMILY)

PLANT AND LEAVES: Lanceleaf Blanketflower is an herbaceous perennial growing 1 to 2 feet tall. Leaves are 2 to 4 inches long, alternate, thick, and with soft hair on both sides. Lower leaves are larger than those higher on the stem.

FLOWERS AND FRUIT: The flower heads have 6 to 10 yellow, white, or pink ray flowers and white, yellow, or purple disc flowers in the center. The ray flowers are tubular at the base but flare out at the top into three deeply cut lobes.

FLOWERING: The flowering season for Lanceleaf Blanket flower begins in April and continues to October.

RANGE AND HABITAT: Lanceleaf Blanketflower is native to the South and the southern Great Plains. In Texas, it can be found in the eastern third of the state, where it grows in open pine forests and grasslands.

COMMENTS: Some authorities recognize three or more botanical varieties based primarily on the varying colors of their ray and disc flower, including: *Gaillardia aestivalis* var. *aestivalis* with yellow ray flowers and purple disc flowers; *G. a.* var. *chrysantha* with yellow ray and disc flowers; and *G. a.* var. *winkleri* with white to pinkish ray flowers and white or yellow disc flowers. *Gaillardia aestivalis* var. *winkleri* is a rare plant of conservation concern from the Pineywoods in east Texas.

Euphorbia antisyphilitica

Candelilla, Wax Plant

EUPHORBIACEAE (SPURGE FAMILY)

PLANT AND LEAVES: Candelilla is a perennial herb with fleshy rhizomes producing clusters of many erect, mostly unbranched, pencil-like stems growing 8 to 18 inches tall, occasionally to 3 feet in height. The stems secrete a fine wax that coats the plant and imparts a bluish bloom to the stem's surface. Very small, fleshy, lance-shaped leaves are formed on new growth but are normally soon shed, giving the plant the appearance that it is leafless.

FLOWERS AND FRUIT: This species is monoecious; that is, it has separate male and female flowers on the same plant. Tiny pale-pink or creamy-white flowers, deep pink in the center and ¹⁄₁₆ to ⅛ inch across, grow near the tips of the stems, often in great numbers. The flowers are followed by tiny rose-pink fruits, three-lobed capsules about ¼ inch in diameter.

FLOWERING: Flowering occurs April to November.

RANGE AND HABITAT: This species can be found in the Chihuahua Desert on limestone soils in south and west Texas, New Mexico, and northern Mexico.

COMMENTS: A high-grade wax is produced by boiling the Candelilla plant in large vats, which we have seen in process on the Mexican side of the Rio Grande. The wax has been used in making candles, soap, ointments, sealing wax, phonograph records, insulation material, shoe polish, floor polish, waterproofing, and lubricants. The specific epithet, *antisyphilitica*, was given because of its purported use in treating venereal disease. Originally common over much of the limestone country in Brewster and Presidio Counties, Candelilla is still abundant in Big Bend National Park, where it is protected and not in danger of becoming extinct through removal of the plants. It prefers the same habitat as sotols (*Dasylirion* spp.) and Lechuguilla (*Agave lechuguilla*).

Ipomoea imperati

Beach Morning Glory

CONVOLVULACEAE (MORNING GLORY FAMILY)
Synonym: *Ipomoea stolonifera*

PLANT AND LEAVES: Beach Morning Glory is an herbaceous perennial vine, growing as stolons—stems that grow on the surface of the soil and root at their nodes—and reaching 15 to 25 feet in length. This species is among the few morning glories that do not twine or climb. The leaves are very fleshy and variable in shape. Some leaves are oblong to nearly circular; others are deeply divided into three to seven lobes.

FLOWERS AND FRUIT: Its flowers are borne singly from the leaf axils. They are large and funnel-shaped, 1¾ to 2¾ inches in diameter. Petals are white with a greenish or lemon-yellow throat in the flower's tube. The flowers wither by midday.

FLOWERING: Flowering occurs during warm or hot weather from April to November.

RANGE AND HABITAT: This is a species of beach dunes and sandy flats. It is native along Texas's coast and eastward to Florida

and south to South America and in scattered locales in the Caribbean.

COMMENTS: Beach Morning Glory and Railroad Vine (*Ipomoea pescaprae*) are ecologically important plant species. Both grow on beach dunes and backshore flats and play a large role in dune development and the prevention of beach erosion. Similar to Beach Morning Glory in several ways and often confused, Railroad Vine is easily distinguished. The oval-shaped leaf of Railroad Vine is not lobed, except for a small indention at its apex, and the plant's flowers are pink.

Agave lechuguilla

Lechuguilla

AGAVACEAE (CENTURY-PLANT FAMILY)
Synonym: *Agave lophantha* var. *poselgeri*

PLANT AND LEAVES: Lechuguilla is an herbaceous perennial shrub with stiff, sharply pointed, erect or ascending leaves to about 2 feet in height. The overall appearance of the plant is akin to a very coarse, well-used broom. Its leaves are leathery and light green to yellowish green with sharply toothed margins.

FLOWERS AND FRUIT: Like its relative the Maguey or Century Plant

(*Agave americana*), Lechuguilla requires 12 to 15 years to store enough food for the production of the large flower stalk, which then grows very rapidly to up to 12 feet tall. The stalk is un-branched and flexible, so that it often bends when it is heavy with buds or flowers, retaining a permanent, graceful arc. The upper part of the stalk is covered with a solid mass of purplish or yellowish flowers that appear greenish white in aggregate. After producing flowers and seeds, the stalk dies.

FLOWERING: Flowering occurs in spring and summer, usually in May and June, after rains.

RANGE AND HABITAT: Lechuguilla is native to the Chihuahuan Desert in Texas, New Mexico, and northern and eastern Mexico. In Texas, it is found in the Trans-Pecos region of the state.

COMMENTS: The plant reproduces by putting out offshoots, which are often eaten by deer and javelinas. Human use is also extensive, as rope, mats, and baskets are made from the fiber, while pulque, mescal, and tequila are made from the fermented sap of the flower stalk. The armature of Lechuguilla is to be respected and often injures horses passing through it. Some natural populations grow so thickly as to be impenetrable.

Silene stellata
Starry Campion, Widow's Frill
CARYOPHYLLACEAE (PINK FAMILY)

PLANT AND LEAVES: Starry Campion is an herbaceous perennial growing from a fleshy taproot. Several stems, unbranched below their inflorescences, typically arise from each crown and grow 12 to 30 inches tall. The leaves are lance shaped, covered in soft, downy hairs beneath, and arranged in whorls,

four leaves per node. The leaves at the middle of the stem tend to be the largest, reaching 4 inches in length and about 1 inch wide. Those lower on the stem have usually withered away by the time the plant flowers.

FLOWERS AND FRUIT: Panicles of pure white, broadly bell-shaped flowers top the stems. The showy flowers, nearly 1 inch in diameter, have five petals that are deeply dissected into up to 12 lobes each, giving them the frilled appearance noted in the common name, Widow's Frill. The bowl-shaped calyx is visible in the flower's throat.

FLOWERING: Flowering occurs any time between May and July.

RANGE AND HABITAT: Starry Campion is most at home in moist woodlands on rich, loamy soils and on native prairies. Its range covers nearly the entire eastern half of the United States but enters Texas only in the northeast corner.

COMMENTS: Starry Campion's showiness makes it a popular cultivated plant, especially for woodland gardens.

Platanthera nivea

Snowy Orchid, Frog Spear

ORCHIDACEAE (ORCHID FAMILY)
Synonym: *Habenaria nivea*

PLANT AND LEAVES: Snowy Orchid is a slender, erect, single-stemmed perennial herb growing up to nearly 3 feet tall. It has two or three leaves near the bottom, 4 to 12 inches long and about ¾ inches wide.

FLOWERS AND FRUIT: Topping the plant's stem is a cylindrical or narrowly pyramidal 4- to 5-inch spike of 20 to 60 closely packed flowers. Flowering proceeds from the bottom upward. Flowers have three snow-white sepals and three like-colored petals. Unusual for orchids, the flowers are not resupinate; that is, their pedicels are not twisted so that the flower is held upside down. Hence, the flower's narrow labellum or lip is located at the top. The slender spur is conspicuous, ¾ inch long, extending more or less horizontally, and curving upward at the end.

FLOWERING: Flowering may occur any time between May and August, with most flowering in June and July.

RANGE AND HABITAT: Snowy Orchid appears intermittently on acidic soils in bogs, swamps, wet pine barrens, and meadows in southeast Texas. Its range extends through all coastal states from Texas to New Jersey and also into Arkansas and Tennessee.

COMMENTS: Snowy Orchid often grows alongside Orange Fringed Orchid (*Platanthera ciliaris*) in Big Thicket bogs and damp areas, though it is also found in other places. Its starkly white flowers make it conspicuous wherever it is found.

Polanisia uniglandulosa

Mexican Clammyweed

CAPPARIDACEAE (CAPER OR SPIDERFLOWER FAMILY)

Synonym: *Polanisia dodecandra* ssp. *uniglandulosa*

PLANT AND LEAVES: Of the five species of *Polanisia*—all native to North America—Mexican Clammyweed is the only perennial. The plant may be multibranched or single stemmed and covered with stalked, glandular hairs. It grows 16 to 32 inches in height. The leaves, on green or purple petioles and about 1½ inches long with three leaflets, are densely arranged along the stem.

FLOWERS AND FRUIT: Showy racemes are clustered at the end of the stems. The petals are white, erect, ⅝ to 1⅛ inch long, and notched at the tip. There are nearly 30 purple stamens per flower, ¾ to 2 inches long, that extend beyond the petals and give the flower a striking deep purple and white effect. Fruits (capsules) are erect, are 2 to 4 inches long, and contain up to 60 iridescent, russet-colored seeds.

FLOWERING: Flowering begins as early as May and continues to October.

RANGE AND HABITAT: Common in west Texas at elevations above 4,000 feet; usually abundant in dry streambeds. Its native range extends into New Mexico and Mexico.

COMMENTS: Clammyweeds are sticky and emit a strong odor when disturbed. Their fetid odor makes them unpalatable to herbivores.

Crinum americanum var. *americanum*

Swamp Lily, Southern Swamp Lily, String Lily

LILIACEAE (LILY FAMILY)

PLANT AND LEAVES: Swamp Lily is an erect herbaceous perennial growing from a bulb 3 to 5 inches in diameter. This species typically forms clumps and often is found in large colonies covering many acres. Leathery, dark green leaves grow directly from the bulb and are 2 to 4½ feet long and 1½ to 3 inches wide.

FLOWERS AND FRUIT: The stout flowering scape is about 1 inch in diameter, 2 to 3 feet tall, with two to five flowers forming a showy umbel at the top. The fragrant flowers are white, sometimes marked with pink. The flowers' six tepals are 3 to 4 inches long and ½ inch wide. They are joined at the base, forming a long tube, but curve backward at the end to form a ball-shaped inflorescence. Stamens extend well outside the corolla, have long anthers affixed in the middle to purple filaments. The fruit is a large, spherical capsule, 1 inch to nearly 2 inches in diameter.

FLOWERING: In Texas, flowering occurs from May to November.

RANGE AND HABITAT: As its common name suggests, Swamp Lily is a native of wet areas. It is common in freshwater marshes and cypress swamps in southeast Texas. It occasionally occurs in northeast Texas, where it is rare. It is native to all coastal states from Texas to North Carolina.

COMMENTS: A botanical variety with umbels bearing six to seven flowers (*Crinum americanum* var. *truabii*) is known from only Hardin and Jefferson Counties in southeast Texas.

Datura wrightii

Angel Trumpet, Sacred Thorn-apple

SOLANACEAE (POTATO FAMILY)

PLANT AND LEAVES: Angel Trumpet is a well-branched and widely spreading herb growing from a perennial rootstock. Its stems are covered in short hairs. The plant is bushy and can reach 3 feet tall and 5 to 8 feet across. Its large, broad leaves are more or less egg shaped, pointed at the tip, 4 to 10 inches long and 3 to 6 inches wide, on short petioles, and with fine hair, especially along the veins.

FLOWERS AND FRUIT: The flowers are mostly pearl white but sometimes have a pale pinkish cast. The petals are united to form a funnel 6 to 9 inches long and 2½ to 4 inches across, opening in the evening and closing by midmorning. The fruit is a large, spiny, spherical to egg-shaped capsule about 1½ inches long.

FLOWERING: Flowering occurs from May to November.

RANGE AND HABITAT: This species' current range in Texas is statewide, though much of that may be due to cultivation. Its original range was probably more limited to the dryer regions of the

state. It is known to be native across the Desert Southwest and in Oklahoma and southwestern Colorado.

COMMENTS: The large, white Angel Trumpet flower can be found from one end of the state to the other and is always a refreshing surprise. Though it grows in varied habitats, one sees it only rarely. On still evenings, moths of the family Sphingidae, known as hawk moths, hummingbird moths, or sphinx moths, are apt to be darting from flower to flower. The whole plant is poisonous, but, because of its foul odor and taste, livestock seldom eat it.

Rhododendron viscosum

Swamp Azalea, Clammy Azalea

ERICACEAE (HEATH FAMILY)
Synonyms: *Azalea serrulata, Rhododendron serrulatum*

PLANT AND LEAVES: Swamp azalea is an erect, irregular branching shrub, growing to 15 to 20 feet tall. The oval-shaped leaves, clustered at the end of branches, are 1½ to 3½ inches long and ⅝ to 1½ inches wide, deciduous, lustrous, green on both sides, and with short stems.

FLOWERS AND FRUIT: Flowering occurs in midsummer, after the leaves are formed. Inflorescences are borne at the ends of stems with clusters of 3 to 15 sweet-scented flowers. The flowers are white with a lavender tube that is slightly enlarged at the base and sticky with glandular hairs, 1¼ to 1¾ inches long, and with five narrow, petal-like spreading lobes. The five stamens extend well beyond the floral tube.

FLOWERING: Swamp Azalea flowers between June and August.

RANGE AND HABITAT: As its common name suggests, Swamp Azalea commonly is found in the swamps, baygalls, pocosins, and other consistently moist woodland areas with acidic soils. It is at home in the Texas Pineywoods, across the South, through the Mid-Atlantic states, and throughout New England.

COMMENTS: A species with an especially agreeable scent, Swamp Azalea fills moist southern woodlands with tantalizing sweetness on warm summer evenings. Its white flowers are especially fragrant during nighttime hours—a good indication that they may be attracting moths and being pollinated by them.

Cephalanthus occidentalis

Buttonbush

RUBIACEAE (MADDER FAMILY)

PLANT AND LEAVES: Buttonbush is a multistemmed perennial shrub usually growing 8 to 12 feet tall but may reach 20 feet in height. Its habit is mostly upright but open and irregular. The plant often looks weedy. The simple leaves are lance shaped with smooth margins, 2 to 8 inches long and 1 to 3 inches wide. The leaves are opposite or often in whorls of three, with prominent veins and rounded at the base.

FLOWERS AND FRUIT: Flowers are clustered in ball-shaped heads, 1 to 1½ inches in diameter, with stamens protruding like pins in a pincushion. The trumpet-shaped white-to-yellowish flower is ¼ to ⅜ inch long, opening into four minute, spreading petal-like lobes. Each small flower has four prominent stamens. Like the flowers, the fruits are held in spherical heads and borne in open clusters of six or more heads. They turn bright reddish orange before finally turning black when mature.

FLOWERING: Flowering occurs from June to September.

RANGE AND HABITAT: Buttonbush is almost always found closely associated with open water and is common on stream and pond banks and in marshes. It usually stands in water, at least part of the time, or in very moist areas. It is common in east Texas and is less frequent farther west. Its native range covers the eastern half of the United States and extends south across much of Mexico and into Central America.

COMMENTS: Honeybees and hummingbirds work the flowers for nectar, and many birds eat the fruit. The bark has been used in the treatment of several types of illness.

Mandevilla macrosiphon

Longtube Trumpet Flower, Plateau Rocktrumpet

APOCYNACEAE (DOGBANE FAMILY)

Synonyms: *Macrosiphonia lanuginosa* var. *macrosiphon*, *Macrosiphonia macrosiphon*

PLANT AND LEAVES: Longtube Trumpet Flower is a small, perennial herb that grows to about 1 foot in height. Leaves are opposite, oval to about 3 inches long, and crowded on the stem. On some plants, the leaves are almost round with broad scallops; on others they have entire margins with a point at the tip. All of them are fleshy with a covering of fine hair on both sides and prominent veins and midrib.

FLOWERS AND FRUIT: A single flower grows at the end of a stem. The corolla is a funnel-shaped tube, 2 to 5 inches long, and gradually spreading to five creamy-white, petal-like lobes; the whole flower is about 1½ inches across.

FLOWERING: This species begins flowering about June and continues to September.

RANGE AND HABITAT: This species is native to Texas and northern Mexico. In Texas, it is found on dry, rocky slopes in the Trans-Pecos and in southern parts of the Edwards Plateau.

COMMENTS: One of four US desert-dwelling species; most of the approximately 175 species in the genus *Mandevilla* are native to the tropics of Central and South America. The exceptionally long tube and large lobes arranged in a pinwheel fashion make this species' flowers particularly notable and attractive.

Rhus virens

Evergreen Sumac

ANACARDIACEAE (SUMAC FAMILY)

PLANT AND LEAVES: Evergreen Sumac is a broadly branching shrub 4 to 8 feet and often just as widely spread. Contrary to the implication of its common name and even though its leaves stay green all winter, this is not an evergreen species. Rather, it is what botanists describe as tardily deciduous. That is, it does shed its leaves each year but, like Live Oaks, sheds them just as new leaves are emerging each spring. Leaves are alternate, odd-pinnately compound, 2 to 5½ inches long, with five to nine fleshy leaflets on stiff stems. The upper surface is dark green and shiny but turns red, yellow, or rusty in the fall.

FLOWERS AND FRUIT: Evergreen Sumac is dioecious; that is, each plant has only male or female flowers. Thus, only plants with female flowers bear fruits. The plant's inflorescences are 2 to 4 inches long and borne at the ends of stout branches. Flowers are fairly inconspicuous and have five white petals. When the plant's showy drupes mature in mid-September, they are dark red, broader than long, and covered with fine hairs, giving them the appearance of sugared candies.

FLOWERING: Evergreen sumac flowers during the summer following rains.

RANGE AND HABITAT: In Texas, this species is found at elevations of 2,000 to 7,500 feet on the Edwards Plateau and the Trans-Pecos ecoregions, on rocky slopes and bluffs. It is also native to southern New Mexico, southern Arizona, and Mexico.

COMMENTS: Evergreen Sumac is an excellent landscape plant in its native range. It will tolerate light shade but resents "wet feet," so it should be planted in well-drained soil if used in the garden.

Thelypodium wrightii

Wright's Thelypody, Wright's Stanleyella

BRASSICACEAE (MUSTARD FAMILY)
Synonym: *Stanleyella wrightii*

PLANT AND LEAVES: Wright's Thelypody is an imposing biennial herb occasionally reaching 7 feet or more in height and with many spreading branches. Basal leaves are large and lobed, sometimes nearly 1 foot in length. Stem leaves are mostly un-lobed and lance shaped and grow to about 6 inches in length.

FLOWERS AND FRUIT: Small white (or rarely lavender) flowers are clustered at the end of the main stem and each branch. In flower the plant is quite showy. Long, narrow siliques, to about 3 inches, follow below the flowers.

FLOWERING: Flowering may begin as early as March but mostly occurs from June to October.

RANGE AND HABITAT: Wright's Thelypody can be found growing in abundance on the rocky slopes of the Davis Mountains. It is at home in the mountains of west Texas, west and north to New Mexico, Arizona, Colorado, and Utah and across northern Mexico.

COMMENTS: The long seed capsules and narrow leaves swaying in the breeze give the plant a delicate, lacy effect. Often having a pyramidal shape, if the flower heads were of different colors, the plant would look like a decorated Christmas tree.

Zinnia acerosa

Desert Zinnia, Dwarf Zinnia

ASTERACEAE (ASTER FAMILY)
Synonym: *Zinnia pumila*

PLANT AND LEAVES: Desert Zinnia is a mounding perennial sub-shrub, growing 4 to 10 inches tall and about 12 inches across with numerous branches and many narrow leaves, ¾ to 1½ inches long.

FLOWERS AND FRUIT: Its showy, 1-inch-diameter flower heads virtually cover the entire plant on most specimens. The heads are borne on short peduncles and have four to seven white or off-white, rounded and partially reflexed ray flowers that are nearly as broad as long. The center cluster of about 10 to 12 yellow disc flowers protrudes noticeably above the heads.

FLOWERING: The long flowering season for Desert Zinnia extends from June to October.

RANGE AND HABITAT: Desert Zinnia calls rocky hillsides on lime-
stone soils in the Big Bend and the Guadalupe Mountains in
Texas home. Its native range extends on both sides of the
United States–Mexico border as far west as southern Arizona.

COMMENTS: Desert Zinnia has a long flowering period. That, along
with its low mounding habit and desert affinity, makes it a
great choice for xeric gardens in general and rock gardens in
particular. *Zinnia acerosa* is the only North American member
of its genus bearing white ray flowers.

Froelichia gracilis

Slender Snakecotton

AMARANTHACEAE (AMARANTH FAMILY)

PLANT AND LEAVES: Slender Snakecotton grows 1 to 3 feet high
usually with several stems branching from the base. Narrow
leaves, often with sinuate margins, are clustered mostly near
the base of the plant. These are covered with soft, minute hairs.

FLOWERS AND FRUIT: The flowers also are almost covered with
these woolly hairs, so that in some cases only the end of the

flower is visible, though this might not be apparent without a magnifying glass. The flowers have no petals, but the black-tipped white bracts give the flower head a black-and-white appearance. The flower head, or cluster, ½ to 1½ inches long, is sometimes attached directly to the stem but more often grows on a peduncle ½ to 5 inches long.

FLOWERING: Flowering occurs from July to September.

RANGE AND HABITAT: The original range of this species, once limited to the middle third of the United States and into Mexico, now extends to nearly all parts of the United States except the western Northern Tier states and the Great Basin. In Texas, Slender Snakecotton can be found in suitable habitat in all parts of the state. It prefers sandy soil and open places with low soil nutrient levels.

COMMENTS: It is commonly found in waste places and disturbance areas and is often considered a weed.

Eriogonum wrightii var. *wrightii*

Wright's Buckwheat, Wright's Bastard-sage

POLYGONACEAE (BUCKWHEAT FAMILY)

PLANT AND LEAVES: Wright's Buckwheat is a woody shrub, 2 to 3 feet tall, with several slender branches. The whole plant is gray, being covered by a felted mat of hairs. At ground level it is surrounded by a thick mat of white leaves about 1 inch long, but those along the stem are narrow and fairly inconspicuous.

FLOWERS AND FRUIT: The white, tubular flowers are in clusters,

usually attached directly to the stem along the upper 2 inches, though some are scattered lower on the branches. Each flower has reddish sepals and bracts and a red stripe on the underside of the petals. On the top of the petals, the stripe is green or greenish red. In cool weather the flowers turn reddish orange.

FLOWERING: Flowering begins in July and continues until October.

RANGE AND HABITAT: Wright's Buckwheat is abundant in west Texas, where it can be found in rocky limestone soils, deserts, and scrublands. Its native range extends west across the Sonora and the Mojave Deserts to California and south across most of northern Mexico.

COMMENTS: This species is often found in association with juniper and sagebrush. With 18 *Eriogonum* species occurring in Texas, one would think that we are buckwheat central. In truth, Texas is a bit of an outlier for this genus since there are nearly 225 species native to North America—mostly found in the western United States and Mexico. The only Texas endemics in the genus are Irion County Wild Buckwheat (*E. nealleyi*), Bush Wild Buckwheat (*E. suffruticosum*), and Granite Mountain Wild Buckwheat (*E. tenellum* var. *ramosissimum*).

Euphorbia bicolor
Snow-on-the-prairie
EUPHORBIACEAE (SPURGE FAMILY)

PLANT AND LEAVES: Snow-on-the-prairie is a taprooted herbaceous annual that grows 1 to 4 feet tall from a single stem and usually branches widely beginning about 1 foot above the ground. Its lower stem is often reddish in color. Its slender upper leaves, 2 to 4 inches long, are green and edged with a narrow band of white. The lower leaves are alternate, grow close to the stem, and lack the white edging. They are 1 to 1¼ inches long. When wounded, the plant exudes a milky sap.

FLOWERS AND FRUIT: The numerous, inconspicuous flowers grow in terminal clusters. They are white and have no petals but are surrounded by five white, rounded, petal-like bracts. Clusters group together to form larger clusters surrounded by numerous leaf-like bracts that are conspicuously white-margined.

The bracts are 1⅛ to 2⅛ inches long and about ¼ inch wide. The fruit is a hairy, three-lobed, rounded capsule about ¼ inch in diameter.

FLOWERING: This species flowers as early as July and as late as October.

RANGE AND HABITAT: The native range of this species is mostly limited to the eastern edge of central Texas and eastward to western Louisiana and southwestern Arkansas. It can be found on the Blackland Prairie ecoregion and areas with clay soils in that range.

COMMENTS: A very closely related and similar-looking species, Snow-on-the-mountain (*Euphorbia marginata*), has broader leaves, especially the bract-like leaves just below the inflorescences. Its lower leaves usually have white margins. Also, though there is some overlap of their ranges on Texas's coastal plain, Snow-on-the-mountain is mostly found on dry prairies west of US Interstate 35. Both species, especially their sap, can cause contact dermatitis for some people who handle them.

Rivina humilis

Pigeonberry, Rouge Plant, Baby-peppers

PHYTOLACCACEAE (POKEWEED FAMILY)

PLANT AND LEAVES: Pigeonberry is a branching perennial herb or subshrub growing from a persistent woody base to about 1 foot in height. Depending on its location, the plant may be erect or spreading and vine-like in habit. Leaf shape is variable, but most are delta shaped or lance shaped with some others

being variously elliptical. The leaf margins are mostly entire but often sinuous or contorted.

FLOWERS AND FRUIT: Inflorescences are mostly erect racemes, 1½ to 6 inches long, usually borne at the ends of branches but sometime arising from a near-terminal leaf axil. They are typically held above the plant canopy. The lovely, star-like flowers, 10 to 50 or more per raceme, are about ¼ inch across, have no petals, but feature white to pink sepals. The fruits are numerous, bright red, and almost translucent, often appearing on the lower part of the stem while the upper part is still in flower.

FLOWERING: In Texas, flowering occurs mostly from July to October. In more southern climes, this species may flower during any part of the year.

RANGE AND HABITAT: Pigeonberry is a shade-loving plant, commonly found growing under the drip line of Live Oak trees in central Texas, south to the Rio Grande, and west to the Trans-Pecos. Its native range extends east to Florida, west to Arizona, and south through Central and South America and the Caribbean.

COMMENTS: This species' berries are a choice food for many kinds of birds. Though very attractive when its bright berries are mature, a happy moment occurs when one gets down on the ground and closely examines Pigeonberry's delicate pink flowers.

Verbesina virginica
Frostweed, White Crownbeard
ASTERACEAE (ASTER FAMILY)

PLANT AND LEAVES: Frostweed is a perennial herb that dies to the ground each winter and produces one to several robust, winged stems as new growth each spring. The stems usually branch in the upper half of the plant. It typically grows to 3 to 5 feet tall but can exceed 8 feet in ideal conditions. Leaves are mostly largish, up to 8 inches long and 5 inches wide, giving the plant a rather coarse and weedy appearance.

FLOWERS AND FRUIT: Flower heads of Frostweed are small but are borne in clusters of several heads and those, in turn, are

borne in loose, corymb-like arrays that may contain hundreds of individual heads. Ray flowers are sparse, usually only three or four per head. Their laminae are white. Disc flowers usually number around 12 per head and are greenish white. The overall visual effect of the plant in flower is underwhelming.

FLOWERING: Flowering may occur as early as July, but most flowering takes place from September to November.

RANGE AND HABITAT: A common constituent of moist bottomlands and mesic uplands, especially under oaks, Frostweed is native to the eastern half of Texas. Its range extends to the lower Midwest, across the South, and as far north as Pennsylvania.

COMMENTS: Though Frostweed has a certain gawky charm, it would be largely unnotable if not for two characteristics. First, when in flower, it is a veritable insect magnet, attracting all manner of buggy creatures. But where it *really* makes its name and its fame is on cold winter mornings when delicate ribbons

of ice burst forth from its stems, decorating the woodlands as if scattered with Christmas gifts tied with pearlescent crystalline bows.

Spiranthes cernua
Nodding Ladies' Tresses Orchid
ORCHIDACEAE (ORCHID FAMILY)

PLANT AND LEAVES: Nodding Ladies' Tresses Orchid is a single-stemmed herbaceous perennial growing 1 to 2 feet in height. Two to six narrow, grass-like leaves are 8 to 10 inches long and grow from the base of the plant's stem.

FLOWERS AND FRUIT: The plant's upright stem is topped by an inflorescence about 6 inches long, bearing 20 to 50 or more flowers. The inflorescence is a narrow spike of three or four columns of pure white or creamy-white flowers spiraling gracefully around the central axis. The individual flowers, about ½ inch long, curve downward slightly; that is, "nodding." The lip is about ½ inch long with a flaring, crimped margin. Often confused with the closely related orchid, Fragrant Ladies' Tresses (*Spiranthes odorata*), this species usually has no fragrance at all.

FLOWERING: In Texas, flowering occurs from October to December. In the more northern parts of its range, it may begin flowering as early as August and be finished by September.

RANGE AND HABITAT: Found in bogs, meadows, and moist woods over most of east Texas, Nodding Ladies' Tresses Orchid's native range covers nearly all of North America east of the Rocky Mountains.

COMMENTS: There are 13 species of orchids in the genus *Spiranthes* that are native to Texas. Most are very similar in appearance when in flower and require very careful examination and consideration of habitat, flower time, and other clues to identify them correctly. Of the 20 genera of orchids native to Texas, only *Spiranthes* can be comfortably considered a common wildflower. Few people would guess that *Spiranthes* flowers are orchids, a fact that may help save them from collectors.

Yellow
Flowers

Lesquerella fendleri

Fendler's Bladderpod, Popweed

BRASSICACEAE (MUSTARD FAMILY)
Synonyms: *Physaria fendleri*, *Vesicaria fendleri*

PLANT AND LEAVES: Fendler's Bladderpod is a perennial herb growing from a woody base. It has several erect, mostly unbranched, silvery pubescent stems 6 to 8 inches high. All the leaves are narrow; some are toothed. The plant's basal leaves are linear or narrowly elliptical, 2 to 3 inches long. Those on the plant's stems are linear and 1 to 2 inches long.

FLOWERS AND FRUIT: The flowers are borne on loose racemes, with four yellow or orangish-yellow petals. The flowers are ¾ to 1 inch in diameter, among the showiest in its genus.

FLOWERING: This species flowers primarily from late January to March, but may flower at any time following rains.

RANGE AND HABITAT: Fendler's Bladderpod can be found throughout west Texas on limestone- or gypsum-based soils in rocky areas, arroyos, and desert scrublands. Its range extends across much of the Four Corners states and south into northern Mexico.

COMMENTS: Fifteen species of bladderpods grow in Texas, and all have pea-sized, bladder-like pods that pop when stepped on, hence the common name Popweed. Fendler's Bladderpod is one of the most abundant perennial mustards and is found throughout the Big Bend area, where it is browsed by deer when other vegetation is scarce.

Gelsemium sempervirens

Carolina Jessamine, Yellow Jessamine

LOGANIACEAE (PINKROOT FAMILY)

PLANT AND LEAVES: Carolina Jessamine is a high-climbing, many-branched, perennial woody vine with stems reaching 20 to 30 feet or more in length. The vine climbs by twining. Young stems often have a waxy bloom on their surfaces. The plant's evergreen leaves are about 3 inches long and 1 inch wide. They are arranged oppositely on short petioles.

FLOWERS AND FRUIT: Two to six yellow, fragrant flowers, 1 to 1½ inches long and 1 inch across, grow from the leaf axils. They are funnel shaped and deeply five lobed at the opening. The

fruit is a small, flattened, oval capsule, ½ to ¾ inch long that, when mature and dry, splits open and releases numerous thin, winged seeds that are scattered by the wind.

FLOWERING: Flowering may begin as early as December but often by January and continuing to April.

RANGE AND HABITAT: Carolina Jessamine is often found in rich, sandy bottomland on woodland margins in southeast Texas. It is common in similar habitat in Arkansas and across the Gulf Coast and Atlantic Coast states to Virginia.

COMMENTS: It is common to see Carolina Jessamine climbing to the tops of pine trees in east Texas, giving the appearance, from a distance, that the tree is in flower. All parts of Carolina Jessamine are very poisonous if ingested, and the sap of the plant causes contact dermatitis for some people.

Tetraneuris scaposa

Four-nerved Daisy, Hymenoxys

ASTERACEAE (ASTER FAMILY)
Synonym: *Hymenoxys scaposa*

PLANT AND LEAVES: Four-nerved Daisy is an herbaceous perennial producing a woody underground caudex from which 50 or more aboveground stems may emerge. Stems may reach about 16 inches in height but are usually less than 1 foot tall. They bear a cluster of stiff, rough, silvery-green, oblanceolate leaves crowded around the base from which grow one to many leafless flower peduncles with one flower head on each.

FLOWERS AND FRUIT: The radiate flower head is about 1½ inches across with 12 or more golden- to butter-yellow ray flowers, each with three small teeth and four purple veins beneath that converge at the tip. The ray flowers often reflex, persist, and turn papery white with age. The flower head's center, composed of disc flowers, is orange to gold in color.

FLOWERING: Four-nerved Daisy may flower year-round; most notable flower displays occur from March to June.

RANGE AND HABITAT: Common on rocky, alkaline soils on the Rio Grande plains, in the Hill Country, and north to the Panhandle.

Its range includes most of the southwestern Great Plains and northeastern Mexico.

COMMENTS: Four-nerved Daisy will flower any time conditions are suitable, and it is often the only native species found flowering in January in central Texas. Four-nerved Daisy gets its name from the four purple veins visible on the underside of the plant's ray flowers.

Vachellia farnesiana

Huisache, Sweet Acacia

FABACEAE (PEA FAMILY)

Synonyms: *Acacia farnesiana*, *Acacia smallii*

PLANT AND LEAVES: Huisache is a perennial, woody shrub or tree. Plants growing along the coast are mostly multistemmed shrubs, but in south Texas arroyos and creek bottoms it makes a spreading tree 20 to 30 feet tall. The plant's branches are armed with pairs of whitish needle-like thorns, up to 2 inches long, at each leaf node. The leaves are bipinnate; that is, they are twice-divided compound leaves. Leaves are 1 to 3 inches long with a gland about midway of the petiole. Each leaf has two to six pairs of pinnae, each bearing 10 to 20 pairs of small, oblong leaflets. The leaves remain green on the tree until a hard frost.

FLOWERS AND FRUIT: The plant's inflorescences are spherical heads of many orange or yellow flowers, about ½ inch in diameter, and borne in clusters from the leaf axils along the plant's stems. Each flower's petals are very short and almost concealed by the many stamens, which are the same color. The flowers are sweetly scented and perfume the air around them. The fruit is a fat legume, 1 to 3 inches long, dark brown or black at maturity.

FLOWERING: Flowering occurs in February and March. In some years, the plant may flower as late as April if a freeze has killed its early buds.

RANGE AND HABITAT: Huisache is common across all of south Texas to the Big Bend. It is also native to Louisiana, Florida, Arizona, and southern California in the United States. Its native range extends south throughout much of Latin America.

COMMENTS: The flowers are quite fragrant and are worked heavily by honeybees, which make excellent honey from its nectar.

Mahonia trifoliolata

Agarita

BERBERIDACEAE (BARBERRY FAMILY)

Synonym: *Berberis trifoliolata*

PLANT AND LEAVES: Agarita is an evergreen, well-branched shrub, usually 3 to 5 feet tall and about as broad, with stiff, spiny, grayish-green or bluish holly-like leaves. They are alternate, 2 to 4 inches long, divided into three leaflets that have three to seven lobes ending in sharp spines.

FLOWERS AND FRUIT: In late winter, it produces large numbers of flowers borne in loose clusters in the plant's upper leaf axils. The flowers, which emit a thickly sweet fragrance reminiscent of saffron, have six reddish-tinged yellow sepals and six golden-yellow petals that form a cup shape around the greenish-yellow stamens and pistils. The lustrous orange-red fruit, often coated in a waxy bloom, is a pea-sized berry.

FLOWERING: Flowering occurs mostly in February and early March but may continue into April. The plant's fruits mature in June.

RANGE AND HABITAT: Agarita grows on dry, stony soil, often in partial shade, over most of the western half of Texas. It also can be found in southern New Mexico, southern Arizona, and in Mexico.

COMMENTS: Agarita flowers are an important source of nectar for bees, and as evidenced by their common occurrence in fencer-ows, the berries are an important food for birds. The plant's roots and stems furnished an excellent yellow dye to early pioneers. Though difficult to collect, the copiously produced fruit is tasty and can be processed to make very fine jelly.

Ranunculus macranthus

Large Buttercup,
Showy Buttercup

RANUNCULACEAE (BUTTERCUP FAMILY)

PLANT AND LEAVES: Large Buttercup is a perennial herb growing 4 to 24 inches tall with several erect stems and a few hairy branches near the top. Leaves have five to seven lobes and are supported on long stalks that clasp the stem. The leaves grow smaller and fewer as they advance upward.

FLOWERS AND FRUIT: The waxy, lemon- or golden-yellow flowers, up to 2 inches across, have 8 to 18 petals, 3 to 5 sepals, many

yellow to yellow-green stamens, and many green pistils. A large, rounded cluster of beaked achenes develops on the flower's receptacle following flowering.

FLOWERING: Large Buttercup may begin flowering in late February but invariably by early March and is usually finished flowering by mid to late April.

RANGE AND HABITAT: Grows in damp soil in central Texas, scattered places in the Trans-Pecos, and along the Rio Grande. A disjunct population grows on moist soils in the mountains of eastern Arizona and continues south through most of the highlands of western and central Mexico.

COMMENTS: Whether it is colloquially called Large Buttercup or Showy Buttercup, *Ranunculus macranthus* is aptly named; it is the largest-flowered *Ranunculus* species in North America. Beautiful when flowering in early spring, it is an excellent landscape plant for areas with moist soils.

Corydalis curvisiliqua
Scrambled Eggs, Golden Smoke, Curvepod
FUMARIACEAE (FUMITORY FAMILY)

PLANT AND LEAVES: Scrambled Eggs is a winter annual producing several erect stems from a fleshy root. It grows 6 to 16 inches high. Its glaucous, blue-green leaves cut deeply into many sections, giving them a lacy or fern-like appearance.

FLOWERS AND FRUIT: Inflorescences are borne at the ends of the stems and have 5 to 15 flowers. The flowers are golden yellow, about 1 inch long, with four petals. The outer two petals enclose the inner two. One petal has a short, straight, saclike spur at the base. The fruit is a curved, upright capsule about 1½ inches long and resembling a green bean.

FLOWERING: A sunny harbinger of spring, Scrambled Eggs is one of our earliest flowering plants. It appears as early as February and may continue to flower until May.

RANGE AND HABITAT: Scrambled Eggs are found on disturbed soils throughout Texas with the exception of the Pineywoods and the Rio Grande Valley. Its native range also covers most of the Great Plains, the southern Rockies, and the Great Basin

COMMENTS: Three other species of this genus may be found in Texas. Golden Corydalis (*C. aurea*) is North America's most common species but in Texas is found mostly in the Trans-Pecos. Mealy Fumewort (*C. crystallina*) is native to northeast Texas and the southeastern Great Plains. Smallflower Fume-wort (*C. micrantha*) is a native of Texas's coastal plain.

Packera tampicana

Yellowtop, Great Plains Ragwort

ASTERACEAE (ASTER FAMILY)

Synonyms: *Senecio greggii*, *Senecio imparipinnatus*, *Senecio tampicanus*

PLANT AND LEAVES: Yellowtop is a winter annual with a basal rosette developing during fall and winter and producing one to several flowering stems in late winter that grow 12 to 18 inches high. Delicate, alternate leaves are usually attached directly to the stem and often eared or clasping. They are pinnately lobed, each leaflet unevenly and roundly lobed.

FLOWERS AND FRUIT: The plants are branched near the top, with all branches forming a more or less flat top with many flower heads on each short stem. The plant's flower heads are approximately ¾ inch across with 8 to 13 bright yellow ray flowers each and 50 to 100 tiny orange-yellow disc flowers crowded in the central disc.

FLOWERING: Yellowtop flowers from February to June.

RANGE AND HABITAT: Yellowtop is usually found in open locations on disturbed soils throughout the southern Great Plains into Mexico and grows in most regions of Texas. It is common on roadsides, along railroad tracks, and on power line cuts.

COMMENTS: This species prefers drier, sunnier locations than its close relative, Butterweed (*Packera glabella*). It often occurs in large stands covering many acres.

Ranunculus hispidus var. *nitidus*

Swamp Buttercup

RANUNCULACEAE (BUTTERCUP FAMILY)
Synonyms: *Ranunculus carolinianus*, *Ranunculus septentrionalis*

PLANT AND LEAVES: Swamp Buttercup is a perennial herb growing from slender roots and spreading by stolons, which root at the nodes, that may extend up to 20 feet long, a feature that is

helpful in distinguishing it from the similar botanical variety, Rough Buttercup (*Ranunculus hispidus* var. *hispidus*), which does not form stolons. Spreading by stolons, Swamp Buttercup quickly forms large colonies. The large leaves are divided into three leaflets, 1 to 3 inches long and wide, with each leaflet having three toothed lobes.

FLOWERS AND FRUIT: The species' flowers have five lemon- or butter-yellow petals that are ½ inch long, broadest near the tip, and with a shiny surface as though they had been waxed. The flowers' five sepals bend backward. After flowering, a cluster of broad, flat achenes with hooked beaks develop on the flower's receptacle.

FLOWERING: Most flowering occurs during March and April but may begin as early as February and continue until July depending on environmental conditions.

RANGE AND HABITAT: Swamp Buttercup lives in continuously wet soil along streams and in ditches in southeast Texas and east across the entire eastern half of North America except New England and the Canadian Maritime provinces.

COMMENTS: There are about 75 species of *Ranunculus* native to the United States and Canada, not including the many subspecies and varieties. Texas can claim about 20 species.

Opuntia humifusa
Low Pricklypear, Eastern Pricklypear, Devil's-tongue
CACTACEAE (CACTUS FAMILY)

PLANT AND LEAVES: Low Pricklypear seldom grows higher than 14 inches, as the stems (pads) tend to lie on the ground. Stem segments are sometimes nearly circular but average about 6 inches long and 4 inches wide. During times of drought stress, the stems' surfaces can become significantly wrinkled. Areoles have numerous glochids but often bear no spines. When present, there may be one to three whitish spines to about 2 inches in length.

FLOWERS AND FRUIT: The flowers are quite attractive, 2 to 5 inches

across, pale yellow to orange yellow or orange yellow with red centers. Anthers are pale yellow, and the stigma is white. Fruits are usually shaped like eggs or fat spindles and rose to maroon to brownish red in color.

FLOWERING: Flowering may begin as early as February and continue until August.

RANGE AND HABITAT: Low Pricklypear is common in sandy grassland, dunes, and rocky barrens across the eastern half of Texas. It can be found in similar habitats in nearly all the states east of the Rocky Mountains and in Ontario, Canada.

COMMENTS: This species has the largest native range of all cacti in the United States.

Baptisia bracteata var. *leucophaea*

Cream Wild Indigo, Plains Wild Indigo

FABACEAE (PEA FAMILY)
Synonym: *Baptisia leucophaea*

PLANT AND LEAVES: Cream Wild Indigo is an herbaceous plant that grows from a widely branched central stem, 12 to 18 inches tall and to about 3 feet across. It arises in early spring each year from an extensive perennial rootstock. The plant's foliage

usually has a blue-green hue. The leaves are alternate, 1½ to 4 inches long, divided into three distinct leaflets, the stipules (leaf-like structures that grow where the leaf is attached to the stem) are so large that they are sometimes mistaken for leaves.

FLOWERS AND FRUIT: This species' long, pendulous inflorescences are showy and when growing along a roadside easily grab the passing traveler's attention. Its rather large, pale-yellow or creamy-white flowers grow in racemes on the upper 10 to 18 inches of the stem, bending toward and often touching the ground. The fruit is a legume, 1 to 2 inches long, and contains 10 to 20 seeds.

FLOWERING: In Texas, Cream Wild Indigo flowers in March and April.

RANGE AND HABITAT: This species can be found throughout the eastern third of the state in open woodlands and pastures and along roadsides. Its native range extends north through the Great Plains.

COMMENTS: This is one of our loveliest and most striking spring wildflowers. Common on east Texas roadsides, it is a "wow, what is that?" species.

Sarracenia alata

Yellow Pitcherplant, Yellow Trumpets

SARRACENIACEAE (PITCHERPLANT FAMILY)

PLANT AND LEAVES: Yellow Pitcherplant is an insectivorous perennial herb. It has one large leaf that forms a tube, larger at the top and sloping toward the base. The upper part of the leaf bends over the opening, as if to protect the tube. The inner surface of the leaf is covered thickly with tiny hairs—all pointing downward—that would make velvet seem rough by comparison. The top part of the leaf has many small glands that exude insect-attracting nectar. When unsuspecting creatures arrive for a meal and touch the side of the tube, they literally hit the skids and go to the bottom, where the plant secretes enzymes that dissolves the soft parts of their bodies and absorbs them.

FLOWERS AND FRUIT: The flowers are yellowish green to light orange and about 1½ inches across. They hang their heads and look directly at the ground. One has to turn their faces up to see what they look like, but they are attractive nonetheless. The flowers have three bracts, five sepals, and five petals. The flower's style has an extraordinary shape, like an umbrella upside down, with a stigma beneath each of the five angles.

FLOWERING: Flowering occurs in March and April.

RANGE AND HABITAT: Yellow Pitcherplant is at home in southeast Texas in damp, boggy areas and in similar habitat as far east as Alabama.

COMMENTS: The Yellow Pitcherplant is one of four species of insectivorous plants in Texas getting part of its food from insects it is able to trap and digest. We have cut their tubular leaves open and counted the exoskeletons of trapped insects, the number ranging from 28 to 45; the odor of the contents was distinctly unpleasant.

Echinocereus dasyacanthus

Texas Rainbow Cactus, Spiny Hedgehog Cactus

CACTACEAE (CACTUS FAMILY)

Synonyms: *Echinocereus ctenoides*, *Echinocereus pectinatus* var. *dasyancanthus*, *Echinocereus pectinatus* var. *neomexicanus*

PLANT AND LEAVES: The Texas Rainbow Cactus has an oval shape when young but soon becomes cylindrical and grows to 15 inches or so in height and about 4 inches in diameter. The stems commonly remain single, but old plants sometimes

branch and form several heads. Each head has 12 to 21 narrow, undulate ribs. Fifteen to 25 spines grow out of the closely spaced areoles, spreading widely and interlacing with spines of other areoles.

FLOWERS AND FRUIT: Flowers are borne on spiny stalks arising near the top of the stem and are about 3 inches in diameter. Tepals may be yellow, orange, or magenta with the outer tepals having a pink central stripe. The tepals are quite long and pointed. Outer tepals are sometimes tinged with magenta on the outside, and inner tepals are green basally. Stamens are cream colored and pistils are green. The fruits are maroon-colored tunas.

FLOWERING: Flowering occurs from March to May. The tunas ripen June to August.

RANGE AND HABITAT: Texas Rainbow Cactus is native to Texas's Trans-Pecos ecoregion west to southeastern Arizona and south to the Mexican states of Chihuahua and Coahuila.

COMMENTS: The multiplicity of flower colors this species displays make it a delight to see but a bit of a head-scratcher for new cactus enthusiasts to identify.

Packera glabella
Butterweed, Cressleaf Groundsel
ASTERACEAE (ASTER FAMILY)
Synonyms: *Senecio glabellus*, *Senecio lobatus*

PLANT AND LEAVES: Butterweed is an herbaceous winter annual with a single striated, often purplish stem growing 1 to 3 feet tall from a rosette of leaves at the base and branching near the top. The alternate leaves are lobed and toothed, ¾ to 2¾ inches long. Their resemblance to the leaves of Garden Cress (*Lepidium sativum*) and Watercress (*Nasturtium officinale*) are the origin of one of its common names, Cressleaf Groundsel.

FLOWERS AND FRUIT: The flower heads are held in loose arrays of 10 to 30 heads. Each flower head is about 1 inch across, with about 10 butter-yellow ray flowers and about 40 tiny orange-yellow disc flowers.

FLOWERING: Butterweed flowers mostly in March but may continue until May.

RANGE AND HABITAT: Native to the Great Plains as far north as South Dakota and eastward across the Mississippi and Ohio River Valleys and throughout the South. In Texas, it is found in moist woodlands, along forest edges, on roadsides, and in fallow fields in the eastern third of the state.

COMMENTS: Butterweed is an attractive plant, especially when it blankets many acres with the sun shining across the plants. Its cress-like foliage is particularly interesting when examining the plant close up.

Senecio ampullaceus

Texas Groundsel, Texas Ragwort

ASTERACEAE (ASTER FAMILY)

PLANT AND LEAVES: Texas Groundsel is an herbaceous winter annual reaching 1 to 2½ feet tall. Leaves are 1 to 3 inches long, toothed to nearly smooth edged with one main vein down the center. The leaf petioles are winged and clasp the stem.

FLOWERS AND FRUIT: The yellow flower heads are borne on stems growing out of the leaf axils near the top of the plant, with two to four flower heads per stem, 1 to 1¼ inches across. There are seven to nine ray flowers per flower head. This and all other species of *Senecio* have narrow, yellow ray flowers, rounded on the end, and yellow disc flowers. Ray flowers are often turned backward, exposing the disc flowers completely.

FLOWERING: The flowering season for Texas Groundsel begins in March and continues to May.

RANGE AND HABITAT: Open places throughout east and south-central Texas.

COMMENTS: The genus *Senecio* is one of the largest genera of flowering plants, with at least eight species occurring in Texas. Many more species once classified in *Senecio* are now placed in the closely related genus *Packera*. The various species can be difficult to separate, as there are many different sizes and shapes of leaves and other minute differences among them. Every part of the state has one or more species of *Senecio*. Common pasture weeds, this and other species of *Senecio* and *Packera* are very toxic to livestock.

Amblyolepis setigera

Huisache Daisy

ASTERACEAE (ASTER FAMILY)

Synonym: *Helenium setigerum*

PLANT AND LEAVES: The annual herbaceous species, Huisache Daisy, is so called because it often grows in thick stands under Huisache trees (*Vachellia farnesiana*) and other chaparral bushes, forming an almost solid blanket of gold. It grows 6 to 15 inches tall, with several rough, hairy branches in the upper part. Leaves are without petioles, the upper ones having lobes at the base that extend almost completely around the stem.

FLOWERS AND FRUIT: The large, yellow flower heads, up to 2 inches across, are borne at the ends of long stems that are bare on the upper portion. The yellow to orange-yellow center is dome shaped, and its disc flowers are velvety. The 8 to 12 ray flowers are up to 1 inch long with three or four lobes at the end. Often the lobed portion is noticeably lighter than the rest.

FLOWERING: Huisache Daisy begins flowering heavily in March and April, with dwindling flowering until June.

RANGE AND HABITAT: Huisache Daisy's native range extends from Texas into northeastern Mexico. In Texas, it can be found in the southwestern half of the state.

Echinocereus viridiflorus var. *cylindricus*

Green-flowered Hedgehog Cactus, Nylon Hedgehog Cactus

CACTACEAE (CACTUS FAMILY)

Synonyms: *Cereus viridiflorus* var. *cylindricus*, *Echinocereus chloranthus* var. *cylindricus*, *Echinocereus viridiflorus* ssp. *cylindricus*

PLANT AND LEAVES: The Green-flowered Hedgehog Cactus usually grows as a single stem, rarely in clusters or mounds, although it is not unusual for colonies of plants to grow in close proximity to one another. The plant's stems are sometimes as much as 3 inches in diameter and 8 inches tall. The stems have about

10 to 20 ribs studded with closely spaced areoles that are each armed with 20 to 30 spines of various colors, often purple or purple tinged, which give the plant a rosy hue.

FLOWERS AND FRUIT: The flowers are about 1 inch long and 1 inch broad, smaller than others in this genus. They vary from yellowish green to brownish and grow well down on the sides, often forming a band around the middle. The fruit is green or purple, small, and spiny, ripening a couple of months after flowering.

FLOWERING: Flowering may begin in March and continue until June, though most flowering occurs during April and May. Flowering outside peak times is dependent on the occurrence of optimal moisture and temperature conditions.

RANGE AND HABITAT: Native to Texas's Trans-Pecos ecoregion, southern New Mexico, and northeastern Mexico in desert scrubland and grasslands on soils of volcanic origin.

COMMENTS: The closely related variety, the Davis' Hedgehog Cactus (*Echinocereus viridiflorus* var. *davisii*), is a Big Bend endemic and a federally listed endangered species. Small and very rare, it grows only on soils of novaculite (a type of quartz) origin and should never be disturbed in its native habitat.

Helenium drummondii
Fringed Sneezeweed
ASTERACEAE (ASTER FAMILY)

PLANT AND LEAVES: Fringed Sneezeweed is an herbaceous perennial growing to about 2 feet in height. Stems are slender and unbranched. Leaves are alternate, thin, and long, becoming mere bracts on the upper half of the plant. The leaves extend down opposite sides of the stem below their point of attachment, making the stems appear winged.

FLOWERS AND FRUIT: There is usually one flower head at the end of each stem with 10 to 16 butter-yellow ray flowers, ¾ to 1 inch long and toothed on the end. The center is composed of golden-yellow disc flowers and is almost spherical.

FLOWERING: Flowering occurs from March to June.

RANGE AND HABITAT: The rather limited native range of this species is centered on the southern Texas–Louisiana border and does not extend outside the two states. In Texas, its range does not go farther west than Houston and no farther north than Lufkin. *Helenium drummondii* grows in moist soils in swamps, wet pine forests, and on pond margins.

COMMENTS: We found Fringed Sneezeweed gracing the edge of a swampy area near Sour Lake in April. The large flower heads at the end of long, leafless stems attract the attention they deserve.

Lindheimera texana

Texas Yellowstar, Texas Star, Lindheimer Daisy

ASTERACEAE (ASTER FAMILY)

PLANT AND LEAVES: Texas Yellowstar is an herbaceous winter annual. Plants are typically 6 to 24 inches tall and widely branched, but very small specimens with a single flower are often seen as well as very large, mounded plants bearing hundreds of flower heads. Stems and branches are hairy. The lower leaves are alternate and coarsely toothed, but the upper ones are opposite and smooth on the edges, 2 to 2½ inches long.

FLOWERS AND FRUIT: There are one to several flower heads in a cluster at the end of each stem. Each cheery flower head usually has five butter-yellow ray flowers, each with two prominent veins and indented at the tip. A few yellowish or brown disc flowers make up the smallish center of the flower head. Flower heads are 1 to 1¼ inches across.

FLOWERING: Flowering begins in March and continues into June.

RANGE AND HABITAT: Primarily a Texas species, where it inhabits woods and prairies with well-drained soils in the central third of the state, Texas Yellowstar also can be found in Oklahoma, Arkansas, Louisiana, and in northern Mexico.

COMMENTS: *Lindheimera texana* was named in honor of Ferdinand Jacob Lindheimer, a nineteenth-century German-born naturalist and plant collector commonly referred to as the "Father of Texas Botany" for his many plant discoveries.

Opuntia engelmannii var. *lindheimeri*
Texas Pricklypear, Lindheimer's Pricklypear
CACTACEAE (CACTUS FAMILY)
Synonym: *Opuntia lindheimeri*

PLANT AND LEAVES: Texas Pricklypear often grows to 5 feet tall. It may be erect or spreading, with a more or less definite trunk. The stem segments (commonly called pads) are green to blue green, round to oval, 4 to 10 inches long. Areoles are 1½ to 2½ inches apart and bear one to six stiff spines and numerous glochids. Spines range in length from ½ to about 3 inches long, sometimes to 4½ inches. They are mostly white or yellowish, occasionally reddish basally and aging dark gray.

FLOWERS AND FRUIT: The flowers, 2 to 5 inches across, are often crowded on the edge of the pad. They have several greenish-yellow sepal-like outer tepals. Inner tepals age from butter yellow to yellow orange to red, often with the whole range of colors on one plant. Stamens are creamy white or yellowish, and the stigma is green. The fruits, commonly referred to as tunas, are egg shaped, up to 3 inches in length, and maroon when mature.

FLOWERING: Flowering begins in March and may continue until June, with most taking place during April and May.

RANGE AND HABITAT: Texas Pricklypear is native to xeric areas or on sandy or gravelly soils in central, south, and west Texas, coastal Texas and Louisiana, and southern New Mexico.

COMMENTS: This and other *Opuntia* species have been exported to Africa and South America for use as cattle fodder and living fences.

Opuntia macrocentra

Purple Pricklypear, Black-spined Pricklypear

CACTACEAE (CACTUS FAMILY)
Synonym: *Opuntia violacea*

PLANT AND LEAVES: The stems of the Purple Pricklypear are upright or spreading, 2 to 3 feet tall but without a trunk-like main stem. The stem sections (pads) are 4 to 8 inches long and usually about ½ inch thick. Sometimes the stems are green but more often they are pinkish purplish overall, especially in the winter and during dry, hot summers. The areoles are about ½ inch apart on small plants but up to 1¼ inches apart on large ones. They are arranged in diagonal lines across the stem segment. There are as few as 1 or 2 or as many as 15 spines per areole—the longest, often russet or black in color, sometimes reaching 4½ inches.

FLOWERS AND FRUIT: This cactus presents a spectacular sight in April, their peak flowering period, with as many as 65 to 70 large flowers on one plant. The flowers are about 3 inches in

diameter with yellow or orangish-yellow tepals that are red basally. Anthers, filaments, and styles are creamy yellow; the stigma is green. The fruit is ¾ to 1½ inches long, round to oval, becoming bright red or orange when ripe.

FLOWERING: Flowering begins as early as March and may continue until June.

RANGE AND HABITAT: In Texas, Purple Pricklypear commonly is found from the Big Bend area, northwest through the Davis Mountains, to the Van Horn area. Its range extends westward across southern New Mexico and southern and eastern Arizona. It is also native to northeastern Mexican states.

COMMENTS: The unusual color of this cactus makes it attractive even when not in flower.

Pyrrhopappus carolinianus

Texas Dandelion, False Dandelion

ASTERACEAE (ASTER FAMILY)

PLANT AND LEAVES: Texas Dandelion, a taprooted annual plant, forms one to several erect stems, 6 to 20 inches long. When broken, its stems and leaves exude a milky sap. Large, deeply lobed or deeply dentate leaves, 2 to 6 inches long, grow from the base of the plant on petioles half as long as the leaves themselves. The few upper leaves are alternate, much smaller, with little dentation.

FLOWERS AND FRUIT: Flower heads are bright lemon yellow and 1 to 1½ inches across. The flower heads of plants in the aster family are called capitula (singular: capitulum). The capitula of Texas Dandelion are borne singly or from two to six in loose arrays. The capitulum of this genus is known as a ligulate head and is composed of only ray flowers.

FLOWERING: The flowering season for Texas Dandelion lasts from March to June.

RANGE AND HABITAT: Texas Dandelion is common in the eastern half of Texas. Its range extends northward to Nebraska, east to Pennsylvania, and south to Florida. It is often found growing in pastures and along roadsides.

COMMENTS: Much like its cousin the introduced weed Common Dandelion (*Taraxacum officinale*), Texas Dandelion also quite happily makes its home in lawns.

Vachellia rigidula

Blackbrush Acacia

FABACEAE (PEA FAMILY)
Synonym: *Acacia rigidula*

PLANT AND LEAVES: Blackbrush Acacia is a stiff, spiny shrub growing 5 to 20 feet high, usually with many stems from the base.
Pairs of needle-like spines, 1 to 2 inches long, arise from the
leaf nodes. This species often forms impenetrable thickets.
The leaves are bipinnately compound, usually having one pair
or occasionally two pairs of compound pinnae, each ⅜ to 1 inch
long, and each bearing three to six pairs of oblong leaflets, ¼ to
⅝ inch long.

FLOWERS AND FRUIT: The flowers appear before the leaves or as
they are developing. Flowers are creamy white to light yellow,
fragrant, in cylindrical clusters, 1 to 3 inches long, growing at
the end of the stems. Individual flowers are very small, with
four or five petals and many stamens, which are the most
prominent part of the flower. The fruit is a narrow legume
about 3 inches long and curved, reddish brown or blackish
when mature.

FLOWERING: Flowering may begin as early as February, usually com-
mencing in March or April and continuing until May or June.

RANGE AND HABITAT: Blackbrush Acacia is common across the South Texas Plains ecoregion, where it grows on dry limestone soils on rocky slopes and in ravines and canyons. Its range extends to the Big Bend and south into east-central Mexico.

COMMENTS: The copious nectar-laden flowers produced by this species are very attractive to honeybees. The bees make an excellent honey from the gathered nectar. The sweet fragrance of the flowers can be detected as one drives the highways of south Texas.

Calylophus berlandieri ssp. *pinifolius*

Pineleaf Squarebud Primrose, Pineleaf Sundrops

ONAGRACEAE (EVENING-PRIMROSE FAMILY)
Synonym: *Calylophus drummondianus*

PLANT AND LEAVES: Pineleaf Squarebud Primrose is a perennial plant growing from a perennial root. It may have one or many stems up to 20 inches long, erect or tending to lie on the ground and forming a loose mound up to 3 feet in diameter. The leaves are usually dark green, very narrow, with sharp-toothed margins, and from 1 to 3 inches long.

FLOWERS AND FRUIT: The floral tube is about ⅗ inch long, flaring out into four yellow, rounded petals up to 1 inch long. The

flowers' eight stamen ring the edges of the floral tube, and the yellow anthers are held above the petals. A single pistil rises from the center of the flower with a rather large, usually yellow, spherical stigma held higher than the anthers. The flowers of most plants are yellow in all their parts. However, in some populations of plants, the floral tube is black. In others, the stigma is black. In others still, both the floral tube and the stigma are black.

FLOWERING: Flowering occurs from as early as late March to early July.

RANGE AND HABITAT: Pineleaf Squarebud Primrose occurs on sandy or rocky soils on the Edwards Plateau and in north-central Texas. Its native range extends into central Oklahoma and south into northern Mexico.

COMMENTS: The flowers of the small portion of plants with black floral tubes and stigmas are dramatic and arresting. They are guaranteed to grab your attention. Since no other *Calylophus* species has this feature, they're also very easy to identify.

Coreopsis lanceolata
Lanceleaf Coreopsis, Lanceleaf Tickseed
ASTERACEAE (ASTER FAMILY)

PLANT AND LEAVES: Lanceleaf Coreopsis is an herbaceous perennial that grows to 1 to 2 feet in height when flowering. It grows in small clumps and may form extensive colonies. Leaves are 3 to 4 inches long, mostly opposite, but sometimes alternate near the top where the leaves are fewer. Some of the leaves are deeply cut, almost forming three leaflets. The comparatively large leaves, stout stems, and large flower heads make this species appear more substantial than other tickseeds.

FLOWERS AND FRUIT: The orange-yellow center of disc flowers stands out distinctly from the gold-colored ray flowers, which appear to be attached just below them. Ray flowers are four lobed with the two inner lobes longer than the outer.

FLOWERING: This species can be seen blanketing prairies and roadsides from March to July.

RANGE AND HABITAT: Lanceleaf Coreopsis is a widespread species, native in the United States to all areas east of the Rocky Mountains except some parts of the northern Great Plains. It has been widely planted and has naturalized in other parts of the country. It can be found in great swaths of golden yellow on roadsides in the eastern third of Texas.

COMMENTS: The showiness of this species and its ease of cultivation have made it a garden favorite. A number of cultivars can be found in horticulture.

Grusonia grahamii

Graham's Dog Cactus, Graham's Club Cholla

CACTACEAE (CACTUS FAMILY)
Synonym: *Opuntia grahamii*

PLANT AND LEAVES: A mature Graham's Dog Cactus appears to be a pile of spines. It has many cylindrical branches and forms mounds to about 8 inches in height. The last joint on the branches is erect and widest near the top, about 2 inches long

or less. It has rough, wart-like structures on the joints, giving the plant a rough, dull appearance. Areoles top narrow tubercles and are dressed in short white or yellowish hairs and bear 5 to 15 spines, up to 2 inches in length, that range in color from white to reddish brown. Areoles on older stems, especially, are usually also well armed with numerous yellowish glochids.

FLOWERS AND FRUIT: The small (to about 2 inches in diameter) but attractive lemon-yellow flowers open in the early afternoon. Yellow anthers are borne on filaments that may be greenish yellow or maroon. The stigma is usually creamy white or pale yellow. Tunas are more or less cylindrical and yellow when mature. They are about 1¼ inches long and also bear glochids but no spines.

FLOWERING: Flowering may occur any time between March and July.

RANGE AND HABITAT: Graham's Dog Cactus can be found on sandy or gravelly soils of the Chihuahuan Desert in the Texas Trans-Pecos, southern New Mexico, and northern Mexico.

COMMENTS: The joints of this plant, like those of other chollas, break off easily and hang on to anything that barely touches them.

Lithospermum incisum
Fringed Puccoon, Narrowleaf Gromwell, Golden Puccoon

BORAGINACEAE (BORAGE FAMILY)

PLANT AND LEAVES: Fringed Puccoon is a perennial, taprooted, widely branching herb dying to the ground each winter and growing from a woody caudex early each spring. It is usually rather sprawling, about 6 to 8 inches tall and sometimes 18 inches across. Stems and leaves are quite hairy, with hairs mostly lying flat against the plant's surface. The leaves at the base of the plant can be 4 inches long or more and up to ½ inch wide. The stem leaves are alternate, 1 to 2½ inches long, narrow but larger near the base with their margins rolled under.

FLOWERS AND FRUIT: Spring flowers are showy and borne in loose

clusters at the ends of the stems. They are trumpet shaped, about 1½ inches long, usually golden or sometimes pale lemon yellow, and with five petal-like lobes that open to about ¾ inch across and have crinkled and fringed margins. Interestingly, these flowers are sterile. The species' fertile flowers are produced in the summer. These flowers are minute, hidden within leafy bracts, and do not open. They are self-fertile; that is, their pistils receive pollen from their own stamens and are not cross-pollinated with other plants.

FLOWERING: Flowering begins in March and continues until July.

RANGE AND HABITAT: Fringed Puccoon, preferring sandy soils, is widespread and common on prairies, roadsides, and open woodlands throughout Texas with the exception of the Pineywoods region, where it is absent. Its range is vast and extends from the eastern Great Plains through the Rocky Mountain states and also north into Canada and south into Mexico.

COMMENTS: In Texas, Fringed Puccoon is the most common and widespread of the 12 *Lithospermum* species native to the state.

Opuntia rufida
Blind Pricklypear
CACTACEAE (CACTUS FAMILY)

PLANT AND LEAVES: Blind Pricklypear has an obvious trunk, with many branches, and grows to 5 feet tall, often forming a rounded clump. Its joints are circular and dull gray green. Stem segments (pads) are large and roundish, to about 10 inches long and 7 inches wide. They are on the thin side when compared with other *Opuntia* species and are covered with numerous areoles with numerous short, reddish-brown glochids. Along with *Opuntia basilaris* of the Mojave Desert, this is one of the few North American pricklypears that bears no spines.

FLOWERS AND FRUIT: Flowers are about 3 inches across, starting yellow and aging to bright red orange, with the full range of colors visible on the same plant at the same time. The fruit is red when mature and about 1 inch long.

FLOWERING: Flowering occurs mostly in March and April but may continue to July.

RANGE AND HABITAT: Blind Pricklypear is at home on desert flats and hills in the Big Bend area and south to Coahuila, Durango, and Chihuahua, Mexico.

COMMENTS: Nature can be brutal. You would suppose that this species' lack of spines would be a positive attribute, but spines are actually a cactus's way of saying, "Stay back!" Without spines to let cattle know when they are getting too close, this species' glochids easily detach into the eyes of grazing cattle, causing severe irritation and ultimately blindness, thus the common name.

Utricularia inflata

Swollen Bladderwort, Floating Bladderwort

LENTIBULARIACEAE (BLADDERWORT FAMILY)

PLANT AND LEAVES: Swollen Bladderwort is a carnivorous perennial aquatic herb. It floats by means of hollow "ribs" that radiate horizontally from the stem at water level, or just below, and are always visible. From the center of these, the erect stem rises up to 6 inches high. From the ribs, which sustain the plant in water, grow large masses of fine, root-like filaments on which there are numerous microscopic bladders and from which the genus gets its name (*utriculus* means "small bladder"). These bladders have a complex and delicate mechanism for catching microscopic animals that brush against them. The prey are digested in the bladders and contribute to the nitrogen needs of the plant.

FLOWERS AND FRUIT: The stem bears 3 to 14 yellow flowers ½ to ¾ inch across. The fruit is a spherical capsule.

FLOWERING: Flowering occurs from March to July.

RANGE AND HABITAT: Swollen Bladderwort grows in freshwater marshes, shallow, sluggish streams, or standing water in roadside ditches from east Texas and along the Gulf Coast and Atlantic Coast to New Jersey.

COMMENTS: There are 10 bladderwort species native to Texas. The plants of this species are the largest in the genus.

Thelesperma filifolium

Stiff Greenthread

ASTERACEAE (ASTER FAMILY)

PLANT AND LEAVES: Stiff Greenthread is a winter annual or short-lived perennial often found growing colonially. Its slender, branched stems, 10 to 30 inches in height, bear leaves divided into thread-like segments to about three-quarters of the plants' overall height.

FLOWERS AND FRUIT: The 2-inch-diameter, radiate flower heads are held above the foliage on delicate, leafless peduncles. In bud, the flower heads nod and are surrounded by spiky phyllaries; when fully opened, they are erect and upright. There are normally eight yellow or golden-yellow ray flowers per head, each terminating in three rounded lobes. The spiky disc flowers making up the maroon-colored centers contrast attractively with the ray flowers surrounding them. The disc flowers in some northern populations are yellow with reddish veins.

FLOWERING: Most flowering occurs March to August but, as conditions allow, may extend into early autumn.

RANGE AND HABITAT: Stiff Greenthread is native on calcareous, sandy, or clayey soil across most of Texas. Its range extends across to the Great Plains as far north as Wyoming and South Dakota.

COMMENTS: Masses of flowering Stiff Greenthread plants waving their maroon and gold colors in an early summer breeze along a Texas roadside are an unforgettable sight.

Mentzelia multiflora

Adonis Blazingstar, Prairie Stickleaf

LOASACEAE (BLAZINGSTAR FAMILY)

PLANT AND LEAVES: Adonis Blazingstar is a perennial herb, 2 to 2½ feet tall, growing from a basal rosette of many leaves. A single main stem with many branches, all grayish white in color, grows from the rosette's center. At the plant's base, the leaves are about 6 inches long. Higher on the plant, the leaves

decrease in size. All leaves are long and narrow with a number of narrow lobes or rounded teeth along the margin.

FLOWERS AND FRUIT: The flowers, about 2 inches in diameter, are quite showy, with 10 spoon-shaped golden-yellow tepals—five sepals and five petals—and many yellow stamens. The sepals are the same color as the petals but usually noticeably narrower. The flowers open in the late afternoon and close in the morning.

FLOWERING: Flowering begins in March and continues until October.

RANGE AND HABITAT: In Texas, Adonis Blazingstar is found in sunny locations on sandy soils from the Panhandle to the Big Bend area. It US range extends through the Four Corner states, north into Wyoming, and west into southern California. It also occurs in the Chihuahuan and Sonoran Deserts of northern Mexico.

COMMENTS: This species, and other members of the genus *Mentzelia*, are noted for their rough, sticky foliage and other parts covered with minutely barbed hairs that help them adhere well to passing animals and especially well to clothing, hence the common name "Stickleaf."

Nuphar lutea ssp. *advena*

Common Spatterdock, Yellow Cow-lily

NYMPHAEACEAE (WATER-LILY FAMILY)
Synonym: *Nuphar advena*

PLANT AND LEAVES: Common Spatterdock is an herbaceous perennial that grows in water to 15 feet deep, though usually shallower. It forms extensive root systems in the mud below the water's surface with large, knobby rhizomes 2 to 4 inches in diameter. It has large floating leaves, 4 to 16 inches across, that are almost circular except for a deep, narrow cut one-third to one-half of the way to the center, where the stout stem is attached. Nearly all the leaves lie on the water's surface or are held slightly above.

FLOWERS AND FRUIT: Flowers are slightly fragrant, more or less spherical, and with their six yellow sepals (green at the base) appearing to be petals curving over the flowers' center. The flowers are about 1½ inches across and held above the water by their stout stems. The 18 true petals are yellow, small, and stamen-like and are mixed with the many stamens in the flower's center and mostly hidden within the enveloping sepals.

FLOWERING: Flowering begins in late March and continues to October.

RANGE AND HABITAT: Widely scattered over east Texas in bayous, ponds, lakes, roadside ditches, and other relatively shallow, slow-moving, or still waterways. Outside Texas, its range extends across the Southeast, the Mid-Atlantic, New England, and most of the Midwest.

COMMENTS: Common Spatterdock is an important food source and habitat constituent for many aquatic species. Pollination is primarily a result of the feeding activity of sweat bees (Halictidae), beetles, and flies. This species' flowers are functionally female on the first day of opening and functionally male thereafter.

Baileya multiradiata

Desert Marigold

ASTERACEAE (ASTER FAMILY)

PLANT AND LEAVES: Desert Marigold normally grows to about 18 inches tall. Depending on conditions, it may act as an annual, biennial, or perennial. Most of the plant's deeply cut, often silvery leaves are clustered near the base.

FLOWERS AND FRUIT: Flower stems are 4 to 8 inches long, usually leafless, and bear golden-yellow ray and disc flower heads, about 1½ inches across, with 25 to 50 lightly toothed ray flowers.

FLOWERING: March to November (following rains).

RANGE AND HABITAT: *Baileya multiradiata* is a common constituent of the flora of the Desert Southwest from Texas to California and into northern Mexico. In Texas, it is found from Big

Bend to El Paso. We have seen it flowering continuously from Shafter to Boquillas Canyon—100 miles or more. Appealing in itself, its appearance was enhanced by being mixed with bluebonnets practically all the way, making both of them more attractive than either would be by itself.

COMMENTS: It is an attractive wildflower that will compare favorably with any of its cultivated relatives and performs well in xeric gardens. The plant is toxic to sheep and, for that reason, is not favored by ranchers.

Eucnide bartonioides

Yellow Rocknettle

LOASACEAE (BLAZINGSTAR FAMILY)

PLANT AND LEAVES: Yellow Rocknettle is a perennial, or sometimes annual, herb. The plant is usually a leafy mound, about 6 inches in height and spread. The leaves are variable but most are more or less round, about 2 to 2½ inches long, and lobed and toothed in varying patterns. The leaves are armed with stinging hairs.

FLOWERS AND FRUIT: The plant produces a number of flower peduncles, but only one flower is borne on each and is held just above the foliage. The flower is striking with five bright yellow

petals. The corolla is funnel-shaped, about 1¼ inches long and nearly 2 inches across. One of this species' outstanding features is the many yellow stamens extending well beyond the rest of the flower, with a tip of yellow pollen on each stamen, giving it a delicate, graceful appearance. The bright, showy flowers open only in bright sunshine.

FLOWERING: Flowering may begin as early as March and continue to as late as November.

RANGE AND HABITAT: There are two botanical varieties of Yellow Rocknettle. *Eucnide bartonioides* var. *bartonioides* is native to the Big Bend portion of the Rio Grande River and downstream to Edwards County. It is also found in Coahuila, Mexico, along tributaries of the Rio Grande. *Eucnide bartonioides* var. *edwardsiana* is native to central Texas and the Edwards Plateau, for which it is named. It has smaller flowers than its western cousin. Both varieties are found exclusively on limestone cliffs or on nearby gravel slopes close to rivers.

COMMENTS: For those fortunate enough to raft or otherwise navigate the Rio Grande, Yellow Rocknettle is always an arresting sight along the way. Its bright and cheery flowers shine like rich veins of gold on the otherwise monochromatic canyon walls along the river.

Thymophylla pentachaeta

Common Dogweed, Five-needle Prickleleaf

ASTERACEAE (ASTER FAMILY)
Synonym: *Dyssodia pentachaeta*

PLANT AND LEAVES: Common Dogweed is a small and erect perennial or subshrub growing 4 to 10 inches tall. Its form is usually rather untidy and is rarely as attractive as its relative, *Thymophylla acerosa*. It has many branches with slender, needle-like leaves, about ½ inch long, divided into narrow lobes tipped with a spine.

FLOWERS AND FRUIT: The flower heads, ½ inch across, are above the leaves at the end of peduncles about 3 inches long. They are yellow and numerous, with prominent, protruding orange-yellow centers.

FLOWERING: The long flowering season for Common Dogweed stretches from March to November.

RANGE AND HABITAT: Common Dogweed inhabits limestone soils in the Rio Grande Valley and west Texas scrublands. It also can be found in similar habitat in northern Mexico and across the Desert Southwest to southern California and Nevada.

COMMENTS: This species' specific epithet, *pentachaeta*, roughly translates from Latin to "five bristles" and refers to the number of lobes on its leaves. While many leaf specimens collected from the four botanical varieties found in Texas will feature 5 segments, others—especially samples taken from our most common variety, *Thymophylla pentachaeta* var. *pentachaeta*—may have as few as 3 but normally will be divided into 9 to 11 segments.

Larrea tridentata

Creosote Bush, Greasewood

ZYGOPHYLLACEAE (CREOSOTE-BUSH FAMILY)

PLANT AND LEAVES: Creosote Bush is a widely branching perennial evergreen shrub growing 4 to 6 feet tall and about as broadly spread. The small, compound leaves, ¼ to ½ inch long, are composed of two leaflets. They are opposite, united at the base, pointed at the tip, dark to yellowish green, strongly scented, and often sticky with resin.

FLOWERS AND FRUIT: The flowers are yellow and usually inconspicuous. Under favorable conditions, they are more prominent, giving the bush a yellowish cast. The flowers' five yellow petals are usually narrow and twisted, ¼ to ½ inch long. A fuzzy, white, five-seeded fruit follows flowering.

FLOWERING: Creosote bush may flower any time following rains but usually flowers each April and May.

RANGE AND HABITAT: This species is a common constituent of all three of the US major deserts: the Chihuahuan Desert in west Texas, southern New Mexico, and southeastern Arizona; the Sonoran Desert of southwestern Arizona and southern

California; and the Mojave Desert of southern Nevada and southeastern California. Additionally, it is widespread across much of Mexico.

COMMENTS: Creosote Bush is one of the commonest plants of the desert, and almost anyone can readily identify it by its utility pole-like odor. A crushed leaf smells like creosote; hence its common name. The plant is an indicator of poor soil and has the ability to survive under extremely unfavorable conditions. This and the fact that it is not eaten by animals enable it to extend its range at the expense of other plants. In addition, creosote plants produce a chemical in roots and leaves that inhibits germination of seeds, thus reducing competition.

Cypripedium kentuckiense
Southern Lady's-slipper, Ivory Lady's-slipper
ORCHIDACEAE (ORCHID FAMILY)

PLANT AND LEAVES: Southern Lady's-slipper is a perennial herb growing as a single, upright stem to as much as 2½ feet in height—taller than any other North American *Cypripedium* species. It often forms extensive colonies. The species has three to five more or less oval-shaped, strongly veined leaves 6 to 8 inches long and about half as wide.

FLOWERS AND FRUIT: In addition to being our tallest species of *Cypripedium*, Southern Lady's-slipper also has the largest flowers in its genus. There is usually one, but occasionally two, flowers per stem. The flower's sepals are mostly greenish yellow and heavily streaked with purplish brown. The dorsal sepal is broader than the two lateral ones and up to 3½ inches long. The lateral petals are colored the same as the sepals but are narrower and attractively twisted. The color of the very large "slipper" or lip of this species ranges from ivory white to pale yellow. The lip's edge ends abruptly at its opening and is not incurved like that of other species.

FLOWERING: Flowering occurs from April to June.

RANGE AND HABITAT: This orchid grows in mature hardwood

forests in east Texas's Pineywoods ecoregion and in a number of unconnected populations as far east as Georgia and Kentucky.

COMMENTS: As rare as this species is in Texas—and it is, indeed—its rarity cannot hold a candle to a related plant, Yellow Lady's-slipper (*Cypripedium parviflorum* var. *pubescens*). A single herbarium specimen of that species was collected in far west Texas early in the twentieth century, and another plant has never been recorded from anywhere else in the state.

Linum berlandieri

Berlandier's Flax

LINACEAE (FLAX FAMILY)

Synonym: *Linum rigidum* var. *berlandieri*

PLANT AND LEAVES: Berlandier's Flax is a branching herbaceous annual. It is common on the prairies of the southern Great Plains. The plant grows 6 to 10 inches tall, depending on growing conditions. The leaves are glossy with a bluish, waxy bloom, alternately arranged, very narrow, and ⅜ to 1 inch long.

FLOWERS AND FRUIT: Each branch has a single open flower on any given day, ¾ to 1 inch across. The five orangish-yellow petals have reddish-orange veins extending from the flower's center about halfway to their margins, giving the flower a two-tone appearance. The flower's five stamens bear yellow anthers.

FLOWERING: This species flowers from April to June.

RANGE AND HABITAT: Berlandier's Flax is a very common constituent of prairies throughout Texas and the southern Great Plains as far north as Kansas. Small populations also occur in southern Nebraska, eastern Colorado, and southeastern New Mexico.

COMMENTS: The flowers of Berlandier's Flax are exceptionally short lived. It is common to find the intact corollas of this species that have fallen from the plant early in the afternoon of the same day they opened. Berlandier's Flax is named in honor of Swiss physician and botanist, Jean Louis Berlandier—one of the giants of Texas botany—who in 1828 and 1829 made the first significant botanical survey of Texas's flora.

Polygala nana
Candyroot, Low Bachelor's Button
POLYGALACEAE (MILKWORT FAMILY)
Synonym: *Pylostachya nana*

PLANT AND LEAVES: Candyroot is a diminutive annual or biennial herb growing from a basal rosette to 4 to 6 inches tall with clusters of a few short stems. The leaves are fleshy and elongate, 1½ inches long and about ¾ inches wide. Nearly all the leaves are basal.

FLOWERS AND FRUIT: The spiky flowers are bright lemon or butter yellow and cluster tightly around the top of the stem in a cylindrical or conical inflorescence 1½ inches long and about ¾ inches wide.

FLOWERING: Flowering occurs from April to June.

RANGE AND HABITAT: Candyroot grows best in moist piney woods or wet meadows in the eastern third of state. It is native across the South, especially along the Gulf coastal plain, but also can be found inland in marshy areas.

COMMENTS: What Candyroot lacks in size it makes up for in showiness. When flowering, it cannot be overlooked. Additionally, when chewed, its root is sugary sweet and tastes of licorice; thus, its common name.

Polytaenia texana

Texas Prairie Parsley, Texas Parsley

APIACEAE (CARROT FAMILY)

PLANT AND LEAVES: Texas Prairie Parsley is a biennial or perennial herb growing from a basal rosette and reaching about 2 feet in height. It has stiff, stout stems that become dry and brown and remain standing through the winter months. The leaves are 1 to 3 inches long and nearly as broad, deeply cut, and lobed. Upper leaves usually have three lobes, lower ones have five.

FLOWERS AND FRUIT: The flowers are small, ¼ inch across, and greenish yellow. They grow in umbels, 2 inches across, branching irregularly from the leaf axils near the top of the plant. Oval, wafer-like, winged seeds follow the flowers.

FLOWERING: Flowering occurs from April until June.

RANGE AND HABITAT: Texas Prairie Parsley is found on prairies, in old fields, along fencerows, and on roadsides throughout the eastern half of Texas. Its native range extends north into southern Oklahoma.

COMMENTS: Recent research by botanist Guy Nesom has shown that most Prairie Parsley plants found in Texas and previously believed to be *Polytaenia nuttallii* are, in fact, *Polytaenia texana*. The native range of *P. nuttallii* barely enters northeast Texas and is unlikely to be encountered anywhere else in the state.

Tetraneuris linearifolia var. *linearifolia*

Fineleaf Four-nerved Daisy

ASTERACEAE (ASTER FAMILY)
Synonym: *Hymenoxys linearifolia*

PLANT AND LEAVES: Fineleaf Four-nerved Daisy is an annual herb producing one to several aboveground stems. It may reach 20 inches in height but is often much smaller. Its leaves are scattered along the stem and are narrowly spatulate to about 2 inches long. Each stem may branch several times with each branched stem terminating in a single radiate flower head.

FLOWERS AND FRUIT: The flower head has 6 to 20 golden-yellow ray flowers. They are toothed, with four veins that converge at the tip. The dome-shaped center of disc flowers is tightly packed and orange yellow.

FLOWERING: Flowering may take place any time conditions are favorable, but most flowering occurs from April to June.

RANGE AND HABITAT: In Texas, Fineleaf Four-nerved Daisy is most common in the southwestern third of the state but is also often found in central and north-central Texas. Scattered populations may be encountered just about anywhere west of the Pineywoods. Its range extends outside Texas northward through Oklahoma and into Kansas and south into northern Mexico.

COMMENTS: When one is walking across a bone-dry desert, where nothing is visible but sand and rocks, and comes across this delicate flower, 5 inches high, it commands attention. We found Fineleaf Four-nerved Daisy between San Vicente and the Chisos Mountains, in Big Bend National Park, in April. They grow larger under more favorable conditions.

Cylindropuntia leptocaulis

Tasajillo, Pencil Cactus, Christmas Cholla

CACTACEAE (CACTUS FAMILY)
Synonym: *Opuntia leptocaulis*

PLANT AND LEAVES: Tasajillo (pronounced: tass-uh-hee-yo) is an upright, spreading, multibranched shrub to 6 feet or more in height. Stem segments are long and cylindrical, about the diameter of a pencil when young and to 1 inch in diameter near the base of large plants. Individual plants may be sparingly to densely spiny, though most stem segments bear glochids and one to three gray or yellowish, barbed spines in apical areola.

FLOWERS AND FRUIT: Flowers are mostly inconspicuous and less than 1 inch in diameter. Tepals are greenish yellow and sometimes have reddish tips. Tasajillo gets its common name, Christmas Cholla, from the bright red fruit it produces late in the year. It is common for new stem segments to grow from the apex of mature fruits.

FLOWERING: Flowering occurs from April to July.

RANGE AND HABITAT: Spread widely over central and west Texas in a variety of habitats, it is often found in fencerows. From Texas, its range spreads west nearly to California and south

to north-central Mexico. Tasajillo often forms impenetrable thickets in the Big Bend country.

COMMENTS: The barbed tips of its spines and the readily disarticulating stem segments allow Tasajillo to be spread readily by passing animals and humans, though the process can be quite painful for the hapless passerby. On the plus side, it is those characteristics that make Tasajillo a good candidate for a security barrier.

Engelmannia peristenia

Engelmann Daisy, Cutleaf Daisy

ASTERACEAE (ASTER FAMILY)

Synonym: *Engelmannia pinnatifida*

PLANT AND LEAVES: Engelmann Daisies are attractive but rough and hairy plants that grow 1 to 3 feet tall. They are herbaceous perennials with leaves that are alternate and deeply lobed, 3 to 12 inches long. The upper leaves often have coarse teeth. Their erect to spreading stems form a rounded crown.

FLOWERS AND FRUIT: Plants are topped by broad clusters of showy golden-yellow flower heads about 1½ inch across. Their 8 to 10 ray flowers are about ½ inch long and are indented at the tip.

FLOWERING: Flowering occurs from April to July.

RANGE AND HABITAT: Engelmann Daisy is native to the central and southern Great Plains, to the grasslands of New Mexico and Arizona, and to northern Mexico. In Texas, it might be encountered growing wild in just about any part of the state but the Pineywoods.

COMMENTS: *Engelmannia peristenia* is monotypic; that is, it is the only species in its genus. The genus was named in honor of the renowned American botanist, George Engelmann. This common plant of the plains and prairies closely resembles the sunflowers (*Helianthus* spp.) but has the daisy characteristic of closing the flower heads at night and opening them in bright sunlight.

Opuntia engelmannii var. *engelmannii*

Engelmann's Pricklypear

CACTACEAE (CACTUS FAMILY)

Synonym: *Opuntia phaeacantha* var. *discata*

PLANT AND LEAVES: Engelmann's Pricklypear is a large cactus that sometimes spreads to more than 8 feet across and almost as tall. Stem segments (pads) are oval, 8 to 16 inches long and 6 to 12 inches wide. Areoles are evenly spaced over the stem surface, with one to four spines and numerous glochids on most areoles. The chalky-white spines vary in length from ½ to about 3 inches long.

FLOWERS AND FRUIT: The masses of yellow to orange flowers it produces will bring one to a stop, no matter how often they are encountered. The fruits, called tunas, are up to 2½ inches long with a deep maroon color that makes the plant attractive after the flowers are gone. They are edible but have too many seeds

to be enjoyed. We once sucked the juice from a dozen of them when very thirsty, and although it helped, we recommend better attention to one's water supply.

FLOWERING: Flowering occurs from April to July.

RANGE AND HABITAT: Engelmann's Pricklypear may be found on deserts, sandy plains, and grasslands in the Trans-Pecos ecoregion. Its range stretches west to California and into Mexico.

COMMENTS: This is perhaps the most abundant pricklypear in West Texas and one of the most attractive when in flower.

Thelesperma simplicifolium
Slender Greenthread
ASTERACEAE (ASTER FAMILY)

PLANT AND LEAVES: Slender Greenthread grows to 12 to 30 inches tall and has many loosely branched stems. Leaves are opposite, 1 to 3 inches long. The lower leaves have three to five narrow segments, but those above have fewer.

FLOWERS AND FRUIT: Flower heads are generally similar to those of *Thelesperma filifolium*, usually with eight yellow ray flowers. However, the disc flowers of this species are mostly yellow or greenish yellow, sometimes with reddish nerves.

FLOWERING: Mostly spring and summer flowering (April to July), it may flower as late as October when conditions allow.

RANGE AND HABITAT: Slender Greenthread is usually found on rocky limestone soils in forest clearings and on road cuts in central and southwest Texas and northeastern Mexico.

COMMENTS: Oddly enough, the overall appearance of this species is stiffer and more formal than Stiff Greenthread (*Thelesperma filifolium*) and, lacking the contrasting colors of the ray and disc flowers, is not as showy. Also, it is not as given to forming extensive colonies as its cousin, so finding a population of plants in flower is always a happy treat.

Agave parryi ssp. *parryi*

Parry's Agave, Century Plant, Maguey, Mescal

AGAVACEAE (CENTURY-PLANT FAMILY)
Synonyms: *Agave scabra*, *Agave huachucensis*

PLANT AND LEAVES: Parry's Agave is one of several related species commonly called Century Plant because it takes so long for it to produce flowers, though under favorable conditions it may

be only 12 to 15 years. For most of its life, the plant is a rosette of thick, fleshy leaves, 1½ to 2½ feet long, with spines along the margins, including one at the end of each leaf that is longer and stronger than the marginal spines.

FLOWERS AND FRUIT: Century Plants are most impressive during the flowering stage, when from the center of the rosette a stalk, 4 to 6 inches in diameter and similar in appearance to asparagus, grows rapidly to a height of 12 to 20 feet, sometimes growing as much as 18 inches a day. From the upper third of this stalk grow stout stems 1½ to 3 feet long, each ending in an upturned cluster (6 to 12 inches in diameter) of yellow tubular flowers. These flower clusters provide a veritable feast for many species of birds, butterflies, and other insects.

FLOWERING: Flowering begins in April and may continue through August.

RANGE AND HABITAT: This stately sentinel of the Chihuahuan Desert is confined almost entirely to that ecoregion in Texas, New Mexico, Arizona, and northern Mexico.

COMMENTS: Leaf fibers of this species have been used for making rope. The plant may also be used in the production of alcoholic beverages.

Opuntia phaeacantha

Tulip Pricklypear, Brown-spined Pricklypear

CACTACEAE (CACTUS FAMILY)

PLANT AND LEAVES: Tulip Pricklypear sometimes grows 2 to 3 feet tall, occasionally even taller, with no trunk and forms dense thickets up to 8 feet across; or, it may remain a low, prostrate plant with most of the stem segments (pads) resting their edges on the ground, never growing taller than 18 inches. The stem segments vary widely. Most of them are flattened, but others

are egg shaped or club shaped, 4 to 9 inches long and 3 to 7 inches wide. The surface is bluish green when young, becoming yellowish green with age. Areoles are ¾ to 1 inch apart. There are usually numerous reddish glochids and from zero to eight brownish or tan spines per areole, most on the distal end of the stem segment, from 1 to 3 inches in length.

FLOWERS AND FRUIT: The particularly attractive flowers are 2 to 3 inches across, bright yellow, often with red to maroon centers and/or red central stripes on the tepals. The stamens are yellowish or cream colored. The style is white and supports a yellow-green stigma. Tunas are barrel shaped and purple when ripe.

FLOWERING: Flowering begins in April and is finished by August.

RANGE AND HABITAT: Tulip Pricklypear can be found in the western half of the state, particularly in the Trans-Pecos ecoregion. A native of deserts, its range extends across the US Southwest and Mexico.

COMMENTS: Among the most common cacti in North America, Tulip Pricklypear is the very embodiment of what most folks think of when they think of a pricklypear cactus.

Rudbeckia grandiflora

Tall Coneflower, Rough Coneflower, Large-flower Coneflower

ASTERACEAE (ASTER FAMILY)

PLANT AND LEAVES: This erect, coarse, tall perennial grows 2½ to 4 feet tall and usually forms colonies. The upper stem and leaves have rough hairs. Leaves at the bottom of the plant have long petioles, but the higher ones attach directly to the main stem. They are 2½ to 6 inches long and half as wide, shallow toothed with prominent ribs.

FLOWERS AND FRUIT: Flower heads have 8 to 12 ray flowers and are ¾ to 1 inch long, yellow, and drooping. The cones are ¾ to 1¼ inches high and are gray green but turning brown as their disc flowers mature.

FLOWERING: The flowering season for Tall Coneflower begins in April and continues to August.

RANGE AND HABITAT: In east Texas, Tall Coneflower's range extends west to Corsicana and Madisonville. Its range extends northward up the western Mississippi River Valley to Missouri and includes a few, scattered locations in the Ohio River Valley. Tall Coneflower prefers dry to mesic meadows with deep soils.

COMMENTS: Honey bees, butterflies, beetles, and other insects feed on the nectar and pollen. This coneflower is a desirable ornamental and performs well in cultivation. Tall Coneflower and the very similar species Giant Coneflower (*Rudbeckia maxima*) are our two largest members of their genus.

Chrysactinia mexicana

Damianita

ASTERACEAE (ASTER FAMILY)

PLANT AND LEAVES: Damianita is a small evergreen shrub that looks like it should be an herbaceous plant. New growth is soft but becomes woody with age. It is a low, mounding plant usually to about 15 inches but may reach twice that height in extreme cases. Its thin stems are covered with short, needle-like leaves.

FLOWERS AND FRUIT: During the flowering season, the shrub is usually covered by a blanket of golden-yellow flower heads about 1 inch in diameter. Its seeds (cypselae) have attached pappi similar to dandelions (*Taraxacum* spp.) and are scattered by the wind.

FLOWERING: Damianita can be found flowering any time from April to September.

RANGE AND HABITAT: Damianita is native to west Texas, southern New Mexico, and the northern half of Mexico. In Texas it can be found in the Trans-Pecos and as far east as the southern Edwards Plateau. This species will not tolerate wet feet and grows on thin, poor, very dry soils.

COMMENTS: Any xeric garden within this species' native range should include Damianita if for no other reason than the wonderful fragrance the plant emits when one works with it. It is especially effective when combined with coarse-outlined plants like cacti and agaves and in drifts among large boulders. Deadheading encourages more flowering and provides an opportunity to enjoy its delicious scent.

Ibervillea lindheimeri

Balsam Gourd, Balsam Apple, Globeberry

CUCURBITACEAE (CUCUMBER FAMILY)

PLANT AND LEAVES: Balsam Gourd is an herbaceous vine that typically climbs by tendrils on nearby vegetation. By chance or by design, it is often found growing beneath deciduous shrubs, into the branches of which it ascends each summer. It is a perennial, with a very large turnip-shaped underground tuber,

to 18 inches in diameter and up to 12 inches deep, from which several narrow stems grow 6 to 10 feet long. Its leaves are 1½ to 3¼ inches long, with three to five broad lobes, deeply cut and fine toothed.

FLOWERS AND FRUIT: This plant has interesting and attractive, but small, tubular flowers with five spreading, hairy lobes, each with two or three smaller lobes at their tips. The flowers are creamy or greenish yellow, about ½ inch wide. The fruit is a gourd (technically, a pepo), 1 to 1⅜ inches in diameter, bright red at maturity, and spherical or somewhat oblong. While developing, the fruit is green with whitish stripes, looking very much like a tiny watermelon.

FLOWERING: Flowering occurs between April and September. The fruit matures September to November.

RANGE AND HABITAT: Balsam Gourd grows in thickets and in open brushland, in old fields and on fencelines in the western two-thirds of Texas. It also can be found in southern Oklahoma and in northern Mexico.

COMMENTS: A chance first encounter with a Balsam Gourd in flower is likely to elicit mild admiration of its dark green foliage and contrasting, spikey yellow flowers. Such an encounter with the plant in fruit, its vine dry and withered and its gourds shining like brilliant scarlet suns under a blue Texas sky and adorning an old barbed wire fence or the branches of a small Texas Persimmon (*Diospyros texana*), will thrill the soul.

Castilleja sessiliflora

Great Plains Indian Paintbrush

SCROPHULARIACEAE (FIGWORT FAMILY)

PLANT AND LEAVES: Great Plains Indian Paintbrush is a perennial herb with mostly unbranched stems growing in clusters from a single crown. Shorter than most of our other paintbrushes, it grows 4 to 12 inches tall, and its stems and leaves are velvety with downy hairs. Most leaves are long, narrow, and undivided, though some upper leaves may have a pair of divergent lobes.

FLOWERS AND FRUIT: In Texas populations, the flowers are yellow green, but the petal-like bracts of most plants, which are the most obvious part of all paintbrushes, are a beautiful rose pink. Unlike many other species of paintbrushes, the flowers of Great Plains Indian Paintbrush extend well beyond the bracts and make up a significant part of the plant's floral

display. In other parts of its range, yellow-bracted plants are more common.

FLOWERING: Flowering may occur any time from April to October, depending on location.

RANGE AND HABITAT: This species is found in central and west Texas and is abundant from Sonora to the Guadalupe Mountains. Its native range is among the largest of paintbrush species and includes all of the United States and Canadian Great Plains and Rocky Mountain regions.

COMMENTS: Great Plains Indian Paintbrush forms root connections to *Juniperus* species and receives a substantial portion of its nutrition through parasitism of those plants.

Ferocactus hamatacanthus

Turk's Head Cactus, Texas Barrel Cactus

CACTACEAE (CACTUS FAMILY)

PLANT AND LEAVES: In its early stages of growth the Turk's Head Cactus is rather round, but it becomes columnar as it ages. Mature plants average about 8 inches tall and 8 inches in diameter, but some specimens may reach 2 feet in height. It usually has a single stem but occasionally will branch. The stems have 13 to 17 large, broad ribs with tubercles up to 2 inches high. From the tubercles grow 8 to 14 outer spines and 4 to 8 central ones. Spines are pinkish or pale yellow, fading to gray with age. Each areole bears an extremely long central spine, up to 6 inches and hooked on the end.

FLOWERS AND FRUIT: The flowers are 2½ to 4 inches tall, nearly as wide, and fragrant. There are up to 30 inner tepals, which are long and wide but pointed at the tip. They are lemon yellow, aging to orangish, sometimes reddish at the base. The anthers are yellow and clustered near the base of the tepals. The stigmas are creamy yellow and are held well above the anthers. Tunas are olive green or maroon when mature.

FLOWERING: Flowering is mostly in the summer but may begin as early as April and continue into fall.

RANGE AND HABITAT: Turk's Head Cactus is a native of the South Texas Plains ecoregion in Tamaulipan thorn scrub and Chihuahuan Desert scrub near the Rio Grande from Brownsville to El Paso and south into northern Mexico.

COMMENTS: Two varieties of Turk's Head Cactus can be found in Texas: *Ferocactus hamatacanthus* var. *hamatacanthus* can be found from the Pecos River and westward, while the range of *F. h.* var. *sinuatus* extends from the Pecos River to near the Gulf Coast.

Oenothera laciniata

Cutleaf Evening Primrose

ONAGRACEAE (EVENING-PRIMROSE FAMILY)

PLANT AND LEAVES: Cutleaf Evening Primrose is an herbaceous
annual or short-lived perennial that grows 4 to 18 inches high,
erect or prostrate on stems up to 24 inches long. Larger plants
are often weakly branched. Leaves are alternate, simple, pinnately cleft into rounded lobes, or sometimes merely wavy
edged or toothed. Usually leaves are about 2 inches long and
½ inch wide, but larger specimens have leaves up to 4 inches
long and about 1 inch wide.

FLOWERS AND FRUIT: The small, pale yellow flowers are borne
singly in the axils, with four heart-shaped petals ⅕ to ⅗ inch
long, eight stamens, and one pistil. The flowers usually fade
to salmon when spent. The flower's four narrow sepals reflex
back against the flower's base. The fruit is a cylindrical capsule
about 2 inches long.

FLOWERING: Flowering occurs April to October.

RANGE AND HABITAT: This species grows well in disturbed ground

throughout the eastern half of Texas and westward to the Trans-Pecos and Panhandle. Cutleaf Evening Primrose can be found throughout the United States east of the Rocky Mountains.

COMMENTS: Though lovely when in flower, Cutleaf Evening Primrose is a somewhat weedy plant that grows in weedy places. It has become a noxious weed in some other parts of the world where it has been introduced.

Parkinsonia aculeata

Retama, Paloverde, Jerusalem-thorn

FABACEAE (PEA FAMILY)

PLANT AND LEAVES: Retama is a large spiny shrub or small tree, as much as 30 feet tall, with long, graceful, slightly drooping branches. A longish spine, sometimes a pair, is borne at each node along the stem. The tough but delicate-looking leaves are unusual. The leaves are compound, almost always bipinnate

with two to six pinnae extending from short petioles, 8 to 15 inches long, and hanging parallel to one another. Each pinna has 20 to 50 leaflets. The leaflets usually fall off during the summer, and the pinnae then carry on the photosynthetic function of leaves as does the green bark on the plant's trunk and branches.

FLOWERS AND FRUIT: The tree's fragrant flowers are borne on racemes to about 6 inches long. They have five bright-yellow petals, ⅓ to ⅔ inch long and about equal in size. One petal has a nectar gland at its base and ages to reddish orange. It remains on the plant longer than the others. The seedpods are 3 to 5 inches long, narrow, and constricted between the seeds.

FLOWERING: Retama has a profusion of flowers through the warm months, especially after rains. The first flush appears in April or May and sporadically until fall.

RANGE AND HABITAT: This species prefers moist, sandy soils and can be found across the southern third of Texas. Its native range extends west to southern Arizona and as far south as Argentina. It has naturalized in suitable habitat along the southern border of the United States from California to South Carolina.

COMMENTS: Retama is a popular ornamental. Though preferring moist soil, it is very drought tolerant and works well in xeric gardens.

Psilostrophe tagetina
Woolly Paperflower
ASTERACEAE (ASTER FAMILY)

PLANT AND LEAVES: Woolly Paperflower is an herbaceous biennial or short-lived perennial. Plants grow in clumps. Leaves are alternate, about 1 inch long and ¼ inch wide. Leaf surfaces are covered with hairs giving the plant a grayish-green color.

FLOWERS AND FRUIT: The flower heads, 1 to 1½ inches across, have three to five ray flowers much broader than long and conspicuously three lobed. Both ray and disc flowers are bright yellow. The flower heads are densely clustered on short branches at the top of stems 6 to 24 inches long. The ray flower laminae

are unusually persistent and stay on the plant even after the seeds are formed, eventually becoming whitish and papery. The fruit of Woolly Paperflower, like other species in its family, is a cypsela, a type of achene.

FLOWERING: Woolly Paperflower may flower any time between April and October.

RANGE AND HABITAT: Native to the Trans-Pecos in Texas, its range extends to Utah and Arizona and south into northern Mexico. It is commonly found on sandy or calcareous soil in grasslands, in saline flats, and among desert scrub.

COMMENTS: This plant is typical of many in the dry Southwest in having a dense covering of woolly white hairs that enable it to withstand arid conditions by reducing the loss of moisture. Woolly Paperflower is easily cultivated and makes a nice addition to xeric gardens in its native range.

Gymnosperma glutinosum
Gumhead
ASTERACEAE (ASTER FAMILY)
Synonym: *Xanthocephalum glutinosum*

PLANT AND LEAVES: Gumhead is an herbaceous perennial that grows 1½ to 2½ feet tall and branches from the base. The lower part of the stem is woody. Leaves are narrow and sticky, 1½ to

2½ inches long, and mixed with clumps of smaller leaves that are alternate (some subopposite) on the same stem.

FLOWERS AND FRUIT: Flower stems are branched at the end of the main stems, with the yellow flower heads in clusters. Individual heads have one or two yellow ray flowers about 1⁄16 inch long and one to three disc flowers.

FLOWERING: Flowering occurs from April to November.

RANGE AND HABITAT: Gumhead is a common native to arid regions of Texas, southern New Mexico, and southern Arizona as well as Mexico and Guatemala. It grows in rocky, dry creek beds, gravelly or sandy soils, and open, mixed hardwood–pine forests. In Texas, it is found in the southern Edwards Plateau and in the Trans-Pecos ecoregions.

COMMENTS: This is not a plant that is likely to top anyone's "most memorable species" list. But its abundance in west Texas makes it one that is likely to make a visitor there puzzle, "I wonder what that is?" Now, you know.

Rhexia lutea

Yellow Meadowbeauty

MELASTOMATACEAE (MELASTOME FAMILY)

PLANT AND LEAVES: Yellow Meadowbeauty is a perennial herb usually growing to about 18 inches tall. It is well branched, having many stems growing out of the leaf axils of the four-sided main stem. The plant's stems are studded with scattered, spreading hairs. Leaves are opposite, about 1 inch long and ¼ inch wide, and attached directly to the stem. They are very slightly toothed, have a deep center vein, and are pointed at the tip.

FLOWERS AND FRUIT: The plant's flowers are about 1 inch across and have four golden-yellow petals. The flowers grow out of the leaf axils on short stems that usually have one or more pairs of leaves. The flower's petals are oval to somewhat diamond shaped. The stamens are straight or only slightly curved, lacking the extreme curve of other species in the genus.

FLOWERING: Flowering occurs during May and June.

RANGE AND HABITAT: Yellow Meadowbeauty is commonly found growing in moist pinelands of east Texas. It is native to similar

habitat along the coastal plains near the Gulf of Mexico and the Atlantic Ocean from Texas to North Carolina.

COMMENTS: The genus name, *Rhexia*, is derived from the Greek word *rexis*, meaning "to rupture." The connection is not certain but may refer to the plant's unusual urn-shaped fruit that releases its seeds by splitting open. This and other species of the genus are buzz-pollinated by bumblebees. This is the only *Rhexia* species with yellow flowers.

Zizia aurea

Golden Alexanders

APIACEAE (CARROT FAMILY)

PLANT AND LEAVES: Golden Alexanders is a showy, erect, multi-branched, perennial herb, usually 1 to 2 feet but up to 4 feet tall. The plant's compound leaves are up to 4 inches long and 5 inches wide with deeply cut, serrate, and sometimes lobed leaflets. Higher on the plant, the leaves diminish in size and in the number of leaflets.

FLOWERS AND FRUIT: The inflorescences are compound umbels with one to three flower stems growing from upper leaf axils. Each umbel bears many bright yellow flowers about ⅛ inch in diameter. Each tiny flower has five sepals, five petals, and five stamens. When in full glory, the inflorescences of this species resemble bursting golden-yellow fireworks.

FLOWERING: Flowering begins in May and can continue until July.

RANGE AND HABITAT: Golden Alexanders is native to moist soils on prairies and old fields and in open woodlands throughout the

eastern third of Texas and from the eastern Great Plains across the eastern half of North America.

COMMENTS: We have found Golden Alexanders scattered over east Texas but more commonly on the northeastern prairies from Bonham eastward. This species is a good choice for moist gardens with some shade and for butterfly gardens within its native range.

Coreopsis tinctoria
Plains Coreopsis, Calliopsis
ASTERACEAE (ASTER FAMILY)

PLANT AND LEAVES: Plains Coreopsis is an erect to sprawling herbaceous annual usually topping out at 1 to 2 feet tall. Leaves are opposite, about 4 inches long, once or twice divided into long, narrow segments. The upper leaves are often undivided. The plant's relatively thin stems allow their lovely flower heads to wave in summer breezes to passersby all along North America's highways and back roads.

FLOWERS AND FRUIT: There are numerous flower heads, 1 to 1¼ inches across, usually with eight yellow ray flowers that have four, sometimes three, prominent lobes, brownish red at the base. Disc flowers are also brownish red, and the whole center

of the flower often looks like beadwork. The ray flowers of some plants lack the reddish base while others may be all red with no yellow at all.

FLOWERING: Plains Coreopsis flowers from May to August.

RANGE AND HABITAT: Though originally native to the Great Plains and the Southeast, Plains Coreopsis is now found across virtually all of North America. Its habit of forming large colonies of plants along roadsides makes it a very popular choice for highway plantings. In Texas, it can be found just about anywhere you look except in some of the drier portions of the Trans-Pecos.

COMMENTS: This is a very common constituent of commercial wildflower mixes. It readily self-sows and regenerates year after year.

Dasylirion leiophyllum

Green Sotol, Desert Candle

LILIACEAE (LILY FAMILY)

PLANT AND LEAVES: Green Sotol is a perennial shrub forming a thick trunk about 4 to 6 inches in diameter and eventually reaching 3 feet in length. Most often upright, some plants recline. The crown at the top of the stem produces about 100 bright green, ribbon-like leaves to 3 feet long and ½ to 1¼ inches wide. The leaf margins are well armed with spiny prickles that curve toward the base of the leaf.

FLOWERS AND FRUIT: This species produces an unbranched flower stalk 7 to 15 feet tall with long, dense clusters of small white or greenish flowers, which appear yellow, on the upper third. The flowers on any given plant will be of one sex, all male flowers on one plant and all female on another.

FLOWERING: Flowering occurs during the warm months of May to August.

RANGE AND HABITAT: Green Sotol is at home on rocky or gravelly slopes and canyons of the Trans-Pecos ecoregion in Texas and in southern New Mexico and northern Mexico.

COMMENTS: In periods of drought, the round, cabbage-like base is sometimes cut up and fed to cattle after the leaves are removed.

It is also a source of alcohol and is used commercially in the production of an alcoholic drink (also called sotol).

A similar and closely related species, Texas Sotol (*Dasylirion texanum*), with leaves armed with prickles that mostly point toward the tip of the leaf, is common in similar habitat on the Edwards Plateau.

Cucurbita foetidissima

Buffalo Gourd, Stinking Gourd

CUCURBITACEAE (CUCUMBER FAMILY)

Synonym: *Pepo foetidissima*

PLANT AND LEAVES: Buffalo Gourd is an herbaceous vine, growing each year from an enormous perennial taproot. The plant's several stems grow rampantly to 10 to 15 feet long. Though well-developed branched tendrils develop at each leaf node and the plant does occasionally climb on fences and twiggy vegetation, the plant usually grows flat on the ground or scrambles over low-growing vegetation. All parts of the plant except petals and fruit are roughly hairy. The leaf is lime green to blue green and covered in silvery pubescence. It is shaped like an elongated heart, pointed at the tip and as much as 12 inches long and 6 inches wide at the base.

FLOWERS AND FRUIT: The large, bell-shaped flowers, 2 to 4 inches long, are yellow to orange, five lobed at the opening, and with stamens that have large anthers deep inside the throat. The fruits are gourds, spherical in shape, 3 to 4 inches in diameter. They are green striped when growing, turning orange to yellow to brown with a hard wood-like rind when mature.

FLOWERING: Flowering occurs May to September. Gourds mature in the fall and early winter.

RANGE AND HABITAT: Buffalo Gourd can be found on prairies, roadsides, dry streambeds, and fields throughout Texas. It is native to xeric soils from the southern Great Plains west to California. It is also native throughout much of Mexico.

COMMENTS: It is unclear whether American Bison browse this plant, so the name Buffalo Gourd is a bit of an unsolved mystery. Another common name, Stinking Gourd, and the specific epithet, *foetidissima*, meaning "stinking greatly," are well earned; when wounded, the leaves and stems of this plant are very unpleasantly odorous.

Rudbeckia hirta

Black-eyed Susan, Brown-eyed Susan

ASTERACEAE (ASTER FAMILY)

PLANT AND LEAVES: Black-eyed Susan is an annual or short-lived perennial growing 1 to 2½ feet tall. Its stems and leaves are covered with coarse hairs. Leaves are alternate, 1 to 4½ inches long, and often lightly toothed. Plants are usually well branched, with each bearing a single flower head.

FLOWERS AND FRUIT: Flower heads of wild-growing plants are 1½ to 2 inches in diameter. Ray flowers are mostly yellow or orangish, often with maroon blotches at the base of the laminae and sometimes drooping at the ends. The center of the disc flowers resembles that of a coneflower, but it is dark brown to nearly black and not so tall.

FLOWERING: The flowering season for Black-eyed Susan begins in May and continues to September.

RANGE AND HABITAT: Widely distributed in prairies and pinelands, it is especially abundant in east and south Texas.

COMMENTS: Black-eyed Susan is the state flower of Maryland. The winning horse of the Preakness Stakes, held each year in Baltimore in May and known as the "Run for the Black-eyed Susans," is traditionally adorned in the winner's circle with a blanket of flowers altered to look like Black-eyed Susans because the race is held too early in the year to use flowers of the actual species. Black-eyed Susan is a very showy and popular garden plant, and many cultivars of various flower sizes and colors have been developed over the years.

Asclepias latifolia

Broadleaf Milkweed

ASCLEPIADACEAE (MILKWEED FAMILY)

PLANT AND LEAVES: Broadleaf Milkweed is an herbaceous perennial with milky sap that grows 1 to 3 feet tall, usually with no branches. The plant bears numerous large, elliptical, waxy green or bluish leaves, 2 to 6 inches long and up to 5 inches wide. They are attached directly to the main stem and are coarse with prominent whitish veins. The ends of the leaves are blunt and often indented.

FLOWERS AND FRUIT: The plant's inflorescences are umbels to about 3 inches in diameter borne in the upper leaf axils and are often nearly hidden by the leaves. The petals of the pale green to yellowish flowers are folded back and appressed to the flower's stem. The fruit is a large capsule that splits open at maturity to release its many seeds. The seeds have a bit of fluff attached to assist them in being borne away by the wind to other areas.

FLOWERING: Flowering may begin as early as May and continue to as late as October.

RANGE AND HABITAT: Though occasional in central Texas, Broadleaf Milkweed is more common in the Panhandle, the Concho Valley, and the Trans-Pecos, where it is common on grasslands between Alpine and Fort Davis and in the lower part of the Davis Mountains. Its native range extends north through the western Great Plains to Nebraska and west through the Four Corners states and into southern California. It can be found on sandy, clayey, or rocky soils of limestone origin.

COMMENTS: Broadleaf Milkweed presents a sort of "alien" presence in prairies and meadows and never fails to intrigue those stopping to wonder at it.

Oenothera rhombipetala

Fourpoint Evening Primrose

ONAGRACEAE (EVENING-PRIMROSE FAMILY)
Synonym: *Oenothera heterophylla* var. *rhombipetala*

PLANT AND LEAVES: Fourpoint Evening Primrose is an herbaceous annual or biennial that grows 2 to 3 feet tall from a basal rosette. It is unbranched and heavily leafed from the ground to

the flower cluster. The plant has an ample coat of short hairs on its stems. Rosette leaves are about 6 inches long and 1 inch wide. Stem leaves are alternate and without petioles, 3 to 5 inches long and about ¾ wide, with wavy edges, and usually somewhat twisted. They decrease in length as they grow higher on the stem.

FLOWERS AND FRUIT: A large inflorescence, up to 12 inches in length, tops the plant's stems. A ring of flowers develops from the base of the spike upward, the inflorescence often appearing to have a lemony halo surrounding the stem. The flowers are bright yellow with four diamond-shaped petals, each about 1½ inches long. Each flower has eight yellow stamens and a very long, yellow pistil terminated by a large, four-limbed style.

FLOWERING: This species' long flowering season lasts from May to October.

RANGE AND HABITAT: Fourpoint Evening Primrose can be found across north Texas, commonly on roadsides. It is a native of the Great Plains and its range includes nearly all of that region.

COMMENTS: It is not possible to observe this plant's wild, spiky habit and its exuberance of lemon-yellow flowers without being charmed. It always looks like a plant that's having a party.

Oxalis stricta

Yellow Woodsorrel

OXALIDACEAE (WOODSORREL FAMILY)

PLANT AND LEAVES: Yellow Woodsorrel is a perennial herb growing from a deep taproot. This plant grows to about 10 inches tall on a branching stem. Stems are usually erect but fall over with age and then grow horizontally. Leaves are alternate and borne on petioles up to 2½ inches long. The leaves are palmately divided into three heart-shaped leaflets, about ½ inch long and wide and green to yellow green, which fold in the evening or when it is cloudy.

FLOWERS AND FRUIT: The yellow flowers are about ½ inch across, with five sepals, five petals, ten stamens, and one pistil. There are two to six flowers on a slender stem borne in the leaf axils. The fruit is a beaked, five-sided capsule. When mature, it explosively bursts open, expelling the tiny brown seeds up to 12 feet away.

FLOWERING: Flowering occurs May to October.

RANGE AND HABITAT: Yellow Woodsorrel is found in open woodlands and meadows, on roadsides in east Texas, and on blackland prairies in north and central Texas.

COMMENTS: The genus name *Oxalis* is derived from a Greek word for "sharp," referring to the sour taste of the leaves.

Senna roemeriana

Twoleaf Senna, Roemer's Senna

FABACEAE (PEA FAMILY)

Synonym: *Cassia roemeriana*

PLANT AND LEAVES: Twoleaf Senna is a somewhat sprawling multistemmed, branched herb growing from a woody perennial root. It grows 1 to 1½ feet tall. The plant bears alternately arranged compound leaves 1 to 2 inches long, each with two lance-shaped leaflets.

FLOWERS AND FRUIT: The plant bears showy clusters of golden yellow, five-petaled flowers about 1 inch across. The fruits are cylindrical legumes, about 1 inch long.

FLOWERING: Flowering mostly occurs from May to October.

RANGE AND HABITAT: Twoleaf Senna can be found on dry, rocky, limestone soils from north-central Texas through the Hill Country and across the Trans-Pecos. Its native range extends into New Mexico and northern Mexico.

COMMENTS: One or more of the 13 *Senna* species native to Texas can be found in all parts of the state. They vary in size, but all of them have compound leaves and yellow flowers with five irregular petals. *Senna roemeriana* is named in honor of German geologist Ferdinand Roemer, who collected many plants in Texas in the mid-nineteenth century. Twoleaf Senna is often found growing alongside Lindheimer's Senna, with which it sometimes hybridizes. Both species are poisonous to livestock.

Tecoma stans

Yellow Bells, Esperanza

BIGNONIACEAE (TRUMPET-CREEPER FAMILY)

Synonym: *Tecoma stans* var. *angustatum*

PLANT AND LEAVES: Yellow Bells is a multistemmed deciduous shrub growing 3 to 10 feet tall with an approximately equal spread. In ideal conditions, the plant can reach 15 feet or more in height. Leaves are opposite, 4 to 8 inches long, with seven to nine narrow leaflets, each leaflet 1½ to 4 inches long, sharply toothed, and glossy.

FLOWERS AND FRUIT: The yellow, trumpet-shaped flowers are interestingly fragrant, 1¼ to 1¾ inches long and up to 2 inches across. Flowers are in a long cluster at the top of the stems.

FLOWERING: This species flowers almost continuously from May to October.

RANGE AND HABITAT: Yellow Bells grows on rocky slopes of the Edwards Plateau and Trans-Pecos ecoregions, including the Davis Mountains where they are a common sight decorating the boulder-strewn hillsides like green and gold bouquets. Its native range extends to Arizona and south throughout Central and South America and the Caribbean.

COMMENTS: This has become a popular landscape plant owing to its pleasing upright habit, dark green foliage, and showy, long-lasting, bright yellow flowers. There are orange-flowered cultivars of this species. In areas with freezing winter temperatures, it dies to the ground but resprouts each spring from the root crown. The sturdy stems of this species were used by desert tribes of Native Americans to make bows.

Xanthisma texanum

Texas Sleepy-daisy, Star-of-Texas

ASTERACEAE (ASTER FAMILY)

PLANT AND LEAVES: Texas Sleepy-daisy is a taprooted annual or occasionally a biennial producing one to three stems branching near the top. It grows 8 inches to 3 feet tall, with alternate leaves attached directly to the stem. The lower leaves are larger, 1½ to 3 inches long, and deeply lobed or toothed. Upper leaves are lance shaped, to about 1½ inches long, and sometimes toothed but not deeply dissected like those near the bottom of the plant.

FLOWERS AND FRUIT: This species' flower heads are about 1½ in diameter and bear 15 to 35 lemon-yellow ray flowers with lance-shaped, unlobed laminae. The flower head's center, composed of up to 200 disc flowers, is typically the same shade of yellow as the ray flower.

FLOWERING: Flowering may occur any time between May and October.

RANGE AND HABITAT: Sandy woods, prairies, fields, and along roadsides throughout Texas except in the northeast and the extreme west. Its range extends well into central and south-western Oklahoma and eastern New Mexico.

COMMENTS: The flower heads of this species remain closed each day until about noon; hence the name "sleepy-daisy." Texas Sleepy-daisy performs well as a garden plant. When inter-planted with other species, its flowers do resemble bright yellow stars scattered in the garden. Thus, Star-of-Texas is also an apt common name for this Texas native.

Zinnia grandiflora
Plains Zinnia, Prairie Zinnia, Rocky Mountain Zinnia
ASTERACEAE (ASTER FAMILY)
Synonym: *Crassina grandiflora*

PLANT AND LEAVES: Plains Zinnia is a multibranched perennial subshrub. It grows in low, rounded clumps about 8 inches high and 8 inches across. Leaves are rough to the touch and linear, to about 1 inch in length.

FLOWERS AND FRUIT: The flower stems branch near the top with one or two flower heads to a stem. Flower heads are ¾ to 1¼

inches across. The three to six butter-yellow ray flowers are almost circular. A small cluster of about 20 yellow, green, or red disc flowers center the head. As the flower head matures and seeds form, the ray flowers cling to the base and, with age, they fade to white and become papery. Their disc flowers age to reddish brown.

FLOWERING: The flowering period of Plains Zinnia is lengthy, stretching from May to October.

RANGE AND HABITAT: This species inhabits prairies and open desert on limestone soils in the western third of Texas. Its native range is centered in New Mexico, and it also can be found growing in Oklahoma, Kansas, Colorado, Arizona, and northern Mexico.

COMMENTS: Plains Zinnia is a little plant with a big name. The specific epithet of its botanical name, *grandiflora*, means "large flowered." For such a diminutive species, its flowers are indeed quite large. In the heart of its range, Plains Zinnias will form "carpet blooms" blanketing the desert in golden yellow. This species is easily confused with the Woolly Paperflower (*Psilostrophe tagetina*). They both grow in clumps, are yellow with a variable number of ray flowers, and become papery as they mature. A distinction easy to recognize is that the ray flowers of the Plains Zinnia are not toothed, while those of the Woolly Paperflower are three toothed.

Aletris aurea

Golden Colic-root, Star Grass

LILIACEAE (LILY FAMILY)

PLANT AND LEAVES: Golden Colic-root is a rhizome-forming perennial herb. It grows 8 to 30 inches tall. The thin, typically yellowish, lance-shaped leaves are 4 to 8 inches long and form a rosette at the base of the stem.

FLOWERS AND FRUIT: The inflorescence is a spike formed on the upper third of the stem. The flowers are cylindrical, yellow to orange, about ¼ inch long, and six lobed at the tip. The flowers' tepals are covered with minute, wart-like bumps. The fruit is a three-chambered capsule.

FLOWERING: Golden Colic-root has a relatively short flowering season that lasts from just June to July in a typical year. Atypically, it can begin flowering as early as February as conditions dictate.

RANGE AND HABITAT: Wet or dry pine flatwoods and waste areas habitats in east and southeast Texas form the western limit of Golden Colic-root's native range. It also can be found in every Gulf and Atlantic Coast state as far east and north as Maryland.

COMMENTS: In general, in order to thrive, members of the genus *Aletris* need periodic fires to reduce competition on the forest floor. Fittingly, Golden Colic-root's specific epithet, *aurea*, which refers to the species' flower color, is derived from the Latin word for gold.

Rhus glabra

Smooth Sumac

ANACARDIACEAE (SUMAC FAMILY)

PLANT AND LEAVES: A bit smallish by *Rhus* standards, Smooth Sumac is a sparsely branched deciduous shrub or small tree usually topping out at about 10 feet in height. In addition to its copious seed production, it spreads by deep rhizomes and tends to form thickets where conditions allow. Its branches are smooth and brittle. Leaves are 10 to 18 inches long, odd-pinnately compound, and with 13 to 31 leaflets, each about 4 inches long and ¾ inches wide and with jagged, toothed margins.

FLOWERS AND FRUIT: Very small flowers grow in branched, pointed, upright clusters, 6 to 9 inches long, at the end of a stout stem. Each flower has five greenish-yellow petals. The

inflorescence of drab flowers is soon followed by a very showy infructescence of orange, red, or reddish-brown drupes. It is the fruits of the Smooth Sumac, not the flowers, that catches one's eye. If left undisturbed, the drupes will remain firmly attached through the winter without noticeable deterioration.

FLOWERING: Flowering occurs during June and July, depending on growing conditions; fruits follow a few weeks later, from late June to August.

RANGE AND HABITAT: It is found in open woods, uncultivated fields and pastures, and fencerows in the eastern third of the state. Smooth Sumac is a climax species of prairies across North America.

COMMENTS: Smooth Sumac is very likely the only tree or shrub species native to all 48 contiguous states of the United States, though it is very rare in California and Nevada. The fruits are a favorite food for wild birds. The showy infructescences can be cut and used in large decorative arrangements.

Gaillardia multiceps

Onion Blanketflower, Gyp Blanketflower

ASTERACEAE (ASTER FAMILY)

PLANT AND LEAVES: Onion Blanketflower is an herbaceous perennial growing 12 to 18 inches tall. It is woody at the base. Its small, ¾- to 2-inch leaves are very narrow, hairy, and alternately arranged along the lower two-thirds of the stem. The tops of flowering stems are mostly leafless.

FLOWERS AND FRUIT: Flower heads terminate stems several inches in length and bear about eight yellow, deeply three-lobed ray flowers. Their dome-shaped centers contain around 90 tiny purple disc flowers.

FLOWERING: Flowering occurs from June to September.

RANGE AND HABITAT: This species' range is confined to gypsum soils and dunes in Texas, New Mexico, Arizona, and northern Mexico. In Texas, it is found in the western Trans-Pecos ecoregion.

COMMENTS: After flowering, Onion Blanketflower's ray flowers fall away, and the brownish red center remains, giving the plant a striking appearance. Owing to the species' requirement for gypseous soils, this is not a good candidate for most gardens. However, it is a joy to find flowering in the sere gypsum dunes of the American Desert Southwest.

Monarda punctata

Spotted Beebalm, Spotted Horsemint

LAMIACEAE (MINT FAMILY)

PLANT AND LEAVES: Like many other members of the mint family, Spotted Beebalm has square stems and is strongly scented. It is a mostly unbranched, short-lived, perennial herb. The plant is 1½ to 3 feet tall and its leaves are 1 to 3 inches long and

opposite. Alternating pairs of 3-inch leaves grow in opposite directions on the stem, with each of them often flanked by a 1-inch leaf on each side.

FLOWERS AND FRUIT: The inflorescence is made up of very small individual flowers with a whorl of large, petal-like bracts, white, green, pink, or purple, just under each whorl of flowers. The two-lipped flowers, ¾ inch long, are yellow with brown dots. The upper lip continues beyond the lower one, which turns downward and is broader.

FLOWERING: Flowering occurs June to September.

RANGE AND HABITAT: Spotted Beebalm can be found in sandy soils virtually anywhere in Texas except the Trans-Pecos. It is native to most of the eastern half of North America.

COMMENTS: Spotted Beebalm is one of our showiest horsemints and makes a very lovely addition to a native garden. Its nectar and pollen make it attractive to a large number of pollinators.

Sesbania drummondii

Rattlebox, Rattlebush

FABACEAE (PEA FAMILY)

PLANT AND LEAVES: Rattlebox is a rank-growing, woody shrub 4 to 15 feet tall. It has a number of widely spreading branches in the upper part, well separated and with few leaves, giving it a rather spare appearance. Leaves are alternate, 4 to 8 inches long on a short stem. They are divided into 12 to 50 oval or lance-shaped leaflets, ½ to 1½ inches long and about ¼ inch wide.

FLOWERS AND FRUIT: The plant's pea-shaped flowers are butter yellow, often with red streaks or a rosy tint. The flowers are borne in pendulous clusters, about 2 inches long, on a thin peduncle about the same length. Each flower has five petals, the top petal being longer than the others and standing erect. The fruit is a winged, four-sided capsule about 4 inches long and ¾ inch wide. When the seeds mature they are loose in the capsule and rattle when shaken, suggesting the name "rattlebox."

FLOWERING: Flowering occurs from June to September.

RANGE AND HABITAT: Rattlebox is common in waste areas along ponds, lakes, streams, and bayous of south and southeast Texas. Its native range extends along the Gulf Coast as far east as the Florida Panhandle.

COMMENTS: This species' somewhat unkempt appearance and its preference for areas inhabited by weedy species give the general notion that this plant is a weed and undesirable. Compounding its negative reputation, its seeds are quite poisonous. However, its flowers are quite attractive and its fruits rather unique and interesting. The dry fruits persist and provide easy identification and ornamentation to the plant long after winter frosts have defoliated its branches. *Sesbania drummondii* is one of numerous species named in honor of Scottish botanist Thomas Drummond, an early Texas plant explorer.

Amphiachyris dracunculoides

Prairie Broomweed, Common Broomweed

ASTERACEAE (ASTER FAMILY)
Synonyms: *Gutierrezia dracunculoides*, *Xanthocephalum dracunculoides*

PLANT AND LEAVES: Prairie Broomweed is densely branched from about halfway up the main stem, with many slender stems and leaves, and somewhat sticky throughout. It is 2 to 4 feet tall and 2 to 4 feet across and grows from one central root.

FLOWERS AND FRUIT: The flower heads are numerous and small, ⅛ to ¼ inch across. It sometimes covers large areas, giving a pleasing yellow cast; however, it is not welcome on the range because it shades the ground, taking both sunshine and much-needed moisture from the grasses.

FLOWERING: The long flowering season of Prairie Broomweed begins in June and continues through October.

RANGE AND HABITAT: This species is a common constituent of prairies from the Ohio River Valley to the southern Great Plains. In Texas, it is widespread across the western two-thirds of the state and is especially common in west Texas.

COMMENTS: Prairie Broomweed is harvested by the truckload in west Texas for use in dried flower arrangements. In the past it was used extensively in making brooms, giving it the common name. Direct exposure with this plant my cause contact dermatitis and also eye and respiratory irritations for humans and livestock. It thrives in times of drought when perennial grasses are not able to suppress it. When present in great quantities, it creates a sort of avocado-hued smoky effect over the prairie.

Berlandiera lyrata

Chocolate Daisy, Chocolate Flower, Lyreleaf Greeneyes

ASTERACEAE (ASTER FAMILY)

PLANT AND LEAVES: An herbaceous perennial, Chocolate Daisy usually grows to 1 to 2 feet in height but may reach 4 feet in some locations. The plant produces multiple branching stems

with variable but often lyre-shaped leaves—thus, the specific epithet of the botanical name.

FLOWERS AND FRUIT: Flower stems branch into corymbose arrays and bear terminal flower heads about 2 inches in diameter with maroon or red disc flowers and yellow ray flowers. The lower surfaces of the ray flowers are marked with maroon veins.

FLOWERING: Most flowering occurs from June to October, but this species will flower just about any time conditions allow.

RANGE AND HABITAT: It can be found in dry, rocky soils and in savannahs in the southern Great Plains and in the foothills of the southern Rocky Mountains and into northern Mexico. In Texas, Chocolate Daisy is native to areas bounding New Mexico from the Panhandle to Big Bend. It can be found as far east as the Concho Valley.

COMMENTS: Chocolate Daisy is infrequently cultivated but deserves a place in xeric gardens owing to its showy nature, long flowering season, and its unusual, chocolate-scented flowers. After flowering, its seed heads make interesting additions to dried flower arrangements.

Chamaecrista fasciculata

Partridge Pea

FABACEAE (PEA FAMILY)
Synonym: *Cassia fasciculata*

PLANT AND LEAVES: Partridge Pea is an annual herb growing 1 to 4 feet tall, averaging about 18 inches. It often occurs in stands of dozens or even hundreds of plants. The plant is erect, often unbranched or with a few branches near the top. The leaves are alternate, 1 to 5 inches long, and have 8 to 14 pairs of leaflets, ¼ to ⅝ inch long. Each leaf's petiole has a small gland containing the only nectar produced by the plant.

FLOWERS AND FRUIT: Several flower buds develop in the leaf axils along the stem. The flowers are irregularly shaped and about 1 inch in diameter. They have five butter-yellow petals with one lower petal larger than the others and the other lower petal oddly cupped and curved toward the flower's center. At the base of two to four of the petals is a distinctive red or purple

M-shaped mark. Each flower has 10 curved stamens, all angled either right or left on each plant. Stamens with yellow anthers have fertile pollen; those with purple anthers have sterile food pollen used by a variety of bee species. The pistil extends conspicuously to the side opposite the stamens.

FLOWERING: Partridge Pea has a long flowering period, extending from June to October.

RANGE AND HABITAT: A nitrogen-fixing species, Partridge Pea is abundant in poor or sandy soil in east and central Texas and spreads rapidly; in some years it covers large areas of uncultivated fields. Its native range covers nearly all of the eastern United States from the Great Plains to the Atlantic Seaboard.

COMMENTS: Though it is not palatable to livestock, Partridge Pea is an important food plant for native bees and also for deer and seed-eating birds.

Echeandia flavescens

Torrey's Crag Lily

LILIACEAE (LILY FAMILY)

Synonym: *Anthericum torreyi*

PLANT AND LEAVES: Torrey's Crag Lily is an herbaceous perennial growing from a corm. It produces a slender, unbranched flowering scape, 1 to 2 feet tall. The very narrow, grass-like leaves, which have finely toothed margins and are about 4 inches in length, are clustered at the plant's base.

FLOWERS AND FRUIT: The orangish or golden-yellow flowers are borne in the topmost ⅓ of the flower scape. A flower's three petals are elliptical or somewhat spoon shaped, while its three sepals are typically a bit narrower but about the same length as the petals. All six tepals (sepals and petals) are the same color and usually have a faint green stripe down the middle. The flower's six stamens are held erect but spreading. The flowers close in the afternoon and open again in the morning. The fruits (capsules) are three-lobed and oblong, resembling a partially deflated football.

FLOWERING: Flowering may begin around the first of June and continue until October. Late-summer flowering is most common.

RANGE AND HABITAT: Torrey's Crag Lily's native habitat is open forest in arid mountains and in desert grasslands. It can be found in the mountains of west Texas, New Mexico, Arizona, and northern Mexico.

COMMENTS: A closely related species, Texas Crag Lily (*Echeandia texensis*), is very similar to Torrey's Crag Lily, but its flowers are usually butter yellow with tepals that curve back and erect stamens that adhere to one another in a point, giving the flower a shooting-star appearance.

Gutierrezia microcephala
Threadleaf Broomweed, Small-head Snakeweed
ASTERACEAE (ASTER FAMILY)
Synonym: *Xanthocephalum microcephalum*

PLANT AND LEAVES: Threadleaf Broomweed is a perennial shrub or subshrub, 1 to 3 feet tall and with many branches, especially in the upper part. It may sometimes reach 3 to 4 feet across

the top of the spreading branches. The plant has a somewhat rounded appearance. The narrow leaves are ½ to 1½ inches long, alternate, and with bunches of smaller, narrower leaves in their axils.

FLOWERS AND FRUIT: Two to six small flower heads are held in clusters at the tips of stems. Each head normally includes only one disc flower and one yellow ray flower. Occasionally, an extra disc and/or ray flower may be present in a head.

FLOWERING: Flowering occurs from June to October.

RANGE AND HABITAT: Threadleaf Broomweed is a common constituent of arid lands from Texas to California and much of Mexico, where it inhabits chaparral, grasslands, and other open areas on limestone and gypseous soils. In Texas, it is found in the Chihuahuan Desert and in nearby areas with suitable habitat.

COMMENTS: In some areas of the western United States, great expanses are covered in bumpy, greenish-yellow mounds of this species. It sequesters selenium in its tissue, which makes the plant toxic to livestock.

Senna lindheimeriana

Lindheimer's Senna, Velvet Leaf Senna

FABACEAE (PEA FAMILY)
Synonym: *Cassia lindheimeriana*

PLANT AND LEAVES: Lindheimer's Senna is a widely branching herb growing from a perennial root. It may reach 6 feet in height but usually grows to about 3 feet tall. Its compound leaves are 3 to 6 inches long with four to eight pairs of leaflets that are oval, sometimes pointed, and covered with soft, velvety hairs.

FLOWERS AND FRUIT: Flowers are bright yellow to orange yellow, about 1 inch across, and clustered at the ends of the stems. The five oval petals are crimped at the edges. The fruits are flattened legumes, ¾ to 1½ inches long. They mature in the fall.

FLOWERING: Flowering occurs for the most part from June to October.

RANGE AND HABITAT: Lindheimer's Senna is common on rocky, limestone soils on the Edwards Plateau and grows widely throughout the Trans-Pecos. It ranges west across southern New Mexico into southeast Arizona and south into northern Mexico.

COMMENTS: Though not symmetrical in habit, Lindheimer's Senna is quite attractive in flower and makes a nice addition to xeric gardens within the species' native range. It sometimes produces sterile hybrids with the closely related Two-leaf Senna (*Senna roemeriana*), and the hybrids have characteristics intermediate between both parents. This species is highly toxic to livestock.

Verbesina encelioides

Cowpen Daisy, Golden Crownbeard, Butter Daisy

ASTERACEAE (ASTER FAMILY)

PLANT AND LEAVES: Cowpen Daisy is an attractive herbaceous annual that grows 2 to 4 feet tall with spreading branches. Its leaves are rough and grayish green. The largest leaves are usually roughly delta shaped, 2 to 3 or even 4 inches long, and half as wide at the base. Smaller leaves are often lance shaped. The margins of all leaves have coarse teeth. The larger leaves of plants in east Texas are often auriculate at the base. The leaves of west Texas plants typically lack "ears."

FLOWERS AND FRUIT: This species' flower heads are held at the end of long, leafless peduncles. They are 1 to 1½ inches across with about 12 ray flowers and 100 or more disc flowers per head. Its ray flowers are butter yellow to orangish yellow, each with four lobes at the end of each lamina; the two inner lobes are slightly longer than the outer ones. The disc flowers are orange, aging to dull greenish or brownish yellow.

FLOWERING: The rather long flowering season for Cowpen Daisy may begin as early as June and continue to October.

RANGE AND HABITAT: Very frequent in disturbed soils throughout most of Texas. Because of its showy nature and because it is often inadvertently transported by farm and ranch operations, Cowpen Daisy is widespread across most of the United States. Its exact native range is undetermined.

COMMENTS: Cowpen Daisy comes by its common name quite honestly, being a very common constituent of barnyard flora across its range.

Wislizenia refracta

Jackass-clover, Spectacle Fruit

CAPPARIDACEAE (CAPER OR SPIDERFLOWER FAMILY)

PLANT AND LEAVES: Jackass-clover is a sturdy annual herb with many branches. It grows 1 to 6 feet tall. Leaves are alternately arranged and often closely spaced on the stem. The leaves, each composed of three 1-inch-long, oval-shaped leaflets, are borne on short petioles. Despite the clover-like appearance of its leaves, this species is unrelated to true clovers (*Trifolium* spp.) and their many near relatives, also known as clovers, which are classified in the pea family, Fabaceae.

FLOWERS AND FRUIT: The yellow flowers, about ½ inch across, grow in racemes covering approximately the upper fourth of the stem. Flowers open beginning at the lowest part of the inflorescence and proceeding upward. The many stamens extend beyond the petals and persist even after the petals wither, giving the flower head a feathery appearance. In ideal conditions, Jackass-clover often grows so thickly that it gives a yellow cast to a considerable area.

FLOWERING: Flowering can begin in June and continue to October.

RANGE AND HABITAT: This species is at home in desert scrubland from the El Paso area westward to Nevada and California and south to Chihuahua and Sonora, Mexico.

COMMENTS: Jackass-clover is toxic to livestock and other grazing animals, but its distastefulness precludes poisonings. Flowers are said to be good nectar sources for honey production.

Helianthus annuus

Common Sunflower

ASTERACEAE (ASTER FAMILY)

PLANT AND LEAVES: Common Sunflower is an herbaceous annual that may grow to 10 feet in height. Its stout, bristly, often purple stem may be 1½ inches in diameter at the base. It is widely branched and may spread 6 to 8 feet across. Leaves are alternate, coarsely toothed, 3 to 6 inches long, broad at the base, and tapering to a fine point. The petiole is often as long as the leaf.

FLOWERS AND FRUIT: Flower heads of wild-growing plants are typically 3½ to 5½ inches across, growing singly at the top of the flower stem. The golden-yellow ray flowers are 1 to 2 inches long, often overlapping. The disc flowers are usually dark brown, and the center is about 1½ inches across.

FLOWERING: Flowering occurs from June to November.

RANGE AND HABITAT: The original native range is unknown but believed to encompass nearly all of the contiguous 48 US states, some of western Canada, and northern Mexico. It can be found in virtually every corner of Texas and grows wherever it finds fairly moist, rich soil.

COMMENTS: The spiral patterns of the disc florets are classic examples of often-observed Fibonacci sequences in nature. A popular garden plant, hundreds of cultivars of this species have been introduced to horticulture. The annual value of Common Sunflower as a US agricultural crop exceeds $500 million.

Thymophylla acerosa

Prickleleaf Dogweed, Texas Dogweed

ASTERACEAE (ASTER FAMILY)

Synonym: *Dyssodia acerosa*

PLANT AND LEAVES: Prickleleaf Dogweed is a diminutive, perennial shrub or subshrub, forming a fairly neat mound 4 to 8 inches tall and about 12 inches across. It grows from a woody stem with several branches near the base and has many slender, sharp-pointed leaves less than 1 inch long.

FLOWERS AND FRUIT: When in full glory, a flowering Prickleleaf Dogweed is a sight to behold. The bright yellow radiate flower heads, less than 1 inch across, are clustered at the ends of short stems. Each flower head bears about 8 tiny, lemon-yellow ray

flowers surrounding a center cluster of about 20 or so pale yellow disc flowers.

FLOWERING: This species will flower any time conditions are suitable, but most flowering occurs in summer and fall (June to November).

RANGE AND HABITAT: Prickleleaf Dogweed is native to limestone and gypsum desert soils from the Concho Valley, through the Big Bend region, and onward west to Nevada and into Mexico.

COMMENTS: The dogweeds are strongly scented plants. Just walking through them stirs up a lingering, unpleasant odor reminiscent of a wet dog. The genus name, *Thymophylla*, refers to the resemblance of its foliage to some species of the culinary herb, thyme. Similarly, the specific epithet for this species, *acerosa*, acknowledges its needle-like leaves.

Pectis angustifolia
Lemonscent
ASTERACEAE (ASTER FAMILY)

PLANT AND LEAVES: Lemonscent is an aromatic, herbaceous annual with a mounding or matted habit. It grows to 1 to 8 inches tall and 12 to 24 or more inches across. The leaves are bright

green, with a strong vein down the center, very narrow, and about ¼ to 1¾ inches long.

FLOWERS AND FRUIT: Flower heads are bunched at the ends of the branches and often completely conceal the plant below. The flower heads are less than 1 inch across and have 8 to 10 short, bright yellow ray flowers and about 10 to 15 yellow disc flowers centrally.

FLOWERING: Lemonscent flowers from June to December.

RANGE AND HABITAT: This is a species of the US Desert Southwest and northern Mexico, where it grows on sandy bars, rocky slopes, open grasslands, and roadsides. In Texas, Lemonscent is found in the Trans-Pecos and along Rio Grande River.

COMMENTS: A crushed leaf has a lemon-scented aroma and is good in tea. The experience of smelling the sweet, lemon fragrance emitted by a large stand of this species after a fall rain is unforgettable.

Helenium amarum var. *badium*
Basin Sneezeweed, Brown Bitterweed
ASTERACEAE (ASTER FAMILY)
Synonym: *Helenium badium*

PLANT AND LEAVES: Basin Sneezeweed is an erect annual, 1 to 2½ feet tall. The threadlike leaves are 1½ to 2 inches long and are concentrated below the naked flower stems, which are 4 to 8 inches long. Its lower leaves are often pinnately lobed.

FLOWERS AND FRUIT: Flower heads are borne at the end of the stems and are 1 to 2 inches across. Ray flowers are yellow and three lobed at the end, generally pointing downward at about a 45-degree angle. The disc flowers are reddish brown and clustered in an almost spherical dome, with the ray flowers attached to the lower side of the sphere.

FLOWERING: Flowering occurs from July to October.

RANGE AND HABITAT: Basin Sneezeweed has a much smaller native range than its sister variety and includes only parts of Texas, southern Oklahoma, and northern Mexico. In Texas, it is often found on sandy soils in the northern and western regions of

the state. The range of its sister variety, *Helenium amarum* var. *amarum*, covers most of the eastern United States as far north as Massachusetts and Wisconsin.

COMMENTS: The common name, Brown Bitterweed, is well deserved. When eaten by cattle, this species imparts a noticeable bitter flavor to the cows' milk, making it unpalatable and unmarketable. Consequently, dairy operators are careful to keep this plant out of their pastures.

Helianthus mollis

Ashy Sunflower, Downy Sunflower

ASTERACEAE (ASTER FAMILY)

PLANT AND LEAVES: Ashy Sunflower is an erect, herbaceous perennial that spreads by rhizomes and often forms dense stands. It reaches 2 to 5 feet in height, branching only in the upper part of the plant. The leaves and stems are covered with velvety hairs. Leaves are sessile or clasping, opposite, 2 to 5 inches long, half as wide, and toothed.

FLOWERS AND FRUIT: Flower heads are 3 to 4 inches across, with 15 to 30 lemon-yellow ray flowers, deeply veined, and about 2 inches long. The numerous central disc flowers start out greenish brown and mature to yellow.

FLOWERING: Flowering begins in July and continues to October.

RANGE AND HABITAT: A native of the prairies of the eastern Great Plains and the Mississippi River Valley, where it prefers dry, sandy, or rocky soils and is commonly found growing on roadsides. It has been introduced to the eastern United States, where it has naturalized, and its range is expanding. In Texas, it can be found on suitable habitat in the eastern third of the state.

COMMENTS: The common name Ashy Sunflower refers to the ashy, gray-green appearance of the plant's leaves. It is easily cultivated but its colonial tendencies and allelopathic properties make a bit of a garden thug.

Xanthocephalum gymnospermoides

Gummy Broomweed, San Pedro Matchweed

ASTERACEAE (ASTER FAMILY)
Synonym: *Gutierrezia gymnospermoides*

PLANT AND LEAVES: Gummy Broomweed is an annual herb. A single-stemmed plant at the base, it is usually well-branched and rounded at the top and grows 1 to 4½ feet tall. Leaves are narrow and 1 to 4 inches long.

FLOWERS AND FRUIT: There are about 20 flower heads to a stem, and they are quite showy when growing in dense masses. Glands on the flower heads' phyllaries produce gummy, sticky secretions. The ray flowers are short, only ½ inch long, and number 50 or more per head. The flower head's center is about ½ inch in diameter and is composed of up to 200 tiny disc flowers.

FLOWERING: Gummy Broomweed flowers when conditions are optimal, any time between July and October.

RANGE AND HABITAT: Seasonally moist forest bottomland, meadows, and arroyos in the Trans-Pecos and northern Mexico.

COMMENTS: The stems of this uncommon species are loaded with volatile resins that make its dead branches very useful as a fire starter, thus explaining the common name San Pedro Matchweed. Gummy Broomweed's botanical name has been revised more than once in recent years. In some publications

it is still placed in the genus *Gutierrezia*. The current genus name, *Xanthocephalum*, is fittingly derived from Greek words meaning "yellow head."

Pericome caudata

Mountain Tail-leaf, Tail-leaf Pericome

ASTERACEAE (ASTER FAMILY)
Synonyms: *Pericome caudata* var. *glandulosa*, *Pericome glandulosa*

PLANT AND LEAVES: Mountain Tail-leaf is a perennial herb or subshrub that grows to 5 feet tall and is often 5 feet across at the top. It is woody at the base, is very leafy, and tends to sprawl. Leaf size and shape vary somewhat across its range, but in Texas the upper leaves are about 1 inch long on short petioles, alternate, triangular, and tapering to a long tip. The lower leaves are much longer and opposite.

FLOWERS AND FRUIT: Each upper branch has one to five butter- or orange-yellow discoid flower heads borne in clusters, each cluster ½ to 1½ inches across, on stems less than 1 inch long that grow from the leaf axils on the main stem. They have many disc flowers but no ray flowers.

FLOWERING: The flowering season of Mountain Tail-leaf runs from July to November.

RANGE AND HABITAT: Mountain Tail-leaf is native on rocky soils and roadsides from Texas and the panhandle of Oklahoma across the Desert Southwest to California and northern Mexico. It grows in the mountains of west Texas. The ones we have seen were at elevations of 4,000 feet or more.

COMMENTS: Early Spaniards called this species *Hierba de Chivato*, meaning "billy goat weed," for its unpleasant odor.

Solidago altissima

Tall Goldenrod, Late Goldenrod, Canada Goldenrod

ASTERACEAE (ASTER FAMILY)
Synonym: *Solidago canadensis* var. *scabra*

PLANT AND LEAVES: Tall Goldenrod is an herbaceous perennial growing 2 to 6 feet tall, with alternate, finely toothed leaves, 3 to 4 inches long, attached directly to the stem or by very short petioles.

FLOWERS AND FRUIT: The golden-yellow, radiate flower heads are about ¼ inch across and crowded on the upper side of each of the many arching branches. The fruits of this and other goldenrod species are cypselae with attached pappi (tiny tufts of whitish hairs) that allow them to be carried by the wind to new locations.

FLOWERING: The flowering period for Tall Goldenrod begins as early as July and continues to November.

RANGE AND HABITAT: Often found on uncultivated land over the eastern third of the state; less frequently to the Trans-Pecos.

COMMENTS: More than 20 species of goldenrod occur in Texas. The innumerable tiny yellow flower heads in plume-like clusters are its most identifying feature. An insect-pollinated genus, goldenrod produces pollen too heavy to be wind-borne though it is often incorrectly identified as a source of pollen allergies.

Grindelia papposa

Spanish Gold, Clasping-leaf Daisy, Goldenweed

ASTERACEAE (ASTER FAMILY)

Synonyms: *Grindelia ciliata*, *Haplopappus ciliatus*, *Prionopsis ciliata*

PLANT AND LEAVES: Spanish Gold is a coarse, bushy annual or biennial growing up to 5 feet tall. It has alternate leaves, 1 to 1¾ inch long and half as wide. They are spiny toothed and clasp the stem halfway around or more.

FLOWERS AND FRUIT: The three to five rows of tough, green phyllaries that surround the flower head are quite attractive when it is in bud. The flower head bears 20 to 30 narrow, pointed, yellow ray flowers and many yellow disc flowers in the center.

FLOWERING: Flowering occurs from August to October.

RANGE AND HABITAT: Spanish Gold is native to the central and southern Great Plains and eastern US Southwest. It has

naturalized in Arizona and California and also through the Mississippi River Valley as far north as Michigan. In Texas, it can be found along roadsides and in grassland and prairies in the northwestern half of the state.

COMMENTS: For many years, the classification of this species has been confused and remains so to this day. Various authors sometimes assign to it any of the synonyms listed on the previous page.

Machaeranthera gracilis

Slender Goldenweed, Grass-leaf Tansy-aster

ASTERACEAE (ASTER FAMILY)

Synonyms: *Xanthisma gracile*, *Haplopappus gracilis*, *Sideranthus gracilis*

PLANT AND LEAVES: Slender Goldenweed is a small, herbaceous, taprooted annual that grows 10 to 15 inches tall. Its many narrow leaves are ⅛ to ¼ inch long, the lower ones shallowly toothed. Stiff branches, 1 to 3 inches long, arise from the upper half of the main stem, each bearing one flower head.

FLOWERS AND FRUIT: Each flower head, ½ to ¾ inch across, has 20 to 30 yellow ray flowers and as many as 100 tiny yellow disc flowers.

FLOWERING: This species' flowering season runs from August to November.

RANGE AND HABITAT: Slender Goldenweed grows on bare rocky or sandy soils in desert areas of the US Southwest and northern Mexico. In Texas, it is common on roadsides in west Texas's Davis Mountains.

COMMENTS: This little plant makes up in numbers what it lacks in size. Sometimes it covers large areas, 1 or 2 acres, with its bright yellow flowers. Many current references place this species in *Xanthisma* and many older references classify it in *Haplopappus*. It seems, though, that this little jewel is marvelously unconcerned with whatever names we contrive to call it.

Viguiera stenoloba

Skeletonleaf Goldeneye

ASTERACEAE (ASTER FAMILY)

PLANT AND LEAVES: Skeletonleaf Goldeneye is a multibranched shrub growing 2 to 5 feet in height and about as broad. Its leaves are deeply divided into linear lobes that give the plant a soft, feathery appearance.

FLOWERS AND FRUIT: The radiate flower heads are about 1 inch across on long, slender peduncles and may be borne as a single head or in clusters of as many as 25 flower heads. About 15 in number, the golden or butter-yellow ray flowers are deeply veined. The centers of the flower heads hold dozens of orangish disc flowers, aging to brownish yellow.

FLOWERING: Flowers sporadically from June to September and then heavily to October.

RANGE AND HABITAT: Skeletonleaf Goldeneye is native on alkaline soils along the Rio Grande River from El Paso to Brownsville and extends farther into Texas in the Big Bend region and in the Concho Valley. However, its Texas and New Mexico populations represent the northern limit of what is essentially a Mexican species.

COMMENTS: Skeletonleaf Goldeneye grows in great abundance in the Trans-Pecos. Its drought tolerance, pruning tolerance, deer resistance, and lovely texture make it a good candidate for xeric gardens.

Helianthus maximiliani

Maximilian Sunflower

ASTERACEAE (ASTER FAMILY)

PLANT AND LEAVES: An unusual perennial, Maximilian Sunflower reaches 2 to 10 feet in height. It spreads by rhizomes. Leaves are long and narrow, up to 10 inches near the bottom and as

short as 2 inches near the top. They are alternate, coarse and hairy, slightly wavy on the edges, often folded lengthwise, slightly toothed, and very pointed.

FLOWERS AND FRUIT: Flower heads, scattered along the upper half of the plant, grow from the leaf axils on short peduncles to about 12 inches long at the lower parts of the plant and to 3 inches near the top. The flower head is usually about 3 inches in diameter (sometimes up to 5 inches), with 15 to 19 lemon-yellow ray flowers, deeply veined and slightly toothed on the tip. The center of disc flowers is 1 inch or more across and green to dark brown.

FLOWERING: Flowering begins as early as June in the northern parts of its range; late September to November in Texas.

RANGE AND HABITAT: Maximilian Sunflower is native to the US Great Plains and Mexico. It has spread by cultivation and is now naturalized in most of the United States and Canada. Originally a constituent of deep, rich prairie soils, it prefers that habitat. Often found on fencerows where its seeds are dropped by birds.

COMMENTS: This species is often eaten by livestock, and its seeds are an important winter food of seed-eating birds like gold-finches and sparrows. Named for German naturalist, Prince Maximilian of Wied-Neuwied.

Viguiera dentata
Plateau Goldeneye, Toothleaf Goldeneye
ASTERACEAE (ASTER FAMILY)
Synonym: *Helianthus dentatus*

PLANT AND LEAVES: Plateau Goldeneye is an erect, multibranched herbaceous perennial, normally 3 to 4 feet tall but may reach 6 feet in height in ideal conditions. The leaves and stems are covered with coarse hair. Leaves are variable, but a typical leaf is broadest at the base with serrate or serrulate margins and is sharply pointed.

FLOWERS AND FRUIT: Flower heads are showy and are borne in clusters of 5 to 10 heads 1 to 1½ inches in diameter and held

in corymb-like arrays, often nearly covering the plant. Each radiate flower head has 10 to 15 golden or orange-yellow ray flowers and dozens of orange disc flowers fading to greenish brown with age.

FLOWERING: This species may flower as early as August, but most flowing occurs in October and November.

RANGE AND HABITAT: Native to calcareous soils on the Edwards Plateau and the Big Bend in Texas, its range extends west to Arizona and south into northern Mexico.

COMMENTS: Though Plateau Goldeneye appreciates moist soils, it is amazingly drought tolerant and happily withstands the most extreme climatic conditions Texas can throw its way. In late summer, it often wilts badly each afternoon and then shows no sign of stress the following morning. Its summer toughness and autumn floral show has made it a favorite for xeric gardens.

Orange
Flowers

Bignonia capreolata

Crossvine

BIGNONIACEAE (TRUMPET-CREEPER FAMILY)

Synonym: *Anisostichus capreolata*

PLANT AND LEAVES: Crossvine is a high-climbing, perennial, woody, semi-evergreen vine. It can grow to the top of a tree, 50 feet or more in height. It spreads by stolons and can form large colonies where conditions are favorable. The leaves are opposite and compound, with leaflets 2 to 6 inches long and about 1 inch wide. The leaves are also a bit odd. Though the leaves appear to be borne in pairs, they're actually trifoliate; that is, they have three leaflets. The terminal leaflet is modified—so modified that it is, in fact, a tendril having a forked end used in climbing and adhering to structures.

FLOWERS AND FRUIT: Crossvine is easy to locate when flowering because it often nearly covers the tops of its supporting trees and cloaks them in orange. The large, attractive, trumpet-shaped flowers, 2 inches long and 1½ inches across, grow in clusters of four to six and are usually deep red on the outside and red to yellowish on the inside, though color variations exist. From a distance, masses of flowers appear to be orange. Some have described the flower's fragrance as like coffee or mocha and nice; others characterize it as odorous and unpleasant. Like other members of its family, Crossvine's fruit is a long, bean-like capsule, 4 to 6 inches long, and contains a large number of wafer-like, winged seeds that are distributed by the wind.

FLOWERING: Flowering begins as early as mid-March and may continue until June.

RANGE AND HABITAT: Crossvine is native to the moist woodlands with rich soils in east Texas and across the South.

COMMENTS: When cut in cross section, the pith in the stem of this species is shaped like a cross; thus, the common name.

Kallstroemia grandiflora

Arizona Poppy, Desert Poppy

ZYGOPHYLLACEAE (CREOSOTE-BUSH FAMILY)

PLANT AND LEAVES: Arizona Poppy is an annual herb, often occurring in clumps. It grows 2 to 3 feet tall and spreads 2 to 5 feet across. The plant has hairy stems. Leaves are opposite and compound, with 5 to 10 pairs of leaflets and no terminal leaflet, about 1 inch long on each side of the rachis.

FLOWERS AND FRUIT: The yellow-orange or sometimes off-white flowers, often 2 inches in diameter, have five sepals, five petals, and ten stamens. Irrespective of petal color, flowers typically have a red center. It is easy to confuse this flower with some of the mallows, but the stamens of mallows often join, forming a column and making the center of the flower very prominent, while the stamens of Arizona Poppy remain separate. The fruit is beaked and has 10 nutlets arranged in a circle and protected by persistent, hairy sepals. The nutlets separate and fall to the ground when mature.

FLOWERING: Flowering may occur any time between March and October, usually following rains.

RANGE AND HABITAT: Arizona Poppy is found in the Trans-Pecos ecoregion of southwest Texas. It ranges west to southern California and northern Mexico. True to its name, it is especially abundant in Arizona where it sometimes occurs in large colonies. It is common in roadside swales, waste areas, and open grasslands.

COMMENTS: Arizona Poppy seeds are a favorite bird food, especially relished by doves. Though its flowers resemble them, it is not related to true poppies, which are in the family Papaveraceae.

Eschscholzia californica ssp. *mexicana*

Mexican Gold Poppy

PAPAVERACEAE (POPPY FAMILY)
Synonym: *Eschscholzia mexicana*

PLANT AND LEAVES: Mexican Gold Poppy is an annual herb growing to about 16 inches tall with many branching stems forming

a somewhat bushy plant. Its leaves, up to 4 inches long, are borne at the base of the plant and on the stems. They are blue green and divided into many narrow segments, giving them a fern-like appearance.

FLOWERS AND FRUIT: The flowers, yellow, orange, or rarely white, are borne at the tops of the stems. They have two sepals that join at the top to form a cap that looks like a wizard's hat, which is pushed off by the expanding petals. Stamens are yellow to orange. The flowers open only in fair weather, remaining closed at night and on cloudy days.

FLOWERING: In Texas, flowering occurs during April and May.

RANGE AND HABITAT: This poppy is fairly rare in Texas. Noted Texas botanist Barton H. Warnock found it on the eastern slope of the Franklin Mountains and below Lajitas, on the lower trail across Mesa de Anguila. However, it is much more common in the Sonoran and Mojave Deserts in the US Southwest and in northern Mexico.

COMMENTS: When the Mexican Gold Poppy is growing in favorable habitats, it spreads over large areas and makes the earth seem as if it had turned to gold. It is closely related to the California poppy (*Eschscholzia californica* ssp. *californica*), which is not native to Texas.

Lantana urticoides
Texas Lantana
VERBENACEAE (VERBENA FAMILY)
Synonym: *Lantana horrida*

PLANT AND LEAVES: Texas Lantana is a multibranched, sprawling, mounded, woody shrub growing 2 to 5 feet high with an about equal spread. The plant is deciduous in all but the Lower Rio Grande Valley, dying to the ground each winter and resprouting each spring. Its young stems are densely hairy and four-angled; the older stems are usually somewhat prickly. The plant has opposite, dark green, broadly lance-shaped leaves, 1½ to 3 inches long and 1 to 2 inches wide. The leaves have coarsely toothed edges and hairy surfaces very rough to the touch.

FLOWERS AND FRUIT: The inflorescences are showy hemispherical

heads of numerous flowers 1 to 1½ inches in diameter and
borne from the upper leaf axils. The flowers in the center of the
inflorescence are usually yellow; those around them are orange
to red. Each flower is funnel shaped, about ¼ inch across at the
opening, and has four rounded petals.

FLOWERING: Texas Lantana flowers most of the year in south
Texas, April to October throughout east and central Texas, and
a little earlier in the Trans-Pecos.

RANGE AND HABITAT: This shrub can be found in the south Texas
thorn scrub country and along the coast to Mississippi and
south to Mexico.

COMMENTS: Texas Lantana is often the first and best choice for
gardeners looking for a drought-tolerant, heat-resistant, deer-
resistant, colorful shrub for their Texas landscapes. Texas

Lantana is Texas tough. Hummingbirds and butterflies find the plant's nectar-laden flowers irresistible. Fruit-eating birds relish its berries.

Phemeranthus aurantiacus

Orange Flameflower

PORTULACACEAE (PURSLANE FAMILY)
Synonym: *Talinum aurantiacum*

PLANT AND LEAVES: Orange Flameflower is a perennial herb growing 4 to 18 inches tall from a woody root. The plant is erect, sometimes unbranched but often branched and spreading at the base. Stems and leaves are fleshy. The leaves are rather flat and narrow, up to about 2½ inches long, alternate, and attached directly to the stem.

FLOWERS AND FRUIT: Flowers are usually produced singly, sometimes in groups of two or three. They are borne on short pedicels emerging from the leaf axils, yellow red to orange red, and with five petals, each ¾ to 1¼ inches long. They open in the

morning or early afternoon and wither by evening. The fruit is a small roundish capsule.

FLOWERING: Flowering occurs April to October.

RANGE AND HABITAT: Orange Flameflower is found on sandy or rocky soil in meadows, plains, chaparral, and other scrubland from central to south and west Texas. Its native range extends west to Arizona and south to northern Mexico.

COMMENTS: Before and after flowering, this species is often lost in the surrounding vegetation and is rarely noticed. But when its fiery orange-red petals unfurl, it is a head-turner. Though small, the flowers are so brilliantly colored that they simply cannot be missed or ignored.

Asclepias tuberosa

Butterfly Weed, Orange Milkweed

ASCLEPIADACEAE (MILKWEED FAMILY)

PLANT AND LEAVES: Butterfly Weed grows 1 to 2½ feet tall. The plant's long taproot is well designed to help the plant thrive

in times of drought but makes the plant difficult to transplant for those wishing to add it to their gardens. The leaves are mostly alternate, 1½ to 4 inches long, pointed, and smooth on the edge.

FLOWERS AND FRUIT: The flowers of all milkweed species are unusual and interesting—even showy—but most are not brilliantly colored. That cannot be said of Butterfly Weed. Its yellow-orange to bright orange umbels of flowers, borne at the top of the plant's stems and 2 to 5 inches across, scream, "Look at me!" So look, we do. We cannot help but look!

FLOWERING: For this species, flowering occurs from May to August.

RANGE AND HABITAT: Butterfly Weed is found on prairies, meadows, and roadsides on sandy, limestone-based soils in east and central Texas. Its native range includes all but about the northwestern third of the United States.

COMMENTS: The leaves of Butterfly Weed are poisonous to most herbivores, but many butterfly species, including the Monarch, feed on the nectar. We have seen up to four different species of butterflies at once on a small plant. Aside from its brilliant flower color, Butterfly Weed is unusual for another reason; unlike other milkweeds, it does not exude a milky secretion when wounded.

Campis radicans

Trumpet Creeper, Trumpet Vine

BIGNONIACEAE (TRUMPET-CREEPER FAMILY)
Synonyms: *Bignonia radicans*, *Tecoma radicans*

PLANT AND LEAVES: Trumpet Creeper is a perennial, woody vine, climbing trees by means of root-like holdfasts. Alternatively, it often creeps on the ground, where it can form large, dense colonies. Leaves are compound and opposite, 8 to 15 inches long, with 7 to 13 coarsely toothed leaflets ¾ to 3 inches long and ½ to 1½ inches wide, olive green, and shiny above.

FLOWERS AND FRUIT: During the heat of summer, clusters of 2 to 12 orange-red, trumpet-shaped flowers adorn new growth at the tops of trees. The flowers are 2 to 3½ inches long with five petal-like lobes. Nonclimbing, ground-dwelling plants rarely

flower. Trumpet Creeper's fruit is a 3- to 5-inch-long, bean-like capsule. When mature, it splits open, releasing to the wind scores of wafer-like seeds, each with a pair of membranous wings that aid in their dispersal.

FLOWERING: Flowering begins in June and may continue until late September.

RANGE AND HABITAT: Trumpet Creeper can be found in rich, moist woodlands in southeast and central Texas. Its range extends across most of the eastern half of the United States.

COMMENTS: This species is frequently cultivated because of its large clusters of attractive, bright red flowers and its appeal to hummingbirds. It is pollinated by them and bumblebees. It is a hardy plant and, unless controlled, can become a pest.

Sphaeralcea angustifolia

Narrowleaf Globemallow, Copper Globemallow

MALVACEAE (MALLOW FAMILY)

PLANT AND LEAVES: Narrowleaf Globemallow is a perennial herb or tender shrub usually growing 1 to 3 feet in height and spread. Exceptional specimens can reach 6 feet tall. The stem and leaves of this species are covered in silvery hairs. This species is distinguished from others by its long, narrow leaves, 1 to 2 inches long, many of them folded in half down the middle, all of them wavy on the edges, and often with a marginal tooth near the base.

FLOWERS AND FRUIT: Narrowleaf Globemallow flowers are arranged in clusters in the leaf axils and may flower at any location along the stem at any time. The wide variety of flower colors of this species is remarkable. Though the flower color is often orange, plants with salmon, red, or pink petals are all common. The flowers' five petals are ½ inch long, and the flowers are cup shaped.

FLOWERING: Flowering occurs from June to November.

RANGE AND HABITAT: In Texas, Narrowleaf Globemallow can be found in desert scrub and on dry prairies from the Concho

Valley and westward through the Trans-Pecos ecoregion and northward through the Panhandle. Its native range extends north to southwestern Kansas, west to California, and south into northern Mexico.

COMMENTS: It is difficult to distinguish one species of globemallow from another because of the slight variations that separate them. They usually flower between June and November and may flower more than once during that time if rains are favorable. We have seen Narrowleaf Globemallow as early as the last half of April. They are abundant in the Davis Mountains.

Platanthera ciliaris
Orange Fringed Orchid, Orange Plume
ORCHIDACEAE (ORCHID FAMILY)
Synonyms: *Habenaria ciliaris*, *Blephariglotis ciliaris*

PLANT AND LEAVES: Orange Fringed Orchid is an herbaceous perennial, often forming large colonies. It produces a single stem that grows 1 to 3 feet tall. Two to four lance-shaped leaves, about 1¼ inches wide and up to 12 inches long, are attached at or near the plant's base and arranged alternately on the stem. Leaves higher on the plant's stem become progressively smaller and are reduced to bracts just below the inflorescence.

FLOWERS AND FRUIT: The very showy inflorescence is a tight cylindrical raceme as much as 3 inches in diameter on the upper 2 to 6 inches of the stem. The individual flowers, 1½ inches long, are dark orange to yellow orange, with a conspicuous spur and a well-developed fringe on the lower lip. The spurs of this species are the longest in the orange-flowered *Platanthera*, longer than its flowers' pedicels. This feature makes the species easily distinguishable from the very similar, though less common, Texas native species Chapman's Orchid (*Platanthera chapmanii*) and Crested Fringed Orchid (*Platanthera cristata*).

FLOWERING: This species can be found flowering from July to September.

RANGE AND HABITAT: Occurs in sphagnum bogs, swamps, marshes, and other moist places in and around pine woodlands in southeast Texas. Its North American range is large; Orange Fringed Orchid can be found in every state east of a line between Texas and Michigan, except Maine.

COMMENTS: This species' height and large inflorescences of orange-yellow flowers make it easy to spot—stunning, in fact. A population of these plants in flower is a sight never to be forgotten.

Ferocactus wislizeni

Fishhook Barrel Cactus, Candy Barrel Cactus

CACTACEAE (CACTUS FAMILY)
Synonym: *Echinocactus wislizeni*

PLANT AND LEAVES: The Fishhook Barrel Cactus is a rounded mound early in life, then oval or cone-shaped, and finally cylindrical. It may grow to 4 feet tall or more and about 2 feet in

diameter. It has 20 to 30 or more vertical ribs extending from the bottom to the top of the stem. The tubercles that make up the ribs are pointed. Emerging from each areole, there are 15 to 20 fine tan or whitish spines surrounding 3 to 5 stouter, pinkish-red spines, 1½ to 4 inches long. A typical areole has 4 stout spines; the upper three are straight and the fourth is usually hooked downward and is much heavier than the other three.

FLOWERS AND FRUIT: The flowers vary in color among shades of yellow, gold, red, and orange and are about 2 inches long and up to 3 inches across. The pointed tepals sometimes have a darker shade of the base color running centrally from base to tip. Fruits are bright yellow, oval, and about 2 inches long and often form a circle around the top of the plant, sometimes covering the plant's summit.

FLOWERING: Flowering may occur any time during summer to fall.

RANGE AND HABITAT: The native range of Fishhook Barrel Cactus extends eastward from southern Arizona, across southern New Mexico, and into Texas only in the vicinity of El Paso. It also ranges into northern Mexico. It prefers deep soil and can be found in desert scrubland, in grasslands, and on the southern slopes of mountains.

COMMENTS: The Fishhook Barrel Cactus is one of our rarest cacti and has the largest stem diameter of all of our cacti.

Red
Flowers

Argemone sanguinea

Red Prickly-poppy

PAPAVERACEAE (POPPY FAMILY)

PLANT AND LEAVES: Red Prickly-poppy is a well-branched annual, biennial, or short-lived perennial herb growing to about 3½ feet tall. It is armed with many small prickles on its stems, lower leaf surfaces, leaf margins, and flower buds. The leaves are deeply lobed with many jagged points on each lobe. Like most other prickly-poppies, the primary and secondary leaf veins are white. The upper leaf surfaces are mostly unarmed.

FLOWERS AND FRUIT: Flowers are 3 to 3½ inches in diameter, have six petals and are borne at the ends of the branches. The petals are variable in color ranging from white, pale lavender, and mauve to blood red. The fruit is a very spiny, elliptical capsule about 1 inch long and ½ inch wide.

FLOWERING: Flowering begins as early as February and continues to April, some plants flowering as late as June.

RANGE AND HABITAT: Found along roadsides and in uncultivated areas in south and southwest Texas and in northern Mexico.

COMMENTS: The traveler between San Antonio and the Rio Grande Valley in spring cannot help but marvel at the large populations of Red Prickly-poppy colonizing the roadsides like great patchwork quilts of white, red, lavender, and a shade of mauve that is rarely seen in nature.

Rumex hymenosepalus

Desert Rhubarb, Canaigre Dock

POLYGONACEAE (BUCKWHEAT FAMILY)

PLANT AND LEAVES: Desert Rhubarb is a perennial herb with tuberous roots. The roots are rich in tannin. The plant's stems are mostly erect and branching, growing 1 to 3 feet tall. The large, fleshy, alternate leaves are often 1 foot long and up to 5 inches wide with crisped or sinuous leaf margins.

FLOWERS AND FRUIT: This species' dark pink flowers (appearing

red in aggregate) are borne in large racemes, 1 foot long or more, and are followed by large masses of pink to reddish-brown, three-winged seeds, which are showier and prettier than the flowers.

FLOWERING: Flowering begins in February and continues until April or May.

RANGE AND HABITAT: It is commonly seen in west Texas sandy streambeds and gulches, though it is also found on well-drained high ground, in fields, and on roadsides. Beyond Texas's borders, Desert Rhubarb's range extends across the US Desert Southwest, north to Wyoming, and south to northern Mexico.

COMMENTS: Related to the nonnative plant Rhubarb (*Rheum rhabarbarum*), Desert Rhubarb's stems and leaves are edible after careful preparation. Its infructescences are lovely used in large flower arrangements.

Echinocereus enneacanthus

Strawberry Cactus, Pitaya

CACTACEAE (CACTUS FAMILY)

PLANT AND LEAVES: The cylindrical stems of the Strawberry Cactus are 3 to 30 inches long and 1½ to 4 inches in diameter. They grow in loose clusters of a few to more than 400 stems. New stems grow as side branches, near the ground, so their first growth tends to be horizontal, later turning upward, giving them a long, curling appearance. There are 7 to 10 ribs on each stem. The plant is bright green with a wrinkled appearance, looking withered in dry periods. The stems are often yellow green in sunny locations. This species' spininess is variable, but in general it has fewer spines and shows more plant surface than most cacti.

FLOWERS AND FRUIT: The red, magenta, or pink flowers are 2 to 3 inches long and about the same in diameter. They have 10 to 20 outer tepals with pinkish, crinkled edges. The inner tepals, 12 to 35, are in one to three rows. Anthers are yellow and pistils are light green with 8 to 12 lobes like most other *Echinocereus* species. The fruit is about 1 inch long, almost round, greenish to brown or purple.

FLOWERING: Flowering may begin in March but mostly occurs in April and may continue until midsummer.

RANGE AND HABITAT: Found in desert and thorn scrubland on the Rio Grande plain from Brownsville to Big Bend National Park and in northern Mexico.

COMMENTS: Passersby cannot help but stop in their tracks to admire and be awed by the colorful extravagance of the stunning floral displays of this species.

Aesculus pavia
Red Buckeye, Southern Buckeye
HIPPOCASTANACEAE (HORSE-CHESTNUT FAMILY)

PLANT AND LEAVES: Red Buckeye is a small, deciduous multi-trunked tree or shrub. Commonly reaching 10 to 15 feet tall with a bit more spread, trees to 30 feet or more are sometimes found. The leaves are opposite and made up of five leaflets joined at a central point on a petiole as long as the leaf. The leaflets are fine toothed, glossy dark green above, and whitish beneath. Autumn comes extraordinarily early for this species, its leaves falling as soon as late July.

FLOWERS AND FRUIT: Red buckeye is a handsome shrub with

showy, spike-like clusters of deep red, pinkish, or sometimes yellow, funnel-shaped flowers. The flower clusters are 6 to 10 inches long, and the individual flower is 1 to 1½ inches long. The fruit is a smooth, brown or greenish brown, leathery capsule containing one or two mahogany-colored, chestnut-like seeds.

FLOWERING: This species flowers between March and May. The fruit matures in the fall.

RANGE AND HABITAT: Red Buckeye is an understory plant commonly found on rich, sandy soils in wooded stream bottoms in east Texas; less frequently found southwest to Uvalde and

along the Red River to Wichita County. It is native across the Southeast and in the southern Midwest. The yellow-flowered botanical variety, *Aesculus pavia* var. *flavescens*, is endemic to the Edwards Plateau.

COMMENTS: The flowers of this species are favored by hummingbirds, and Red Buckeye is among the species critical to the birds' survival, flowering at the time of their arrival from their energy-depleting spring return trip from Central and South America.

Castilleja indivisa

Texas Indian Paintbrush, Entireleaf Indian Paintbrush

SCROPHULARIACEAE (FIGWORT FAMILY)

PLANT AND LEAVES: Texas Indian Paintbrush is an unbranched but multistemmed annual or biennial growing from a single crown. The plant grows to 6 to 16 inches tall. Leaves are 1 to 4 inches long, alternate, and with plain or sometimes wavy margins. Unlike the leaves of most other *Castilleja* species, Texas Indian Paintbrush leaves are unlobed.

FLOWERS AND FRUIT: Flowers with the attending floral leaves, called bracts, grow around the upper 2 to 7 inches of the stem.

The intense red-orange color for which the plant is noted is coloration of its floral bracts, which almost hide the inconspicuous cream-colored flowers. White- and yellow-bracted forms are uncommon but not rare.

FLOWERING: Flowering occurs from March to May, with the best displays in April.

RANGE AND HABITAT: Common in sandy soil, especially in fields and on roadsides, from northeast to southwest Texas. Its native range extends into Louisiana.

COMMENTS: Texas Indian Paintbrush, along with Texas Bluebonnet (*Lupinus texensis*) and Indian Blanket (*Gaillardia pulchella*), is one of the "big three" spring wildflowers in much of Texas, especially the central and eastern regions of the state. In bluebonnet country, large fields of red and blue, sometimes with a sprinkling of the white flowers of prickly poppies, are an impressive sight. This species is hemiparasitic; that is, it derives part of its nutrient requirements by parasitizing other plants—often grasses—via root connections. The plant will grow, but poorly, without any help from a host plant, but you can be sure that robust specimens you see are tapped into some nearby plants' roots.

Glandulicactus uncinatus var. *wrightii*

Chihuahuan Fishhook Cactus, Brown-flowered Hedgehog Cactus

CACTACEAE (CACTUS FAMILY)
Synonyms: *Sclerocactus uncinatus* var. *wrightii*,
Ferocactus uncinatus var. *wrightii*

PLANT AND LEAVES: Chihuahuan Fishhook Cactus is unbranched, oval or cylindrical in shape, and up to 12 inches tall and 4 inches across but often about half that size. It has 9 to 13 tall, conspicuous ribs separated by broad grooves. The surface is bluish green. There are 8 to 12 heavy spines at each areole. The upper four are straight and flattened, about 1 to 2 inches long, but the lower ones are somewhat shorter and nearly round, curved at the tips. There is one central spine, 2 to 4 inches long, very heavy, and often twisted and hooked at the tip.

FLOWERS AND FRUIT: Flowers are maroon to reddish brown, funnel shaped, and up to 1¼ inches long and about 1 inch across. The petals are sometimes slightly pointed at the tip; others are squared off. Stamens are yellow. The stigma is dull

brownish orange with about a dozen lobes. Tunas are bright red at maturity.

FLOWERING: Flowering begins as early as March and continues to May.

RANGE AND HABITAT: As its name implies, Chihuahuan Fishhook Cactus is a Chihuahuan Desert native of Trans-Pecos Texas, southern New Mexico, and northern Mexico. It can be found in desert scrubland and arid grasslands and on rocky hillsides.

COMMENTS: The identity of this taxon has long been in flux and has, at various times, been placed in the cactus genera *Sclerocactus*, *Ferocactus*, *Echinocactus*, *Echinomastus*, and *Ancistrocactus*.

Lonicera sempervirens

Coral Honeysuckle, Trumpet Honeysuckle, Woodbine

CAPRIFOLIACEAE (HONEYSUCKLE FAMILY)

PLANT AND LEAVES: Coral Honeysuckle is a woody vine, evergreen in much of Texas. It climbs by twining and produces stems that may climb 20 feet more. The stems may be green or red and herbaceous when young but after one growing season become woody with shredding, gray, papery bark. Leaves are opposite and range in shape from narrow and lance shaped to egg shaped and nearly 3 inches long and 2 inches wide. The pair of leaves just below an inflorescence is rounded and perfoliate; that is, the bases of the two leaves are fused to one another and encircle the stem. The leaves are thick, white on the underside, and depending on conditions, pale green to dark green above.

FLOWERS AND FRUIT: Borne at the apex of the stems are two to four loosely stacked clusters of 8 to 20 trumpet-shaped flowers, each 1½ to 2 inches long and with five small, rounded, flaring lobes. The lowest clusters flower first, then the next, and so

on toward the end of the stem. Its flowers are scarlet red to rose red on the outside and red, bright orange, or yellow in the throat. The flower's yellow stamens protrude beyond the petals. The plant produces clusters of red berries, which mature in the fall.

FLOWERING: This species flowers March to May and sometimes produces flushes of flowers at any time during the year. Its berries ripen in September and October.

RANGE AND HABITAT: It is common in the eastern half of Texas and the eastern half of the United States.

COMMENTS: Coral Honeysuckle is a very popular garden plant because it is easy to grow, fast growing, and spectacularly showy when in flower. Bird-loving gardeners appreciate its attractiveness to hummingbirds. Evening visits by hummingbird moths are also exciting to observe.

Spigelia marilandica
Pinkroot, Indian Pink
LOGANIACEAE (PINKROOT FAMILY)

PLANT AND LEAVES: Pinkroot is an erect, clump-forming, herbaceous perennial, 1 to 2 feet tall, with wiry, mostly unbranched stems that tend to be four-sided near the top. The leaves are opposite and, having no petioles, are attached directly to the stem. They are lance shaped, 1 to 4 inches long, the largest about 2 inches wide, and with smooth margins.

FLOWERS AND FRUIT: The flowers are arranged in racemes along the last 2 inches or so of the arching stem, which ultimately curves downward at the tip. All the flowers grow on the top side of the stem in the same manner as freesias. The lowest flowers open first and continue toward the stem's apex. The flower is narrow and tubular, 1½ inches long, ending in five narrow and pointed petal-like lobes, yellow on the inside and bright red on the outside of the tube. While the five yellow stamens gather just outside the opening of the flower's lobes, the pistil's yellow style extends well beyond and makes the flower evocative of a shooting star.

FLOWERING: Flowering occurs from March to May.

RANGE AND HABITAT: Pinkroot prefers moist, rich woods. Found along the eastern edge of the state, from Woodville to the Big Thicket, and eastward to the Louisiana state line. Pinkroot is rather rare in Texas and more common in Louisiana. Its native range extends north throughout the southern Midwest and east across the South to as far north as Maryland.

COMMENTS: Pinkroot is a species that grabs your attention and elicits admiration the first time you see it in flower and every time subsequent to that. It is a true woodland jewel.

Echinocereus coccineus

Scarlet Hedgehog Cactus, Claret-cup Cactus

CACTACEAE (CACTUS FAMILY)

PLANT AND LEAVES: Scarlet Hedgehog Cactus is a clumping species with 100 or more stems forming a dense, rounded mound up to 3 feet in diameter in older plants. The longest stems may reach 16 inches and are usually about 3 or 4 inches in diameter. Each stem is divided by 6 to 14 ribs, with 10 ribs being common. Spines are longish, 5 to 15 per areole, often red or yellow with black tips when fresh, fading to gray with age.

FLOWERS AND FRUIT: The bright red-orange, 2½-inch-diameter

flowers often cover the entire plant. The numerous flowers emerge near the tops of the stems from the previous year's areoles, all at about the same height, giving a full view of all the flowers at one glance. Anthers are usually purplish, rarely yellow. Tunas are about 1½ inches long and usually brownish red when mature two or three months post-flowering.

FLOWERING: Flowering occurs any time between March and June.

RANGE AND HABITAT: Scarlet Hedgehog Cactus is at home on a variety of soils on the Edwards Plateau, the Trans-Pecos, and across the US Desert Southwest. Its native range extends into northern Mexico.

COMMENTS: The cup-shaped flowers of this species and the closely related *Echinocereus triglochidiatus* give each species the common name Claret-cup Cactus. The native range of *E. triglochidiatus* is now believed not to extend as far east as Texas.

Echinocereus russanthus

Rusty Hedgehog Cactus

CACTACEAE (CACTUS FAMILY)

PLANT AND LEAVES: Rusty Hedgehog Cactus stems grow to 10 inches tall and 2 to 3 inches in diameter. The plants sometimes branch and form clusters of as many as a dozen stems. Each

has 13 to 18 ribs. Stems are heavily covered with a mass of inter-locking bristle-like, slender spines radiating in all directions. Central spines, especially younger ones, are usually longer and maroon colored.

FLOWERS AND FRUIT: Flowers are small, about 1 inch long and ½ inch across. Tepals are rust red (some are greenish) with darker central lines and fading at the edges; they are pointed at the ends. The tepals' characteristics make the flowers appear to be made of feathers. Anthers are numerous and creamy white to greenish yellow. Stigmas are lime green with a variable number of lobes.

FLOWERING: Flowering may begin in March and continue until June with most flowering taking place during April and May.

RANGE AND HABITAT: Native to the Big Bend, where it grows on rocky slopes.

COMMENTS: It grows from the Chisos Mountains in Big Bend National Park northwest to Study Butte. Some investigators have considered this species to be a variety of *Echinocereus chloranthus*.

Penstemon murrayanus

Scarlet Penstemon, Cupleaf Beardtongue

SCROPHULARIACEAE (FIGWORT FAMILY)

PLANT AND LEAVES: Scarlet Penstemon is a perennial herb that grows to about 3 feet high with multiple, unbranched reddish stems arising from a crown. Its leaves are oppositely arranged and attached directly to the stem. The bases of the upper leaves are fused and form a cup around the stem that holds water. Leaves are smooth on the edges and have a downy covering.

FLOWERS AND FRUIT: The flowering upper portion of the stem is often over 1 foot long, with a profusion of tubular, scarlet flowers about 1 inch long. The flower's tube opens into five petal-like lobes. Stamens extend beyond the flower, and the fifth stamen, which has no anther, is lightly bearded. The fruit is a "beaked" capsule, about ¾ inch long.

FLOWERING: Flowering occurs from March to June.

RANGE AND HABITAT: Scarlet Penstemon grows on sandy soils in pine woods and open prairies over most of east Texas. Its native range extends into Louisiana, Arkansas, and Oklahoma.

COMMENTS: Plants with red, tubular flowers are usually well adapted for pollination by hummingbirds, which are particularly attracted to the color red. The very showy Scarlet Penstemon is no exception and is an important nectar source for nesting Ruby-throated Hummingbirds. The genus *Penstemon* is among the largest in North America, with 250 species. At least one species is native to every US state except Hawaii. Texas can claim 24 species as its own, with all parts of the state except the Lower Rio Grande Valley having a good representation of native beardtongues.

Phlox drummondii
Drummond's Phlox, Annual Phlox
POLEMONIACEAE (PHLOX FAMILY)

PLANT AND LEAVES: Drummond's Phlox is an herbaceous, annual species forming large colonies. The plant's hairy stems are mostly upright, from 4 to 20 inches tall. The stems may be branched or unbranched. Leaves low on the plant are opposite but become alternate on the upper half of the stem. The leaves are hairy and lance shaped; having no petioles, they are attached directly to the stem and sometimes clasp the stem.

FLOWERS AND FRUIT: The flowers are borne in clusters of two to six flowers. Flower color varies widely, with red, purple, pink, white, and multicolored forms common. The five sepals form a tubular shape for the flower, but the petals lie flat and are wider at the tip. Stamens are inconspicuous.

FLOWERING: Flowering occurs from March to June.

RANGE AND HABITAT: The flowers often form solid blankets of color in fallow fields, along roadsides, and in other uncultivated areas. Though much cultivated and widely naturalized across the southeastern United States, this species was apparently an endemic of east and central Texas.

COMMENTS: There are many species of *Phlox* in Texas, and one or more can be found in almost any part of the state. It is difficult for the amateur to distinguish the different species but fairly easy to recognize the genus. *Phlox drummondii* is named in honor of Scottish botanist Thomas Drummond, who gathered

seeds of the plant near Gonzales in 1834. They were sent to England, where the plants grown from these seeds were soon introduced into horticulture and quickly became garden favorites. They were described as brilliant rose red, with purple in some and darker red "eyes" in nearly all. Wild Drummond's Phlox still grows in great profusion in the area where Thomas Drummond collected seeds.

Hesperaloe parviflora

Coral Yucca, Red Yucca, Redflower False Yucca

AGAVACEAE (CENTURY-PLANT FAMILY)

PLANT AND LEAVES: Coral Yucca is a shrubby herbaceous perennial with narrow, stiff, evergreen leaves all arising from the plant's base and about 3 feet long. Its leaf margins fray, with interesting, persistent threadlike curled margins clinging to them. The overall appearance of the plant is of a spiky mound.

FLOWERS AND FRUIT: Arching inflorescences (often several) extend well above the leaves (to about 6 feet in height) and bear tubular flowers on short branches. Flowers are about 1 to 1½ inches in length, typically salmon red on the exterior and yellow inside.

FLOWERING: May occur any time but primarily from March to July.

RANGE AND HABITAT: This species is native to Texas and Coahuila, Mexico. In Texas, it is found in the southwestern Edwards Plateau ecoregion.

COMMENTS: Coral Yucca is attractive, has a long flowering season, is easy to propagate from seeds and grow in the landscape, and is very tough and drought tolerant once established. Thus, it is a very popular addition to xeric gardens and in roadside plantings across the southwestern United States. The closely related species, *Hesperaloe funifera*, is a somewhat larger, coarser plant overall with less showy, purple-tinged greenish-white flowers. Its US range is similar to that of Coral Yucca.

Ratibida columnifera

Mexican-hat, Long-headed Coneflower, Thimbleflower

ASTERACEAE (ASTER FAMILY)
Synonym: *Ratibida columnaris*

PLANT AND LEAVES: Mexican-hat is a taprooted, herbaceous perennial that typically reaches 2½ to 3 feet in height. Leaves are alternate, 2 to 4½ inches long, deeply cut into five to nine narrow segments. Both leaves and stems are somewhat rough, with the upper third of the stem bare.

FLOWERS AND FRUIT: One to 15 radiate flower heads are held well above the leaves. The laminae of the ray florets are ¾ to 1 inch long and quite variable in color from plant to plant. The ray

flowers are often pure butter yellow, but plants bearing flowers with orange-red to maroon bases are very common. An occasional plant will display velvety, maroon-colored flowers with little or no yellow at all. The ray florets of most plants reflex downward, giving the flower heads a rocket-like appearance. The head's center, which bears the disc florets, is erect and thimble-like, 1 to 2 inches long, and gray green, turning brown as it matures.

FLOWERING: March to July, or as late as November, depending on rains.

RANGE AND HABITAT: Fields, roadsides, and open woods from east Texas through the Trans-Pecos and to the Panhandle, it is widespread and very common across the state. Likewise, this species can be found across nearly all of North America.

COMMENTS: We have photographed the eye-catching Mexican-hat in many parts of the state. In east Texas, this species often grows to 3½ feet tall.

Salvia coccinea

Scarlet Sage, Tropical Sage, Blood Sage

LAMIACEAE (MINT FAMILY)

PLANT AND LEAVES: Scarlet Sage is an erect herb, unbranched to widely branched, softly hairy, 1 to 4 feet tall, and with square stems. It is an annual and dies to the ground with the first freeze, but roots may persist and produce new stems following mild winters. Leaves are opposite, simple, 2¾ inches long and 2 inches wide, and with a blunt tip. It is lightly scalloped to sharply toothed with a petiole 1½ to 2 inches long.

FLOWERS AND FRUIT: Flowers grow in whorls at nodes along the upper few inches of the plant's stems. They are usually scarlet to dark red, with five petals united to form a two-lipped flower, ¾ to 1 inch long, the lower lip notched. There are two stamens and one pistil. White- and pink-flowered forms are common.

FLOWERING: Flowering occurs from March to August.

RANGE AND HABITAT: Scarlet Sage grows primarily in woods on

sandy soils near the Gulf Coast but inhabits similar habitat in scattered locales throughout east Texas. Its native range extends along the coast to Florida, where it grows throughout the state.

COMMENTS: Scarlet Sage is an excellent, easy-to-cultivate choice for a woodland garden within its native range.

Erythrina herbacea

Coral Bean, Cherokee Bean

FABACEAE (PEA FAMILY)

PLANT AND LEAVES: Coral Bean is a perennial shrub with several unbranched stems dying to the ground most winters and re-sprouting from the crown each spring. In areas without winter freezes, the plants can reach 15 feet in height, though in most parts of its Texas range it tops out each year at about 4 to 6 feet high. The plant's stems are well armed with very sharp, curved prickles. Leaves are alternate, scattered along the stem,

and with three leaflets forming the leaf, which is triangular in shape and often prickly beneath. The leaves are 3 to 5 inches long and 3½ to 4 inches wide.

FLOWERS AND FRUIT: The spike inflorescences, shaped like tall pyramids 12 inches or more long, are borne at the tops of the stems. The scarlet-red to rose-colored flowers are long and narrow and curve upward. There are five united sepals and five petals 1½ to 2 inches long, with the upper petal wrapped around the other four. The pod is blackish when mature, constricted between the bright red seeds, and up to 8½ inches long.

FLOWERING: This species flowers April to June.

RANGE AND HABITAT: Coral Bean is native to moist soils on the Texas coastal plain and the Pineywoods. Its range extends east to North Carolina.

COMMENTS: One's attention is caught by the large, scarlet seeds, which are prominently displayed after the seedpod opens in early fall. The seeds are firmly attached to the pod by a sturdy

⅛-inch long thread and will remain in place for months. This makes them excellent for floral arrangements, especially since the color does not fade. These seeds are poisonous, however, so care should be taken when using the fruit in floral displays where curious youngsters can reach them.

Fouquieria splendens

Ocotillo, Devil's Walking Stick

FOUQUIERIACEAE (OCOTILLO FAMILY)

PLANT AND LEAVES: Many people have mistaken Ocotillo for a cactus; it grows in the same habitat and has so many thorns. It is, in fact, a soft-wooded shrub with wand-like stems branched at the base and growing gracefully to as much as 20 feet. Leaves are alternate and leathery, ½ inch long or more; when they fall, the strong, durable petiole remains. The plant adapts well to drought conditions, shedding its green leaves when under moisture stress. The stem then takes over their function, but if the drought continues and becomes severe, the stem turns brown as though it were dead.

FLOWERS AND FRUIT: Even during times of drought, Ocotillo will annually produce brilliant red, intricate flowers, which give no indication at all of any stress. The flowers are in dense clusters at the end of the stems.

FLOWERING: The normal flowering period is from April to June, but with good rains, the plants will produce flowers well into the fall.

RANGE AND HABITAT: Ocotillo is a native of the Chihuahuan Desert in west Texas, southern New Mexico, and north-central Mexico and the Sonoran Desert in southern Arizona, southern California, and northwestern Mexico. It is commonly found on rocky slopes west of the Pecos River.

COMMENTS: Ocotillo is quite attractive and has been used widely as an ornamental in arid areas. It has been so widely used, in fact, that its wild populations have been decimated in much of its native range by unscrupulous plant dealers. This species should not be purchased from any but very reputable plant nurseries. The collection, sale, or possession of wild-grown Ocotillo in Arizona is prohibited by state law.

Gaillardia pulchella

Indian Blanket, Firewheel

ASTERACEAE (ASTER FAMILY)

PLANT AND LEAVES: Indian Blanket usually occurs as an annual but may persist for two or more years. The plant is widely branched at the base and grows 1 to 2½ feet tall. Lower leaves typically have few teeth. A botanical variety of south Texas, *Gaillardia pulchella* var. *australis*, has shallowly pinnately lobed lower leaves. Upper leaves are alternate, 2 to 2½ inches long, and smooth, but the lower ones have a few teeth.

FLOWERS AND FRUIT: Flower heads are 1½ to 2 inches across, one on each main stem, which may be 4 to 8 inches long. A typical flower head has 10 to 20 ray flowers, usually brick red basally and marked with brilliant yellow on the ends of the rays, forming a yellow band along the outside. The disc flowers on most plants are brownish red, with the middle flowers tinged yellow.

FLOWERING: Flowering occurs from April to June.

RANGE AND HABITAT: Native to the Southeast, the central and southern Great Plains, and northern Mexico but has

naturalized over much of North America where suitable habitat exists. In Texas, it is common in sunny areas with sufficient rainfall throughout the state.

COMMENTS: Indian Blanket is a beautiful and impressive flower that grows along roadsides and in fields and pastures, sometimes covering large areas. We have seen 40 acres of these colorful flowers in a nearly pure stand. It is also a good garden flower. The flowers of this species may appear in a dizzying array of colors and forms. Many unusual variants have been selected for horticulture.

Malvaviscus arboreus var. *drummondii*

Turk's Cap, Red Mallow

MALVACEAE (MALLOW FAMILY)
Synonym: *Malvaviscus drummondii*

PLANT AND LEAVES: Turk's Cap is a deciduous perennial shrub that usually grows 2½ to 3½ feet tall but occasionally will reach 10 feet in height. It often forms extensive colonies, spreading by stolons. The stems freeze to the ground in hard winters, and several erect, unbranched, dark green stems grow from the crown in the following spring. Leaves are alternate, with petioles 1½ to 4 inches long. The leaves are 3 to 5 inches long and about as wide, with three shallow lobes, coarse hair above, and velvety below. The margins are shallowly toothed.

FLOWERS AND FRUIT: Turk's Cap gets its name from its vague similarity to a Turkish fez. The broad, red petals remain closely wrapped around one another at the base but spread somewhat toward the end. Each flower's staminal column extends considerably beyond the petals. The flowers, ¾ to 1½ inches long, grow singly in the leaf axils or, sometimes, in clusters at the ends of the stems. The edible but mealy red fruit, which resembles a little apple, is about ½ to ¾ inch wide and half as high. It matures in late summer or early fall, after flowering is complete.

FLOWERING: Flowering occurs more or less continuously from April to October.

RANGE AND HABITAT: Abundant in east, central, and south Texas in open woods, along streams, or in damp or shaded areas.

COMMENTS: Turk's Cap will grow in full sun but is an excellent small- to midsized shrub for shady areas and is one of the few native plants that will flower throughout the summer there. However, it can be a bit of a garden thug and will spread aggressively if conditions are favorable.

Ipomopsis rubra
Standing Cypress, Red Texas Star
POLEMONIACEAE (PHLOX FAMILY)

PLANT AND LEAVES: Standing Cypress is a biennial herb usually growing as a single erect stem, 2 to 5 feet tall. The stems are usually unbranched, pale green, and very leafy. The leaves are divided into five to seven threadlike segments, vaguely resembling the lacy leaves of the unrelated Cypress tree.

FLOWERS AND FRUIT: The bright red, tubular flowers are more than 1 inch long and have five spreading petal-like lobes. On the inner surface they are pale orange-red with dots of darker red. The flowers, which resemble those of the also unrelated, nonnative species Cypress Vine (*Ipomoea quamoclit*), are closely clustered along the upper part of the stem. Peach-, yellow-, and orange-colored forms are sometimes seen.

FLOWERING: Flowering occurs May to August.

RANGE AND HABITAT: Standing Cypress is found on dry, rocky, or sandy soils in east and central Texas. Its native range extends across the southern United States to North Carolina.

COMMENTS: Standing Cypress often forms large colonies and presents a spectacular sight when in flower. This species is easily cultivated in the garden. If a plant's single stem is pinched early in the growing season, the plant will readily branch and produce a cluster of vertical, flowering stems.

Silene laciniata ssp. *greggii*

Cardinal Catchfly, Mexican Campion

CARYOPHYLLACEAE (PINK FAMILY)

PLANT AND LEAVES: Cardinal Catchfly is a perennial herb growing from a thick, fleshy taproot. The plant is usually in the 10- to 15-inch range but can reach nearly 4 feet tall in extreme cases. The crowns of some plants can produce multiple stems, though most are mostly unbranched or branched only near the top. Leaves are opposite, narrow, slightly wavy, and 1½ to 2½ inches long.

FLOWERS AND FRUIT: The flowers are a fiery scarlet. The flowers are sometimes borne singly but often in inflorescences growing from the leaf axils, with one to three (occasionally as many as five) pairs of flowers held above the foliage on pedicels up to 2 inches long. The sepals are united, forming a tube 1 inch long that encloses the flower, which opens out flat into five petal-like lobes. Each lobe is deeply cut into four narrow sections, giving the flower a fringed effect. A whitish ring at the center surrounds the stamens and pistil. The stamens have greenish anthers.

FLOWERING: The flowering period for Cardinal Catchfly begins in May and ends in October.

RANGE AND HABITAT: Mountains of west Texas. It also can be found in western New Mexico and eastern Arizona and in northern Mexico.

COMMENTS: This eye-catching wildflower is found in the same

general habitat preferred by the Giant Crested Coralroot Orchid (*Hexalectris grandiflora*)—under oak or madrone trees in the mountains from 5,000 to 6,000 feet. We found it in the Davis Mountains on the upper reaches of Limpia Creek. Cardinal Catchfly is so called because it generally has sticky bands around the stem between the upper leaves on which small insects are often caught; however, this is not an insectivorous plant—it does not digest the insects.

Bouvardia ternifolia
Scarlet Bouvardia, Firecracker Bush
RUBIACEAE (MADDER FAMILY)

PLANT AND LEAVES: Scarlet Bouvardia is a multibranched perennial shrub growing 2 to 4 feet tall and almost as broad. Its habit is loose and somewhat rangy. Leaves are narrowly to broadly lance shaped, ¾ to 1¾ inches long, and grow in whorls of three or sometimes four.

FLOWERS AND FRUIT: The inflorescences are clusters of 4 to 12 very showy scarlet flowers borne at the ends of the stems. The flowers are tubular, about 2 inches long, separating into four short, petal-like lobes at the end. The fruit is a two-valved capsule containing many small, winged seeds.

FLOWERING: Flowering occurs May to November.

RANGE AND HABITAT: Scarlet Bouvardia is found on dry, neutral to acidic soils in the mountains of west Texas at elevations of 4,000 to 6,000 feet. It is native westward to Arizona and south throughout most of Mexico.

COMMENTS: The red flowers of the Scarlet Bouvardia will catch the eye quickly in the mountains of west Texas. It is a nice accent plant in the garden with appropriate soil but will not survive hard freezes. Hummingbirds love nectaring at its flowers. The specific epithet, *ternifolia*, refers to the plant's whorls of three leaves along its stems.

Lobelia cardinalis

Cardinal Flower

CAMPANULACEAE (BELLFLOWER FAMILY)
Synonyms: *Lobelia fulgens*, *Lobelia splendens*

PLANT AND LEAVES: Cardinal Flower is an erect perennial herb growing 1 to 4 feet tall and occasionally to 6 feet. The plant's dark green leaves are lance shaped with toothed margins, 4 to 8 inches long and 1 to 2 inches wide.

FLOWERS AND FRUIT: The spectacular inflorescence of Cardinal Flower sometimes stretches 2 feet or more at the top of the stem. Each scarlet, tubular flower is 1½ to 2¼ inches long, opening into five petal-like lobes that are two lipped; the upper two lobes are longer and narrower than the lower three. There are five stamens with light-gray anthers that contrast sharply with the scarlet-red flower.

FLOWERING: This species flowers from May to December, depending on location and available moisture.

RANGE AND HABITAT: Cardinal Flower can be found in swamps and on the banks and sandbars of streams anywhere in Texas, but it occurs primarily in east Texas. Its native range extends across the United States, and it is absent only in the Pacific Northwest.

COMMENTS: Often Cardinal Flowers are worked heavily by the sulphur butterflies, but with its brilliant red, long-tubed flowers it could not have been better designed for its primary pollinator in the eastern United States, the Ruby-throated Hummingbird.

Ipomoea cristulata
Scarlet Morning Glory, Trans-Pecos Morning Glory
CONVOLVULACEAE (MORNING GLORY FAMILY)

PLANT AND LEAVES: Scarlet Morning Glory is an annual vine with several stems that climb by twining and may reach 5 to 10 feet

long. Its alternately arranged leaves are deeply divided into three or five lobes—occasionally, seven lobes. The leaves, with their finger-like lobes, give the plant an interesting, tropical appearance.

FLOWERS AND FRUIT: The flowers of Scarlet Morning Glory are often scarcer than on many other morning glory species. They are scarlet or orangish red and borne singly or in small clusters of two or three flowers—only one opening at a time—on long peduncles that rise above the foliage. The flowers are salverform; that is, each has a long, narrow tube that abruptly widens flat at the end. The flower's tube is ¾ to 1½ inches long and opens to about ½ inch across. Unlike most other morning glories, the flowers of this species remain open all day. After flowering, the peduncles curl back toward the foliage, helping to protect the developing fruit, a capsule that will contain up to four hard, black seeds when mature.

FLOWERING: This species flowers as early as July and may continue to flower until November.

RANGE AND HABITAT: Scarlet Morning Glory is found on sandy soils in canyons, ravines, and rocky slopes in the Davis Mountains and elsewhere in the Trans-Pecos. It is also native to New Mexico and is widespread in Arizona and northern Mexico.

COMMENTS: This species' flower is very similar—and often confused with—the nonnative but widely cultivated species, Scarlet Creeper (*Ipomoea coccinea*), which has unlobed leaves. Scarlet Morning Glory is the only bright red morning glory native to Texas.

Salvia regla

Mountain Sage

LAMIACEAE (MINT FAMILY)

PLANT AND LEAVES: Mountain Sage is an open-branched, deciduous, perennial shrub growing to about 6 feet tall and spreading nearly as wide. Leaves are usually pale green, alternate, egg shaped, ½ to 1 inch long, and with scalloped margins. They are about as wide at the base as they are long. The leaves' lower surfaces are studded with small orange glands.

FLOWERS AND FRUIT: The shrub's showy flowers are borne in clusters in the leaf axils near the ends of the stems. There are masses of crimson, two-lipped flowers, about 2 inches long. They last for several days. The sepals also are tinged with red.

FLOWERING: Flowering occurs from July to December.

RANGE AND HABITAT: In Texas, Mountain Sage's native range is limited mostly to Big Bend's Chisos Mountains. The large majority of its range is found in Mexico, where the species is also a colorful part of mountain flora.

COMMENTS: The late Texas botanist Barton H. Warnock, rightly called the Mountain Sage one of the most beautiful shrubs in the Chisos Mountains. It reaches its peak after most other flowers are on the wane, thus giving this attractive plant center stage. We photographed many of them at elevations from 5,000 to 7,000 feet in late September. Fortunately, for late-traveling hummingbirds flying south during their annual fall migration from North America to Central and South America, Mountain Sage provides an important and much-needed energy source along the way when few other plants are flowering.

Purple Flowers

Houstonia pusilla

Tiny Bluet, Star Violet

RUBIACEAE (MADDER FAMILY)
Synonym: *Hedyotis crassifolia*

PLANT AND LEAVES: Tiny Bluet is a colony-forming, annual herb growing 1 to 5 inches tall with several branches. The opposite leaves are not more than ½ inch long and ¼ inch wide.

FLOWERS AND FRUIT: Tiny Bluet's flowers are held above the foliage. They have purple-blue, lavender, or occasionally lilac or white flowers, ¼ to ⅓ inch across, that grow singly on the tips of fine peduncles that emerge from the leaf axils. Each flower consists of a narrow tube crowned by four lobes that spread sharply at right angles. The fruits are small globular capsules, borne in pairs.

FLOWERING: Flowering occurs from February to April; it is sometimes a year's first species to be seen flowering.

RANGE AND HABITAT: Tiny Bluet can be found in open meadows, roadsides, forest margins, and waste areas throughout east Texas. Its native range includes the Southeast and all but the most northern reaches of the Midwest.

COMMENTS: Though very small, Tiny Bluets sometimes color a field blue. Their cheery little four-lobed flowers remind one of twinkling starlight. Their diminutive stature means that they are best appreciated while lying flat on the ground on one's belly and examining them up close.

Viola bicolor

Wild Pansy, Field Pansy

VIOLACEAE (VIOLET FAMILY)
Synonym: *Viola rafinesquei*

PLANT AND LEAVES: Wild Pansy is an annual herb growing from 1 to 4 inches tall. Leaves grow in clusters on the stem and vary in shape from long and narrow to spoon shaped to oval with smooth edges to deeply lobed.

FLOWERS AND FRUIT: One or two flowers emerge from the leaf

axils, held well above the foliage on long nodding peduncles. Flower color varies from cream white to pale lavender to deep violet.

FLOWERING: Flowering occurs from February to April but mostly in March.

RANGE AND HABITAT: Wild Pansy grows in sandy soil on roadsides, in lawns, and in fields all over east Texas. Its native range includes most of the eastern half of the United States.

COMMENTS: This is one of the smallest of Texas violets. Wild Pansy grows in east and northeast Texas, usually flowering in early March. We always seem to have a special appreciation for it because it is one of the very early flowers to announce the arrival of spring. It is difficult to understand how anyone could dislike this cheery little wildflower, but because it commonly appears in lawns, it is the sworn enemy of many who want pristine expanses of grass. So sad.

Pinguicula pumila
Small Butterwort, Bog Violet
LENTIBULARIACEAE (BLADDERWORT FAMILY)

PLANT AND LEAVES: Small Butterwort is a perennial herb forming a rosette of leaves from which one to several erect, flowering scapes grow 6 to 8 inches tall. The leaves are lime green or yellowish and nearly round, though usually curled inward along the margins, giving them a triangular appearance. They are fleshy and feel greasy to the touch.

FLOWERS AND FRUIT: The 1 to 10 scapes each bear a single whitish, pale pink or pale violet flower. The flowers are about ¾ inch long, funnel shaped with red streaks in the throat, somewhat two lipped, and with five petal-like lobes and a yellowish spur at the base, similar to the spurs on a violet or a larkspur flower.

FLOWERING: Flowering begins as early as February and may continue until June.

RANGE AND HABITAT: Small Butterwort inhabits bogs, seepages, and other moist soils in pine woods from southeast Texas across all the Gulf and Atlantic states to South Carolina. It also occurs in the Bahamas.

COMMENTS: The sticky surface of this species' leaves trap small insects. Once trapped, the plant's leaves curl over the hapless creatures and slowly digest them. Small Butterwort is the only member of its genus native to Texas. Ten species in the related genus *Utricularia* (bladderworts) can be found in Texas. One species in the unrelated genus *Sarracenia* (pitcherplants) and four *Drosera* species (sundews) complete the contingent of Texas's insectivorous plants.

Erodium texanum

Texas Heron's-bill, Texas Stork's-bill

GERANIACEAE (GERANIUM FAMILY)

PLANT AND LEAVES: Texas Heron's-bill is a biennial or rosette-forming winter annual. This low-growing plant produces horizontal stems that can be 15 inches long or more. Leaves are opposite with long, often red, petioles. The leaves are ½ to 2 inches long, more or less triangular or heart shaped, and sometimes with three to five large lobes and numerous small rounded lobes. It is common to see that one or more of the oldest leaves on a plant has turned bright red, giving the plant a festive appearance.

FLOWERS AND FRUIT: The flowers are often deep wine red or magenta in color—sometimes purple or pink—and are borne in clusters of two or three. They have five petals and are about 1 inch in diameter. The stamens have prominent yellow anthers. Flowering responds to light, the flowers opening late in the day and closing in the morning, except when it is cloudy. The fruit is long and narrow, 1 to 2 inches long. When mature, the fruit splits and the seeds, with long coiled tails, are released. With

changes in humidity, the seeds' tails uncoil and recoil and, in doing so, drill the seed into the ground.

FLOWERING: Flowering occurs between February and May.

RANGE AND HABITAT: Texas Heron's-bill is most abundant in central Texas but extends westward to the Trans-Pecos and north to southern Oklahoma. Its native range reaches as far west as southern California and south into northern Mexico.

COMMENTS: Species of the genus *Erodium* have 5 stamens, which easily distinguishes it from members of the related genus *Geranium*, which have 10 stamens.

Streptanthus platycarpus

Broadpod Twistflower

BRASSICACEAE (MUSTARD FAMILY)

Synonym: *Erysimum platycarpum*

PLANT AND LEAVES: Broadpod Twistflower is an annual herb with upright, branching stems that reach about 3 feet in height. Its stems and leaves are glossy and essentially hairless. Leaves are alternate and nearly round, and the lower part clasps the stem. They range from 1 to 6 inches in length.

FLOWERS AND FRUIT: Inflorescences are showy and are borne in

racemes at the ends of each of the plant's stems. Bell-shaped, dark purple sepals surround four lavender or purple petals, the flower spreading flat, 1 to 1½ inches across and suggesting the face of an old windmill. Long, thin capsules, to about 4 inches long, soon follow flowering.

FLOWERING: Flowering may occur from February to June, most taking place during March and April.

RANGE AND HABITAT: Grows on bluffs, roadsides, and other rocky locations on limestone soils in the Trans-Pecos ecoregion. Broadpod Twistflower also can be found in nearby Coahuila, Mexico.

COMMENTS: *Streptanthus platycarpus* is one of five species in its genus native to Texas. A close relative, *Streptanthus bracteatus* (Bracted Twistflower), a central Texas endemic, is listed by the Center for Plant Conservation in its National Collection of Endangered Plants and should be protected wherever it is found.

Corallorhiza wisteriana

Spring Coral-root, Wister's Coral-root

ORCHIDACEAE (ORCHID FAMILY)

PLANT AND LEAVES: Spring Coral-root is a perennial herb containing no chlorophyll. It gets all its nutrition by utilizing soil-borne fungi to reap nutrients from the roots of nearby plants. Sometimes solitary, it often forms colonies. When not flowering, the plant is completely subterranean. Being without chlorophyll, it has no need for leaves and thus, it has none.

FLOWERS AND FRUIT: The flowering scape is purplish brown to yellowish, 5 to 18 inches tall, the top third being a raceme with 5 to 25 scattered flowers. Flower corollas are no more than ¼ inch across. They have three sepals and three petals, mostly purplish brown (occasionally yellow) and sometimes greenish near the tips; the lip is white, usually heavily spotted with purplish brown, and curved sharply downward.

FLOWERING: Often early flowering, it begins appearing in February, but some flowering plants may be found as late as August.

RANGE AND HABITAT: In southeast Texas, on the edges of swamps

and other moist areas. Spring Coral-root is a wide-ranging species and can be found across North America wherever moist hardwood forests with rich soils occur.

COMMENTS: Most orchids of the genus *Corallorhiza* have no chlorophyll and cannot make their own food. Therefore, they depend on symbiotic relationships with soil fungi to acquire nutrition from other plants. A notable exception is Yellow Coral-root (*Corallorhiza trifida*), which does have chlorophyll and manufactures some of its food needs but still gets most of its nutrients from other plants through the intermediate mycorrhizal fungi.

Viola missouriensis

Missouri Violet

VIOLACEAE (VIOLET FAMILY)

Synonym: *Viola sororia* var. *missouriensis*

PLANT AND LEAVES: Missouri Violet is a stemless perennial herb, spreading by rhizomes as well as by seeds. All of its leaves are basal and produced by the plant's crown. It is one of the most robust of our native violets, forming clumps 6 inches or more in diameter. The heart-shaped leaves, as many as 30 per plant, are coarsely toothed and up to 3½ inches long and 2½ inches wide. They grow from the plant's base on long petioles.

FLOWERS AND FRUIT: The flowers, about ¾ inch across, are borne on long nodding peduncles that hold the flowers nestled just atop the foliage. They have five petals, like most other violets, deep to pale violet in color and mostly white or greenish white at the base. The two lateral petals are bearded. They and the lower petal are lined with purple streaks that aid pollinating insects in finding the flower's nectar. A short, rounded spur extends behind the flower.

FLOWERING: Flowering occurs during March and April.

RANGE AND HABITAT: Missouri Violet can be found on rich soil along river and stream banks in forested areas in the eastern third of Texas. Its native range extends north through the central Great Plains and throughout the Mississippi and Ohio River Valleys.

COMMENTS: Walking through the woods in early spring, one is not surprised to see the Missouri Violet pushing its way up through dead leaves or other vegetation, rarely more than two or three plants in one place.

Viola pedata
Birdfoot Violet
VIOLACEAE (VIOLET FAMILY)

PLANT AND LEAVES: Birdfoot Violet is a stemless, perennial herb. It is one of the largest Texas violets, 4 to 6 inches tall. The leaves, almost round in outline, are ¾ to 2 inches across and deeply cut into three to five segments, and these again narrowly lobed.

The width of the lobes is variable, but on plants with very narrow leaf lobes, the leaves really do resemble bird feet, for which the species gets its common name.

FLOWERS AND FRUIT: Logic would lead you to believe that *Viola bicolor* would be our native species that bears bicolor flowers. That logic would be incorrect. Birdfoot Violet is the species that often shows off two-tone flowers. Its flowers are pale to dark purple, broad, flat, 1 to 1½ inches across. They have five petals, the two upper ones smaller than the lower three, very often deep purple and sometimes white. The lower three petals are usually lavender and have the dark purple streaks that are common to most violets. There are five stamens with brilliant orange anthers. The flowers of this species have no hairs at the bases of its petals.

FLOWERING: Flowering occurs during March and April.

RANGE AND HABITAT: Birdfoot Violet's native range barely enters our state, but there is a healthy population of this species in southeast Texas. It is native on dry soils across the South and up the eastern seaboard to New Hampshire. It is also very common throughout the Mississippi and Ohio River Valleys and in the eastern Great Plains.

COMMENTS: The greatest concentration of Birdfoot Violets we have seen was on the banks of Village Creek in the Big Thicket area, where it almost covered the bank for 300 feet.

Nama hispidum

Sand Bells, Bristly Nama, Purple Mat

HYDROPHYLLACEAE (WATERLEAF FAMILY)
Synonym: *Nama foliosum*

PLANT AND LEAVES: Sand Bells is an herbaceous, widely branching annual. In times of sufficient rainfall, it grows as a low mound or mat, 2 to 6 inches high and up to 12 inches across. The plant has a pungent odor. The leaves are narrow, about ½ inch long, and covered in hairs. Their margins curl under on either side.

FLOWERS AND FRUIT: The bell-shaped flowers are held more or less upright and grow in crowded clusters at the ends of the

plant's several stems. They open into five petal-like lobes, ½ inch across, mostly purple or pinkish violet but white in the throat. The stamens are yellow.

FLOWERING: Flowering most commonly occurs from March to May.

RANGE AND HABITAT: In Texas, Sand Bells is most common in the Trans-Pecos, but it can be found just about anywhere in the western two-thirds of the state with sandy soils, especially along rivers and streams. Its range extends west to southern California and south into the northern Mexico deserts.

COMMENTS: In years of ample rainfall, Sand Bells seems to cover the earth with purple, but in dry seasons it may be evident by only a single flower, nearly hiding the poor plant supporting it.

Xylorhiza wrightii

Big Bend Woody-aster, Gyp Daisy

ASTERACEAE (ASTER FAMILY)
Synonym: *Machaeranthera wrightii*

PLANT AND LEAVES: Big Bend Woody-aster is a woody perennial or subshrub growing to about 16 inches tall when in flower. Its stems, which branch in the lower portion of the plant, are woody near the base and are covered with sticky hairs. Leaves

are numerous and mostly clustered near the base of the plant; they are widest near the tip and sometimes have spiny teeth.

FLOWERS AND FRUIT: The flower heads are borne on long, mostly leafless peduncles. Very large for any species in the genus *Xylorhiza*, the flower heads can be nearly 2 inches in diameter and are usually slightly cupped during flowering. Each head bears 20 to 30 usually pale lavender ray flowers about ¾ of an inch long. Some individuals may have purple, violet-pink, or even white ray flowers. Disc flowers are yellow.

FLOWERING: Big Bend Woody-aster flowers from March to May and sporadically as late as October.

RANGE AND HABITAT: The gypseous west Texas and northern Mexican soils, where other desert-dwelling plants such as yucca and Creosote Bush (*Larrea tridentata*) share its habitat, lend this species another common name, Gyp Daisy.

COMMENTS: Big Bend Woody-aster is a showy desert species that closely resembles Tahoka Daisy (*Machaeranthera tanacetifolia*), to which it is closely related. In fact, this species was, for years, placed in the genus *Machaeranthera*.

Astragalus mollissimus

Woolly Locoweed

FABACEAE (PEA FAMILY)

PLANT AND LEAVES: Woolly Locoweed is a short-lived perennial herb arising from a taproot and a woody crown. The plant grows 12 to 18 inches tall and up to 3 feet across, with many sprawling branches that turn upward, forming a rounded clump. The stems and leaves are covered by downy hairs, giving the plant a silvery-blue hue and a soft-textured appearance. The leaves are compound and narrow, 6 to 10 inches long, with 10 to 30 oval leaflets diminishing in size toward the apex.

FLOWERS AND FRUIT: The flowers are borne in clusters on an upright inflorescence on the upper 2 to 4 inches of the stem. They have five sepals and five usually lavender-to purple and sometimes yellowish petals. The banner petals arch backward. The fruit is an oblong pod resembling a fat, hairy cashew that is shed and falls to the ground before later splitting open and releasing its seeds.

FLOWERING: Flowering occurs from late March to June.

RANGE AND HABITAT: This species prefers desert or semidesert habitats in open scrublands and prairies. In Texas, it occurs

from the Edwards Plateau to the Davis Mountains but is rare in the Chisos. It can be found on the western Great Plains and west across the Four Corners states, where it is common.

COMMENTS: In general, members of the genus *Astragalus* that are poisonous to livestock are called "locoweeds," while the harmless ones are called "milkvetches." The locoweeds cause a slow poisoning of horses, sheep, and cattle but are especially harmful to horses, causing staggering and some paralysis. They have an unpleasant taste, fortunately, and animals have to be starved in periods of drought before they will eat them. Members of the related genus, *Oxytropis*, are also called locoweeds.

Astragalus nuttallianus

Turkey Pea, Texas Pea, Small-flower Milkvetch

FABACEAE (PEA FAMILY)

PLANT AND LEAVES: Turkey Pea is a highly variable species of herbaceous annual or winter annual. Its stems are lax and vine-like to about 18 inches long. It usually appears in large masses, sometimes covering many acres. The leaves are odd-pinnate, ½ to 2½ inches long, with 7 to 19 narrowly elliptical leaflets, each about ¼ to ½ inch long.

FLOWERS AND FRUIT: The flowers are held above the foliage in one- to four-flowered inflorescences and radiating laterally from the top of a stout peduncle. The flowers range in color from white to lilac pink to blue or a very pretty deep violet. The brightly colored varieties often have a white "eye." The fruit is a narrow legume, short but of various lengths depending on the variety.

FLOWERING: This species flowers in the spring, the timing depending on the variety and seasonal environmental factors.

RANGE AND HABITAT: Turkey Pea is widespread across Texas. Its native range includes the southern Great Plains, the Four Corners states, southern Nevada, southern California, and northern Mexico.

COMMENTS: A prairie awash in a sea of blue and white sparkling flowers is a spectacle not to be forgotten. This is a very

common but highly variable species with eight botanical varieties recognized in the United States, five in Texas, each with slight variations of stem hairiness, leaflet shape, or flower and fruit characteristics. It is a good idea to have a botanist's loupe in one hand and a good botanical key in the other when attempting to identify the varieties of this species.

Tradescantia gigantea

Giant Spiderwort

COMMELINACEAE (SPIDERWORT FAMILY)

PLANT AND LEAVES: Giant Spiderwort is a perennial herbaceous monocot. Plants are usually erect clusters of stems 10 to 36 inches tall. The leaves are spirally arranged, narrowly lance

shaped to about 16 inches long with somewhat inflated sheaths clasping the stem.

FLOWERS AND FRUIT: Umbel-like clusters of many flowers make up the inflorescence. There are one to three narrow, leaf-like bracts just beneath the inflorescence. The flowers have three sepals, three petals, and six yellow stamens. Petal color is usually dark purplish blue, but lavender-, pink-, fuchsia-, and white-flowered forms are all common. Flower color may be, in part, indicative of soil pH with purple-flowered plants more common on acidic soils and pink flowers produced on plants growing on alkaline soils.

FLOWERING: An early species, Giant Spiderwort begins flowering in March and can continue until June.

RANGE AND HABITAT: Very nearly a central Texas endemic, a few populations can be found in northeast Texas. Wherever it grows, it prefers sunny spots in moist, open woods and prairies, on rocky hillsides, and on roadsides.

COMMENTS: *Tradescantia* species are given to hybridizing when two species are growing in close proximity. Thus, positive identification of a species is often difficult, if not impossible. Giant Spiderwort's limited native range, its unusual size, and its large, many-flowered inflorescences make identifying it relatively easy.

Callirhoe involucrata
Winecup, Purple Poppymallow
MALVACEAE (MALLOW FAMILY)

PLANT AND LEAVES: Winecup is mat-forming perennial herb to about 1 foot high and growing from a stout taproot. Its widely branching stems are sprawling and will extend up to 4 feet in length. They often have a purplish tint and have many white hairs. The leaves are alternate on long petioles. They are more or less round in outline, 2 to 4 inches in diameter, with five to seven deeply cut palmate lobes, which are each further cut at the end into several smaller, narrow lobes.

FLOWERS AND FRUIT: The flowers are borne singly on long peduncles that emerge from the leaf axils. The have five rounded,

overlapping, usually purple-colored petals that form cup- or bowl-shaped flowers that give the plant its common name. A mostly white staminal column that bears both the white stamens and the flower's pinkish style arise from the center of the flower. White- and pink-flowered specimens are sometimes found.

FLOWERING: Flowering begins as early as March and continues until around the end of June.

RANGE AND HABITAT: Winecup prefers dry, rocky soils on limestone substrate but is common on grassy roadsides, in meadows, and on prairies throughout all but the most western parts of Texas. It is native throughout the Great Plains as far north as Nebraska and Iowa.

COMMENTS: There are six species of winecups native to Texas. All but one, Annual Winecup (*Callirhoe leiocarpa*), are perennials.

Sophora secundiflora

Texas Mountain Laurel, Mescal Bean

FABACEAE (PEA FAMILY)

Synonyms: *Dermatophyllum secundiflorum, Calia secundiflora*

PLANT AND LEAVES: Texas Mountain Laurel is a large evergreen shrub or small tree, usually 10 to 15 feet high but sometimes as much as 30 feet tall or more. The plant's twigs are velvety and smooth, but the surfaces of older branches and the trunk are scaly or furrowed with dark, grayish-brown bark. It has dark

green, glossy, leathery compound leaves 4 to 6 inches long, with seven to nine oval leaflets, each about 1½ inches long.

FLOWERS AND FRUIT: The dense clusters of flowers have a strong, sweet fragrance, which some people find disagreeable but others like. There is considerable variation in the color of the flowers from white to pink, lavender, and deep purple. The fruit is an oddly-formed legume with a velvety surface. The rather ugly fruit, however, contains brilliant red beans with a very hard seed coat.

FLOWERING: In central Texas, this species is among the earliest shrubs to flower, usually in March. Some flowering may occur as late as June.

RANGE AND HABITAT: Grows on limestone soils from central Texas to the Chisos Mountains and in the Davis Mountains. The lion's share of its native range is in north-central Mexico.

COMMENTS: Texas Mountain Laurel is a beautiful and much-loved landscape plant. It grows relatively fast and produces handsome flowers with a very strong, grape soda fragrance. The seeds are poisonous if ingested and toddlers should be kept away from them.

Glandularia bipinnatifida

Prairie Verbena

VERBENACEAE (VERBENA FAMILY)
Synonym: *Verbena bipinnatifida*

PLANT AND LEAVES: Prairie Verbena is an erect to sprawling widely branching perennial herb, 6 to 16 inches tall and up to 3 feet in diameter. The lower branches sprawl or creep along the ground and take root wherever a joint touches, forming dense colonies. The stems are densely hairy. Leaves are opposite and deeply cut several times on both sides of the midrib; they are 1 to 3½ inches long and 1½ inches wide on a petiole 1 inch long.

FLOWERS AND FRUIT: The lavender to pinkish-purple flower clusters grow at the ends of the stems. Individual flowers are about ½ inch long and ½ inch in diameter, with five sepals and five petal-like lobes.

FLOWERING: Flowering occurs from March to July.

RANGE AND HABITAT: This species is common across all of Texas except the Pineywoods. Its native range extends north to South Dakota, west to Arizona, and south throughout much of Mexico and into Guatemala.

COMMENTS: Prairie Verbena is one of the most abundant and familiar wildflowers of Texas, growing throughout most of the state. It is also one of the first to attract attention in early spring, when it flowers along roads, in fields, and in open woods under widely varying conditions.

This species' little flowers produce abundant nectar and feed many hungry pollinating insects and hummingbirds. For that reason and for its heavy flowering, it makes a very fine garden plant.

Clematis crispa

Swamp Leatherflower, Curly Clematis

RANUNCULACEAE (BUTTERCUP FAMILY)

Synonym: *Viorna crispa*

PLANT AND LEAVES: Swamp Leatherflower is an herbaceous perennial vine that from its roots each spring climbs to as much as 10 feet, clinging to whatever surrounding vegetation is available, often shrubs and young trees. Like other *Clematis* species, its leaf petioles and leaf rachises act as tendrils, twisting themselves around adjacent plant stems for support. Its leaves are opposite and very variable in morphology, even on a single plant. Some leaves are simple, others have 2, 3, or up to 10 leaflets of widely varying shapes and sizes.

FLOWERS AND FRUIT: The pinkish-purple flowers grow on a naked stem and hang upside down. They have no petals, but the petal-like sepals are joined in a way that gives them the shape of an urn. They separate into four petal-like lobes at the rim, where they are wavy and crimped, curling backward and to the side. The fruit is a cluster of achenes with long, curving feathery tails. Together, they make an attractive, wispy ball that persists on the vine for months.

FLOWERING: Flowering begins as early as March and may continue until October.

RANGE AND HABITAT: The only native clematis that not only tolerates wet soil but thrives in it, Swamp Leatherflower can be found in marshy areas of southeast Texas and across the Southeast in every coastal state to Virginia. It is also native to the wet lowlands bordering the Mississippi River and its tributaries as far north as southern Illinois, where it is listed by the state as an endangered species.

COMMENTS: These beautiful flowers seem to do their best to conceal themselves by habitat and design, growing low and looking downward, but they are a rewarding "find" when one runs across them.

Machaeranthera tanacetifolia

Tahoka Daisy, Tansy Aster, Tansyleaf Tansyaster

ASTERACEAE (ASTER FAMILY)

Synonyms: *Aster tanacetifolius*, *Machaeranthera coronopifolia*, *Machaeranthera parthenium*

PLANT AND LEAVES: Tahoka Daisy is a bushy, multibranched, sometimes sprawling annual or biennial that grows 8 to 15 inches high. Leaves are alternate, the upper ones pinnately divided, the lower ones twice divided. Bracts are green and feathery.

FLOWERS AND FRUIT: Flower heads are at the end of the branches and are 1¼ to 2 inches across with 15 to 25 lavender ray flowers. Upwards of 150 yellow disc flowers make up the large central disc of the flower head.

FLOWERING: Flowering begins as early as March and may continue to October.

RANGE AND HABITAT: An open grassland and scrubland species of the western Great Plains from Texas to Alberta, the US Desert

Southwest, and Mexico, Tahoka Daisy prefers sandy or rocky, well-drained soils in sunny areas. In Texas, it is a native of the western third of the state and is often found on roadsides, in dry creek beds, and in other disturbed soils.

COMMENTS: The large, showy flower heads of Tahoka Daisy and its ability to thrive in arid conditions make it an excellent choice for xeric and rock gardens within its native range. The common name Tahoka Daisy was given to it in the early 20th century by a citizen living near Tahoka, Texas, who was an enthusiastic supporter of the species.

Quincula lobata

Purple Groundcherry

SOLANACEAE (POTATO FAMILY)
Synonym: *Physalis lobata*

PLANT AND LEAVES: Purple Groundcherry is a sprawling perennial herb with stems 1 foot or more in length that grows almost flat on the ground. Leaves are alternate, 1½ to 3 inches long and not quite as broad, often with wavy margins that are coarsely toothed or deeply cut with rounded lobes.

FLOWERS AND FRUIT: The flowers are purple with a darker purple, star-shaped pattern in the center. They have five united petals that open out to form a flat surface about ¾ inches across. The flowers have five stamens with yellow anthers. The fruit is a berry, orange when mature, and surrounded by a papery husk formed by the united lobes of the flower's sepals.

FLOWERING: Flowering occurs from March to October.

RANGE AND HABITAT: Purple Groundcherry grows from central Texas west through the Trans-Pecos and the Panhandle. Its native range extends north in the western Great Plains to Kansas and Colorado and west to southern California.

COMMENTS: Having a large, water-storing root, Purple Groundcherry is not much affected by drought and flowers with great abandon in the most sere summers. It would be good as a garden flower, especially in areas of little rainfall. Once lumped into the genus *Physalis*, this species is now the sole representative of the genus *Quincula*.

Solanum elaeagnifolium

Silverleaf Nightshade, Prairie Berry, White Horsenettle

SOLANACEAE (POTATO FAMILY)

PLANT AND LEAVES: Silverleaf Nightshade is a branching perennial herb growing 1 to 3 feet tall from a long, fleshy taproot. Both the stems and the leaves are covered in silvery hairs. The leaves are lance shaped, 2 to 4 inches long and about 1 inch wide, with wavy edges.

FLOWERS AND FRUIT: Flowers are violet purple or occasionally white, about ¾ inch across, with five petal-like, triangular lobes that are joined at the base. The flowers have the prominent, bright yellow stamens that distinguish all the horsenettles. The yellow fruits resemble small tomatoes and remain on the plant for months.

FLOWERING: Flowering occurs from March to October.

RANGE AND HABITAT: This species is found over most of Texas, where it seems to prefer waste areas and disturbed sites. It will thrive in very dry areas. Though it has spread to much of the southern half of the United States, its US native range is more limited and originally extended only as far east as Louisiana and Arkansas, north to Kansas and Colorado, west to Arizona, and as far south as Chile and Argentina.

COMMENTS: Silverleaf Nightshade gets its name from its covering of silvery hairs, among which are the nettle-like prickles. The specific epithet, *elaeagnifolium*, in its botanical name references its leaves' resemblance to the leaves of Silverberry shrubs (*Elaeagnus* spp.). The leaves and the fruits of Silverleaf Nightshade are toxic if ingested.

Wisteria frutescens

American Wisteria, Texas Wisteria

FABACEAE (PEA FAMILY)

Synonym: *Wisteria macrostachya*

PLANT AND LEAVES: American Wisteria is a woody, deciduous, high-climbing vine with multiple stems reaching up to 40 feet long. Leaves are alternate and odd-pinnate, to about 12 inches long, divided into 9 to 15 lance-shaped leaflets, to about 2½ inches long.

FLOWERS AND FRUIT: The flowers are in large, pendulous racemes, 4 to 6 inches long. Individual flowers are nearly 1 inch long and are lilac or bluish purple and quite sweetly fragrant.

FLOWERING: Flowering occurs April to June, occasionally to August.

RANGE AND HABITAT: American Wisteria grows in thickets and woods and along streams. Widespread in the eastern third of Texas, its native range covers nearly the entire eastern half of the United States.

COMMENTS: We have seen it at old abandoned home sites where it filled several trees, making it look, at first glance, as if the trees were blooming. American Wisteria is a less robust-growing plant than its more commonly grown relatives, Chinese Wisteria (*W. sinensis*) or Japanese Wisteria (*W. floribunda*). It is also much less likely to destroy an arbor or choke to death a tree upon which it is climbing—a very common problem with its Asian cousins. Thus, though a bit less floriferous, it is usually a more mannerly and better choice for gardens.

Arisaema triphyllum
Jack-in-the-pulpit
ARACEAE (ARUM FAMILY)
Synonyms: *Arisaema quinata*, *Arisaema atrorubens*

PLANT AND LEAVES: Jack-in-the-pulpit grows from a corm and is a perennial herb. A stem emerges from the ground in spring producing one or two three-lobed leaves on the typical species (*Arisaema triphyllum* ssp. *triphyllum*) and five-lobed leaves on *Arisaema triphyllum* ssp. *quinatum*.

FLOWERS AND FRUIT: A spathe emerges from the junction of the leaves and forms a kind of tube, the tip of which curves over the spadix within. The spathe is often very showy, sometimes colored purple with white or green stripes. The spadix is club shaped with flowers borne on its lower section. A variety of flies, thrips, and springtails are known pollinators. Immature

green berries turn red when mature. After flowering and fruiting the plant dies to the ground each winter.

FLOWERING: Flowering occurs from April to June. Fruits are mature in late summer.

RANGE AND HABITAT: Jack-in-the-pulpit prefers light shade and grows in moist to wet, rich soils across the eastern half of North America. It is found in suitable habitat most anywhere in the Pineywoods of east Texas.

COMMENTS: Fresh plant material contains calcium oxalate crystals and is harmful or fatal if eaten by humans. Birds eat the plant's ripe berries.

Castilleja purpurea

Prairie Indian Paintbrush, Downy Indian Paintbrush

SCROPHULARIACEAE (FIGWORT FAMILY)

PLANT AND LEAVES: Prairie Indian Paintbrush is an herbaceous perennial with unbranched, multiple stems growing from a single crown. The stems reach 6 to 18 inches tall with soft hairs throughout, giving the plant a grayish cast. The leaves are alternate and attached directly to the stem. They are deeply dissected into one or two (rarely three) pairs of narrow lobes.

FLOWERS AND FRUIT: The flowers are borne in spikes on the upper third of the stems. The flower color is mostly creamy but insignificant to identification, being mostly obscured by the plant's colorful floral bracts. Three different botanical varieties of this species occur in Texas; each has its own range of bract colors. *Castilleja purpurea* var. *purpurea* has mostly purple, pink, or purplish-red and sometimes white bracts. *Castilleja purpurea* var. *lindheimeri* has orange bracts, and *Castilleja purpurea* var. *citrina* bears bracts in various shades of yellow.

FLOWERING: Flowering occurs from April to June.

RANGE AND HABITAT: Prairie Indian Paintbrush favors rocky limestone soils and is found in open grassland and on roadsides from Texas's central Rio Grande plain to the Oklahoma border in the north-central part of the state. Its native range extends north through the middle of the Great Plains to southern Kansas.

COMMENTS: Where the ranges of the varieties overlap a great variety of colors can be found. In short, if you can think of a bract color that you've seen on any other *Castilleja* species, chances are there are specimens of this species with bracts of that same hue.

Physostegia intermedia

Spring Obedient Plant, Slender False Dragonhead

LAMIACEAE (MINT FAMILY)

PLANT AND LEAVES: Spring Obedient Plant is a perennial herb that spreads by rhizomes and grows 1 to 5 feet tall. Its stem is square, solitary, and slender, usually unbranched. Leaves are somewhat fleshy, opposite, sparse, 2 to 3 inches long, narrow, and lance shaped. Leaf margins are usually wavy.

FLOWERS AND FRUIT: Flowers are pink or lavender with purple spots and streaks, up to ¾ inch long, and attached directly to the stem. The flowers are two-lipped with an inflated throat; the upper lip is unlobed; the lower lip is three-lobed and spreading, with a broad middle lobe. There are four stamens.

FLOWERING: This is an early flowering species with sometimes

spectacular shows of pink or lavender flowers from April to June.

RANGE AND HABITAT: Spring Obedient Plant grows in consistently moist areas, often growing as an aquatic in shallow water. It is commonly found in wet roadside ditches, along bayous, and on pond margins in the eastern third of Texas. Its native range extends north through the eastern Great Plains to Kansas and in the Mississippi River Valley as far north as Kentucky.

COMMENTS: Flowers of the genus *Physostegia* grow straight up and down the stem on all four sides and at right angles to it. They may be moved laterally (like the pages in a book), and will remain in the new position; thus, the common name "obedient plant."

Neolloydia conoidea

Texas Cone Cactus, Chihuahuan Beehive Cactus

CACTACEAE (CACTUS FAMILY)
Synonyms: *Echinocactus conoideus, Mammillaria conoidea*

PLANT AND LEAVES: Texas Cone Cactus is a low-growing plant, egg shaped at first, later becoming cone-like, about 4 inches tall and almost 3 inches across. It often produces two or three side branches that may emerge from the base of the plant or farther up the side of stem. The surface is dull green, often swaddled in cottony hairs, and has several rows of pyramid-shaped tubercles about ½ inch high. There are 10 to 16 whitish spines, often having black tips, that are straight and rigid, radiate outward, and lie flat on the stem; in the center there are 1 to 4 spines, ⅜ inch to 1 inch long, that project outward. These are black when young, fading to gray.

FLOWERS AND FRUIT: The flowers are violet or violet pink, 1 to 2 inches across, about 1 inch deep, and opening out widely. The tepals are long and pointed. Anthers are yellow orange, and the stigma is multilobed and creamy white. Tunas ripen around November and are round, yellowish green or reddish, later turning brown.

FLOWERING: Flowering begins in April and continues to July.

RANGE AND HABITAT: Texas Cone Cactus is primarily a Mexican species, its range crossing the Rio Grande River between Del Rio and Boquillas. It prefers limestone soils in desert scrub.

COMMENTS: Only one of three varieties of this species occurs in Texas, *Neolloydia conoidea* var. *conoidea*. The other two varieties are Mexican endemics.

Triodanis perfoliata

Venus' Looking Glass

CAMPANULACEAE (BELLFLOWER FAMILY)

Synonym: *Specularia perfoliata*

PLANT AND LEAVES: Venus' Looking Glass is an erect, unbranched, herbaceous annual, growing 6–24 inches tall from a taproot. The plant's single stem has whitish, hairy veins running the length of it. Leaves are alternate and heart shaped, about 1 inch wide, with gently scalloped or indented margins. Their bases clasp the stem, forming a partial envelope.

FLOWERS AND FRUIT: One to three flowers are borne in each leaf axil, with only one opening at a time. The flowers lower on the plant are smaller than those above, are shaped differently, and have only three sepals; their petals do not open. Those flowers are self-fertile, with pollen passing from the anthers to the pistil within the flower. The flowers higher on the plant are larger, about ½ inch across, with five sepals and five lavender or violet, narrow, pointed petals united to form a slender tube that flares out nearly flat at the opening. The pistils on the upper flowers extend beyond the petals and have three-lobed, white stigmas.

FLOWERING: In Texas, this species flowers from April to July.

RANGE AND HABITAT: Venus' Looking Glass prefers poor soils where competition is suppressed. It is often found in old fields, prairies, and open woods in the eastern half of the state and west to the Trans-Pecos. It is a little plant with an impressive native range, covering nearly every US state and all but the Canadian Great Plains provinces. Southward, its range extends to Argentina.

COMMENTS: The fruit of this species is interesting. When the seeds are mature, pores in the sides of the fruiting capsules break open. As wind jostles the plant, the tiny seeds within the capsule are scattered hither and yon.

Cirsium texanum

Texas Thistle

ASTERACEAE (ASTER FAMILY)
Synonym: *Carduus austrinus*

PLANT AND LEAVES: Texas Thistle is a biennial or perennial that grows 2 to 5 feet tall without branches or sparingly branched near the top. The numerous leaves are alternate, 4 to 9 inches long, smaller on the upper third of the stem. Leaves are green above and white below, with a woolly texture on the underside. The leaves' bases are auriculate clasping; that is, they have ear-like lobes that wrap around the plant's stem. The irregular lobes have spines at the tip but few elsewhere on the leaf.

FLOWERS AND FRUIT: There is one flower head to a stem, with no ray flowers but numerous disc flowers that are deep rose lavender. The phyllaries on the attractive, hemispherical involucre are each topped with a whitish glutinous ridge. These vertical streaks are sticky and efficiently capture insects that feed on the plant or prey on pollinators.

FLOWERING: Texas Thistle flowers from April to August.

RANGE AND HABITAT: Texas Thistle is native to the southern Great Plains, the US Chihuahuan Desert, and northern Mexico. In Texas, it can be found over most of the state except for the

Pineywoods in the east and much of the Rolling Plains and far western Trans-Pecos in the west.

COMMENTS: Bumblebees are especially fond of this species, and it is an important nectar source for them and other bees, butterflies, and hummingbirds. Painted Lady butterfly caterpillars feed on the leaves of Texas Thistle.

Clematis pitcheri

Purple Leatherflower, Bluebill

RANUNCULACEAE (BUTTERCUP FAMILY)
Synonym: *Viorna pitcheri*

PLANT AND LEAVES: Like a number of other native clematises, Purple Leatherflower is a rather delicate, perennial vine, climbing by means of clasping tendril-like leaf petioles and leaf rachises. New growth emerges from the plant's crown each year and quickly grows up to 12 feet in height, clinging to nearby vegetation. Leaves are opposite, most divided into two to four pairs of lateral leaflets and a terminal leaflet that are marked on the underside by a prominent raised network of veins.

FLOWERS AND FRUIT: Flowers are urn shaped and nodding on long, slender stems from the leaf axils. They are lavender to frosty pink on the outside and dark purple, red, or sometimes whitish on the inside. The four sepals are petal-like, thick, and united at the base; they are recurved or only lightly spreading near the tip; petals are absent. The many stamens and pistils are packed inside the flower. The infructescence is a ball of tailed achenes, but unlike many other clematises the tails of this species are not feathery but bare.

FLOWERING: Purple Leatherflower can be found in flower any time from April to September.

RANGE AND HABITAT: A wide-ranging species, Purple Leatherflower can be found across most of Texas, in thickets and along woodland edges. Its native range extends northeast from Texas in a wide swath to the southern tip of Lake Michigan.

COMMENTS: Purple Leatherflower, along with its close relative Scarlet Leatherflower (*Clematis texensis*), prefers similar habitat in moist, but not wet, rocky soil in partial shade.

Linum lewisii

Prairie Flax, Blue Flax

LINACEAE (FLAX FAMILY)

PLANT AND LEAVES: Prairie flax grows 18 to 20 inches tall. It rarely stands straight up but rather leans at an angle. The stem is leafy when the plant is young, gradually losing most of its leaves as it matures. Leaves are narrow and about ¾ inch long.

FLOWERS AND FRUIT: Flowers are about 1 to 1½ inches across, pale or bright purplish blue with a small yellow "eye." Each flower has five petals with veins a darker shade of blue. Each stem produces several flowers, opening from the bottom upward. We have never seen more than one flower at a time open on any stem. The seeds are produced on the lower flowers while those above continue to open.

FLOWERING: This species flowers from April to September.

RANGE AND HABITAT: In Texas, Prairie Flax can be found in the Trans-Pecos. The species is native to the western half of the United States, west of the Great Plains, and also much of Canada and northern Mexico.

COMMENTS: We have seen several instances in which the wind had blown the flower off its stem and all the petals remained attached to each other with a hole in the center that had surrounded the stamens. If handled carefully, such detached flowers remain intact.

Ruellia caroliniensis

Carolina Wild Petunia

ACANTHACEAE (ACANTHUS FAMILY)

PLANT AND LEAVES: Carolina Wild Petunia produces herbaceous, branched stems each spring from perennial crowns and grows 12 to 24 inches tall. Its opposite leaves are lance shaped and 2 to 3½ inches long with margins that are wavy or vaguely toothed.

FLOWERS AND FRUIT: Flowers—each of which is open but one day—are trumpet shaped, five lobed, and usually lavender or purplish blue and occur singly or in small clusters in the upper leaf axils. The calyces and bracts below the flowers have needle-like lobes and are helpful field identification features for this species. The fruit, which contains about five seeds, is a small football-shaped capsule.

FLOWERING: Among the native members of its genus, Carolina Wild Petunia is one of the first to flower. Flowering begins in April and can continue to September.

RANGE AND HABITAT: *Ruellia caroliniensis* prefers well-drained soils in open woodlands and along roadsides. It can be found in suitable habitat in east Texas and is endemic to the United States, east of the Great Plains.

COMMENTS: Carolina Wild Petunia is 1 of 14 species of *Ruellia* native to Texas. Though their flowers resemble those of garden petunias (family Solanaceae), *Ruellia* species are unrelated. This and related species make fine garden plants for partly shady areas. It is very attractive to most pollinators and is the larval food plant for several native butterflies.

Ruellia nudiflora

Violet Wild Petunia

ACANTHACEAE (ACANTHUS FAMILY)

PLANT AND LEAVES: Violet Wild Petunia is an herbaceous perennial that resprouts each year from a somewhat woody base. Its stems are erect to somewhat sprawling, 1 to 2 feet tall, with few branches. The leaves are gray green in color, opposite, 2 to 5 inches long, with slightly toothed margins, narrowed at the base, and on short petioles.

FLOWERS AND FRUIT: Flowers are produced in panicles or occasionally singly at the tops of the stems. They are trumpet shaped and lavender or purple. The five-lobed flowers may be nearly 2 inches across at the opening. Compared with other species, the sepals and bracts below the flowers are quite small, and the flowers appear to be "naked" on the inflorescence. The flowers open shortly after sunrise, lasting only one day. The fruit is a football-shaped capsule bearing four or five seeds.

FLOWERING: Flowering occurs from April to as late as September.

RANGE AND HABITAT: Common in open woods or prairies in east, central, and south Texas, its native range extends as far south as Costa Rica and north to southern Arizona.

COMMENTS: Violet Wild Petunia has flowers much like those of the unrelated cultivated garden petunia (family Solanaceae).

Dyschoriste linearis

Snake Herb, Narrowleaf Snake Herb, Polkadots

ACANTHACEAE (ACANTHUS FAMILY)

PLANT AND LEAVES: Snake Herb is a perennial plant, often forming spreading mounds to 1 foot or more in diameter. As the common name suggests, it is an herbaceous plant. Several erect stems, 6 to 12 inches tall, grow from the root of this plant. The branches and stems are covered with stiff, coarse hairs. The leaves are opposite, ¾ to 2¾ inches long, and attached directly to the four-sided stem.

FLOWERS AND FRUIT: The flowers are more or less two lipped with two lobes on the upper lip and three lobes on the lower. Flowers are ½ to 1 inch long and up to 1 inch across, lavender to purple with a white throat, and with variously shaped purple markings at the lobes' bases and in the flowers' throats. The flowers grow in the leaf axils on very short stems and are somewhat tucked in between the leaves, scattered here and there on the main stem.

FLOWERING: Flowering begins around April and may continue after rains through the warm months to October.

RANGE AND HABITAT: Snake Herb can be found on well-drained,

calcareous soils on rocky outcrops, grassy hillsides, and alluvial flats in the western two-thirds of Texas and also in southern Oklahoma and northern Mexico.

COMMENTS: Snake Herb is a good choice for a groundcover in a partially shaded garden. Very drought tolerant, it will grow in full sun but prefers some afternoon shade. Its common name is a mystery; the plant is not known to be either attractive or repellant to snakes.

Guaiacum angustifolium

Texas Lignum-vitae, Guayacan

ZYGOPHYLLACEAE (CREOSOTE-BUSH FAMILY)
Synonym: *Porlieria angustifolia*

PLANT AND LEAVES: A leafy, compact evergreen shrub, Texas Lignum-vitae rarely grows higher than 6 feet, though under favorable conditions it may grow twice that high. It is often darker than surrounding shrubs, owing to the stems being covered with dark green leaves. Leaves are pinnately compound, about 1 inch long, and with four to eight pairs of small, leathery leaflets, each about ½ inch long and ⅛ inch wide.

FLOWERS AND FRUIT: The plant's flowers, which have five petals, are violet to purple, about 1 inch across, and with prominent yellow anthers. The flowers are followed by small, heart-shaped capsules that burst open at maturity, exposing two shiny, scarlet-red seeds.

FLOWERING: Flowering begins in April and may continue until October.

RANGE AND HABITAT: Texas Lignum-vitae is native to west and southwest Texas and to northern Mexico. It is most at home at elevations below 4,000 feet, though we have photographed healthy specimens in the Chisos Basin on the slopes of Pulliam Mountain.

COMMENTS: The bark of the roots is sometimes used as soap for washing woolen goods, as it does not fade colors. Texas Lignum-vitae is a favored nectar source for honeybees. It performs well in xeric gardens and rock gardens and as hedges in its native range.

Krameria lanceolata

Trailing Ratany, Trailing Krameria, Prairie Sandbur

KRAMERIACEAE (RATANY FAMILY)

Synonym: *Krameria secundiflora*

PLANT AND LEAVES: Trailing Ratany is an herbaceous perennial growing from a thick, woody root. Its stems lie flat on the ground or sometimes scramble over low vegetation. One to several freely branching, slender stems emerge from each plant's crown. They are usually 1 to 3 feet but sometimes grow up to 5 feet long. Silky, gray, appressed hairs are found on all parts of the plant. The leaves are very narrow and about ¾ inch long.

FLOWERS AND FRUIT: At first sight, many mistake Trailing Ratany's flowers for orchid flower, which they resemble. Its showy flowers are borne singly on short stems. They are about 1 inch across, with five purple to wine-red sepals usually mistaken for petals. The flowers' actual petals can be easily overlooked.

Somewhat lost in the flower's center, they are very small and tinged with green. The upper three petals are united. The fruit is a very hard, spiny bur, about ⅜ inch in diameter.

FLOWERING: Flowering may occur any time from April to October.

RANGE AND HABITAT: This species is common in most of Texas except the Pineywoods region. Its native range extends north to Kansas and Colorado, west to New Mexico and Arizona, and south to northern Mexico.

COMMENTS: Trailing Ratany is easily overlooked as it lives prostrate on the ground or snaking its way through grasses and low vegetation. Once seen, though, something about its flowers always compels a closer look. This is not the sandbur of the grass family (*Cenchrus* spp.); however, stepping barefoot on one of its burs is every bit as painful.

Lythrum californicum

California Loosestrife

LYTHRACEAE (LOOSESTRIFE FAMILY)

PLANT AND LEAVES: California Loosestrife is an herbaceous perennial with thin, widely branched, four-sided stems 8 inches to 2 feet tall growing from woody rhizomes. The alternate leaves are narrow, without petioles, and about 1 inch long and ⅛ inch wide.

FLOWERS AND FRUIT: There are four to six pinkish-purple flowers, sometimes more, open at any one time along the upper third of each stem. The sepals form a short tube for the flowers, which open out into six soft petals, ¾ to 1 inch across.

FLOWERING: Flowering occurs between April and October.

RANGE AND HABITAT: Like most other members of its family, California Loosestrife can usually be found in close association with water. It is commonly found in moist soils along pond, marsh, and stream margins in the western two-thirds of Texas. Its native range extends north to Kansas and west to California and northwestern Mexico.

COMMENTS: A Eurasian relative of this species, Purple Loosestrife (*Lythrum salicaria*), is one of North America's most problematic invasive wetland weeds. Unlike that species, California Loosestrife is much more mannerly and does not take over waterways. Despite its clear preference for wet feet, the native species will perform well in the garden if regular water is provided.

Monarda citriodora

Lemon Beebalm, Plains Horsemint

LAMIACEAE (MINT FAMILY)

PLANT AND LEAVES: Lemon Beebalm is an herbaceous annual with several upright, seldom-branched stems that grow 1 to 2½ feet tall. In Mexico, it may act as a short-lived perennial, but in Texas, it has one season and is done. The stems are square in cross section with numerous downwardly curved hairs. Its leaves are opposite, narrow, up to 2½ inches long, and slightly toothed.

FLOWERS AND FRUIT: The green, leaf-like bracts taper to a spine-like tip and bend downward. They are located under the clusters of flowers that surround the stem at intervals (typical of the horsemints). The five small petals are white or lavender, often dotted with purple. They are united to form a two-lipped flower 1 inch long with two stamens.

FLOWERING: Flower may occur from May to August; commonly from May to June.

RANGE AND HABITAT: Lemon Beebalm is common in old fields and on prairies and roadsides. It prefers rich soils but grows with abundance on dry, open, rocky ground as well. It can be found in sunny areas across Texas. Its native range includes much of the southern Great Plains and the southwestern desert regions as far west as Arizona and south into central Mexico.

COMMENTS: We found Lemon Beebalm still healthy in late September (because of good rains) at 6,000 feet elevation in the Chisos Mountains. The crushed leaves of this species often emit a pleasant lemony fragrance.

Passiflora incarnata

Maypop, Purple Passionflower

PASSIFLORACEAE (PASSIONFLOWER FAMILY)

PLANT AND LEAVES: Maypop is an herbaceous vine with stems up to 8 feet long growing from a perennial rootstock. It commonly climbs by tendrils over fences and bushes or runs along the ground. The leaves are alternate, to about 6 inches long, and with deeply divided lobes that look almost like three leaflets.

FLOWERS AND FRUIT: The flower is mostly lavender or purple and about 3 inches across. Its structure looks more alien than earthly. The fruit is oval and green, larger than a hen egg. When it ripens, the outside skin becomes light tan or yellow, somewhat deflated, and tough.

FLOWERING: Flowering occurs from May to August.

RANGE AND HABITAT: Maypop can be found in scattered sunny locations in east Texas. It is especially common on disturbed soils and on old field fencelines on roadsides. Its native range encompasses the southeastern Great Plains and the southeastern United States to as far north as Illinois and New Jersey.

COMMENTS: The genus *Passiflora* has more than 500 species, nearly all of which are native to the tropics of South and Central America and Asia. There are six species native to Texas. Plants of this genus are the sole larval food of the Gulf Fritillary butterfly (*Agraulis vanillae*). This species may be the cold hardiest of all passionflowers. Maypop pollen attracts many insects, and its fruit is attractive to many animals. The sweet pulp within the fruit is delicious eaten fresh and is sometimes processed to make jelly.

Ipomoea cordatotriloba var. *cordatotriloba*

Tievine, Purple Bindweed, Wild Morning Glory

CONVOLVULACEAE (MORNING GLORY FAMILY)
Synonym: *Ipomoea trichocarpa*

PLANT AND LEAVES: Tievine is an herbaceous vine growing each year from a stout, perennial root. It can and sometimes does also grow as an annual vine. The several stems of the vine reach up to 15 feet long, usually creeping along the ground or climbing by twining on low vegetation, fences, or other suitable supporting structure. The species' specific epithet, *cordatotriloba*,

is apt, as it bears leaves of two very different shapes: cordate, or heart-shaped, and trilobate, or three-lobed. Some leaves may have five lobes, and all leaves are arranged alternately on the stem.

FLOWERS AND FRUIT: This species flowers copiously. The funnel-shaped flowers are orchid colored with a deep purple center, 1 to 1½ inches across and about the same length. A star-shaped pattern of lines is evident in the flower's petals. There is often a faint, whitish area around the flower's center.

FLOWERING: Flowering occurs May to October.

RANGE AND HABITAT: Tievine is found in old fields, on roadsides, and in disturbed areas in the eastern third of the state. From Texas, its native range extends east along the US coast to North Carolina and also north into Arkansas.

COMMENTS: Morning glories are lovely, colorful vines and have long been favorites of gardeners looking for floriferous climbers. However, these rampant vining species do not endear themselves to everyone, especially farmers, who consider them aggravating and costly weeds. In two states—Arkansas and Arizona—most or all members of *Ipomoea*, including native species, are officially listed as noxious weeds. Tievine is one of at least 30 species native to North America, with no fewer than 24 of them Texas natives. The very closely related *Ipomoea cordatotriloba* var. *torreyana* is native to central and west Texas.

Dalea frutescens
Black Dalea
FABACEAE (PEA FAMILY)

PLANT AND LEAVES: Black Dalea is a perennial, semi-evergreen, low, mounding shrub that usually grows 1 to 2 feet tall but may reach 3 feet in height and spread to 5 feet. The plant is hairless throughout. It has red stems and is fairly densely branched. The leaves are smallish (to about 1 inch in length), grayish green, and compound with 11 to 17 oval leaflets, each about ¼ to ½ inch long. The leaves have glands on the lower surface that contain a fragrant oil. When crushed, the leaves emit a pleasant scent.

FLOWERS AND FRUIT: The flowers are held in tight clusters at the ends of the stems. Flower petals are magenta colored and the banner petal is white.

FLOWERING: Flowering occurs from June to October.

RANGE AND HABITAT: Black Dalea can be found on dry soils from the Hill Country through the Trans-Pecos and into southern New Mexico. Its range extends south into northern Mexico.

COMMENTS: Like the similar species Feather Dalea (*Dalea formosa*), Black Dalea makes a nice addition to dry gardens. It is a more handsome plant than Feather Dalea, especially when pruned in winter to maintain a compact shape, but it is not quite as showy when in flower. The flowers of this species are magnets for bees and butterflies.

Leucophyllum frutescens

Cenizo, Purple Sage, Barometer Bush, Texas Ranger

SCROPHULARIACEAE (FIGWORT FAMILY)

PLANT AND LEAVES: Cenizo is a well-branched but dense evergreen shrub with gray stems. It grows 5 to 8 feet tall and about 5 feet wide and is the most common of three *Leucophyllum* species

native to Texas. The leaves are variably light gray green, the relative amount of gray or green varying from plant to plant. The silvery gray color of the plant's stems and leaves gives rise to the name Cenizo, meaning "ashy." The leaves are opposite, whorled, or alternate.

FLOWERS AND FRUIT: The rose-pink to orchid-rose or occasionally white flowers have five sepals and five petals, which form a funnel-shaped flower about 1 inch across at the opening. The fruit is a minute capsule, about ⅕ inch long and rarely noticed.

FLOWERING: This species flowers any time from June to October following rains or sometimes in response to an increase in humidity.

RANGE AND HABITAT: Cenizo is native from central Texas southwest to the Big Bend area and south to Mexico.

COMMENTS: This plant is often used as an ornamental in xeric gardens and probably should be used even more. It is relatively fast growing and has few pest or disease issues. A nice-looking, naturally rounded shrub year-round, when in flower, which is typically several times each summer, it can be stunningly beautiful.

Vernonia baldwinii

Western Ironweed

ASTERACEAE (ASTER FAMILY)

PLANT AND LEAVES: Western Ironweed is a perennial herb that grows 2 to 4 feet tall. It has numerous dark green, mostly ovate leaves, 3 to 6 inches long and up to 1½ inches wide, that are attached directly to the stem. It branches considerably in the top few inches of the stem.

FLOWERS AND FRUIT: Western Ironweed flower heads are discoid, having no ray flowers. Its heads are clusters of stunning, fuchsia-purple disc flowers held in corymb-like arrays. Buds are cream colored with a rosy glow before opening.

FLOWERING: May flower any time during summer and fall (June to November).

RANGE AND HABITAT: Historically a constituent of the Great Plains flora, Western Ironweed can still be found in prairie remnants on field margins and especially along roadsides, where it never fails to be noticed. Frequent in north-central Texas, Edwards Plateau, and plains country; infrequent in east Texas. Its native range extends northward throughout the Great Plains to South Dakota and Minnesota.

COMMENTS: Though coarse in outline, Western Ironweed's show-stopping flower color makes this plant worthy of cultivation. One or more species of ironweed, all with similar flowers, may be found in all parts of the state.

Dalea formosa

Feather Dalea, Featherplume

FABACEAE (PEA FAMILY)

PLANT AND LEAVES: Feather Dalea is a colony-forming, perennial shrub that normally grows 2 to 3 feet tall and rarely to 6 feet. The plant looks a bit unkempt with branches that are thin, contorted, widely spreading, and not at all uniform in length. Leaves are very small, usually less than ½ inch long, with 5 to 11 tiny, glandular leaflets.

FLOWERS AND FRUIT: Flowers are borne in loose, head-like clusters of 2 to 12 flowers at the ends of each stem and twig in hairy cups made up of bracts. Flower petals are deep purple or magenta, and the banner petal is often a nicely contrasting yellow or cream color.

FLOWERING: This species may begin flowering as early as April but mostly flowers July to October.

RANGE AND HABITAT: Feather Dalea is native to the western third of Texas, from the Rio Grande to the Panhandle, where it is found on dry, rocky soils. It is commonly found scattered

across the Trans-Pecos region and throughout the Chihuahuan Desert and the Sonoran Desert in New Mexico, Arizona, and Mexico.

COMMENTS: When not flowering, the plant is not particularly attractive or even noticeable, but when it flowers, it is a showstopper. Then, the plant is nearly blanketed with bright purple and yellow flowers. This species is an important food plant for wildlife. It is an excellent choice for a xeric garden within its native range.

Liatris elegans

Pinkscale Gayfeather, Elegant Blazingstar

ASTERACEAE (ASTER FAMILY)

PLANT AND LEAVES: Pinkscale Gayfeather is a slender, unbranched perennial arising from a large, rounded corm. It grows 1 to 4 feet tall. Its narrow leaves, much like pine needles, are about 3 inches long and whorled around the stem.

FLOWERS AND FRUIT: The flower spike is 6 to 20 inches long, flowering from the top downward. Flower heads bear four or five purple to pale lavender-pink disc flowers, about ½ inch long. There are no ray flowers, but long, petal-like bracts the same color as the disc flowers are often mistaken for them.

FLOWERING: August to October (September and October in Texas).

RANGE AND HABITAT: Native to dry, sandy prairies and open pinelands in US states along the Gulf of Mexico, Oklahoma, Arkansas, Georgia, and South Carolina. In Texas, it can be found in the eastern and southeastern third of the state.

COMMENTS: Individual plants in this genus are easily recognizable as being members of *Liatris*, but determination of species name often requires some botanical knowledge and a good botanical key. In Texas, there are no fewer than 16 species of gayfeathers, most of which are very similar in appearance.

Eryngium leavenworthii

Leavenworth's Eryngo, False Purple Thistle

APIACEAE (CARROT FAMILY)

PLANT AND LEAVES: Leavenworth's Eryngo is an herbaceous annual that grows 1 to 3 feet high, often in dense masses. In early August the foliage is gray green, but it gradually takes on a purple hue by September. The deeply lobed leaves surround the stem, clasping it, and the leaf segments have many spiny

teeth. A tuft of small, rigid, spiny leaves grows out of the top of the flower head.

FLOWERS AND FRUIT: The flower heads resemble miniature purple pineapples. They are up to 2 inches long and when fully developed, the bracts and the stamens are all purple. The flower heads are held vertically and grow on short stems in the forks of the branches.

FLOWERING: Flowering takes place in late August and September.

RANGE AND HABITAT: A native of the southern Great Plains, Leavenworth's Eryngo is commonly found in old fields, along roadsides, and in waste areas. It is abundant in central and north Texas. It also grows in Oklahoma and Kansas.

COMMENTS: *Eryngium* species are not true thistles, but anyone familiar with this spiny plant will easily understand how it got the name. The flowers are often used in dried arrangements. It is desirable to wear a thick pair of gloves if one cuts the flowers.

Physostegia virginiana ssp. *praemorsa*

Fall Obedient Plant, Blunt False Dragonhead

LAMIACEAE (MINT FAMILY)
Synonym: *Physostegia praemorsa*

PLANT AND LEAVES: Fall Obedient Plant is an erect perennial herb that spreads by rhizomes and is mostly 1 to 2 feet tall, occasionally reaching 4 feet in height. Unlike some other obedient plants, it has no branches in the upper part. Leaves are opposite, 1 to 2¾ inches long and ½ inch wide or less. The leaves on the lower part of the stem are larger. The upper ones are sharply toothed. There are many large, showy flowers on the upper portion of the stems.

FLOWERS AND FRUIT: The stems are terminated with vertical spikes of many large, showy flowers. The flowers are 1¼ inches long, pinkish lavender, and lightly spotted within with lines of rose-purple dots. The two-lipped flowers have four stamens and are inflated at the throat.

FLOWERING: Flowering occurs from August to October.

RANGE AND HABITAT: Fall Obedient Plant can be found on consistently moist to wet soils in scattered locations in east Texas. Its native range extends across the Southeast and through the eastern Midwest.

COMMENTS: This is the only fall-flowering Texas *Physostegia* species. The odd characteristic that gives obedient plants their common name is the phenomenon that if a flower is pushed to one side it will remain in place and not spring back as would normally be expected.

Symphyotrichum patens var. *patens*

Late Purple Aster

ASTERACEAE (ASTER FAMILY)

Synonyms: *Aster patens, Aster amplexicaulis*

PLANT AND LEAVES: Late Purple Aster is an herbaceous perennial that grows 1 to 3 feet tall and is easily recognized by its short, broad, rough leaves, which are attached directly to the stems. Leaves are arranged alternately along the stem.

FLOWERS AND FRUIT: The showy flower heads of Late Purple Aster are borne in arrays of up to five per cluster. Ray flowers vary in color from violet to mauve to pale pinkish white. Disc flowers are typically yellow but may be creamy white and may turn purple with age.

FLOWERING: Late Purple Aster may flower any time from August to December. Most flowering occurs September to November.

RANGE AND HABITAT: Dry woodlands throughout east and central Texas. Outside Texas, its range covers virtually all of the United States east of the Mississippi River as well as the southern and south-central Great Plains.

COMMENTS: After a taxonomic review, botanists determined that all but one North American native aster species (the northern alpine native, *Aster alpinus*) must be assigned to a new genus. Thus, most former North American members of the genus *Aster* are now classified—like Late Purple Aster—in *Symphyotrichum*. Other species were transferred to *Eurybia, Machaeranthera, Oclemena, Xylorhiza,* and other genera.

Pink
Flowers

Drosera brevifolia

Dwarf Sundew, Red Sundew

DROSERACEAE (SUNDEW FAMILY)

Synonym: *Drosera annua*

PLANT AND LEAVES: Dwarf Sundew is an annual, rosette-forming, insectivorous herb to about 4 inches tall when flowering. The rosette is usually about 1 inch in diameter, lying flat on the ground. The plant's leaves are wedge or paddle shaped, usually pink or red or occasionally green, their upper surfaces covered in sticky, glandular hairs that trap small insects. Once trapped, the hapless creature is enfolded by the leaf and digested by the plant's exuded enzymes.

FLOWERS AND FRUIT: The sticky, glandular scape—diagnostic for this species—rises about 4 inches above the rosette and produces as many as six flowers, only one opening at a time. The flowers are about ¾ inch in diameter, usually pale pink, sometimes white, and with five nearly circular petals.

FLOWERING: Flowering begins as early as February and may continue to as late as June.

RANGE AND HABITAT: Dwarf Sundew grows on moderately moist to dry sand in open woodlands and in meadows in east and southeast Texas and along the Gulf Coast as far south as Corpus Christi. Mostly found in areas along or close to a coastline, its native range extends along the Gulf Coast and the Atlantic Coast to Virginia. However, it spreads far inland in some areas and can be found throughout Louisiana, much of central Arkansas, and in isolated populations in Tennessee and Kentucky.

COMMENTS: *Drosera* is one of the four genera of insectivorous plants in Texas, each of which has its own way of catching its prey. One butterwort (*Pinguicula* sp.), ten bladderworts (*Utricularia* spp.), and one pitcher plant (*Sarracenia* sp.) are the other native Texas bug-eating plants. Most can be found in Texas only in the eastern portion of the state.

Cercis canadensis

Redbud, Eastern Redbud, Texas Redbud, Mexican Redbud

FABACEAE (PEA FAMILY)

PLANT AND LEAVES: Redbud is a small, deciduous tree or shrub with a spreading, rounded crown up to 30 feet tall and a trunk diameter up to 10 inches. It usually grows as a single-trunked tree, branching near the ground. Its spread often exceeds its height. It has alternate, rounded, heart-shaped leaves, 2 to 3 inches across.

FLOWERS AND FRUIT: Each spring, this is one of Texas's earliest-flowering woody plants. The flowers are actually pinkish purple, somewhat redder in the bud. They are ¼ to ½ inch long, with five pea flower-shaped petals. The flowers grow in clusters and appear before the leaves. When the plant is weakened by adverse conditions, such as old age or drought, the flowers often grow directly from the main trunk and large limbs. Being a member of the pea family, Redbud's fruit is a leathery legume, 2 to 4 inches long and about ½ inch wide, containing three to five seeds. They are often red or purple and very showy during development.

FLOWERING: Flowering occurs in March to April. The fruit matures in the fall.

RANGE AND HABITAT: Redbud can be found in most areas of Texas except in the southern, western, and northwestern extremes. It is common from the Pineywoods to the eastern Trans-Pecos. It is primarily an understory tree found in woodlands across most of the eastern United States.

COMMENTS: Though all botanical varieties are lumped together here, those considering use of this Redbud in their landscape should choose the variety best suited to their area. In general, that would be: Eastern Redbud (*Cercis canadensis* var. *canadensis*) in east Texas, Texas Redbud (*C. c.* var. *texensis*) in central and north Texas, and Mexican Redbud (*C. c.* var. *mexicana*) in west Texas.

Rhododendron canescens

Piedmont Azalea, Honeysuckle Azalea, Hoary Azalea

ERICACEAE (HEATH FAMILY)

Synonym: *Azalea canescens*

PLANT AND LEAVES: Piedmont Azalea is a showy shrub with open branching, usually to about 10 feet though some specimens can approach 20 feet in height. The bark on older trunks is often shredding. Leaves are deciduous, alternate, and clustered, 1½

to 4 inches long and ¾ to 1¼ inches wide. They are firm and thick, with a dark green upper surface and pubescent below.

FLOWERS AND FRUIT: The glandular-sticky flowers have a pleasant but faint, often musky, fragrance. They are 1 to 2 inches in diameter and borne in whorl-like clusters. The flowers open just as new leaves begin to emerge in spring. Flower color ranges from dark shell pink to white (rarely). Flowers are trumpet shaped, about 1 inch long, and flare into five petal-like lobes. The outside of the tube is often a darker shade of pink than the rest of the flower. There are five stamens, 1 to 1¾ inches long, that extend well beyond the flower lobes, and a pistil equal to or exceeding the stamens in length.

FLOWERING: Flowering typically begins in late March and continues until late April.

RANGE AND HABITAT: Piedmont Azalea is native to mixed woodlands in moist soils near swamps and along streams in the southeastern corner of Texas. Its range extends across the US Southeast.

COMMENTS: Because this species' flowers appear before its leaves have expanded, the spring floral show in the South's woodlands is usually spectacular.

Phlox roemeriana
Golden-eye Phlox, Roemer's Phlox
POLEMONIACEAE (PHLOX FAMILY)

PLANT AND LEAVES: Golden-eye Phlox is an herbaceous winter annual growing 3 to 12 inches tall. The stem and leaves are coarsely hairy. The plant has narrow, lance-shaped leaves that are mostly opposite near the plant's base but alternately arranged on the upper reaches of the stem. The largest leaves may be 2 inches long and ½ inch wide.

FLOWERS AND FRUIT: The flowers are borne in small clusters in the upper leaf axils. Flowers have five pink to purple petals united to form a tube that is slightly shorter than the length of the corolla lobes. The petals open out almost flat and have a conspicuous yellow "eye" bordered by white. Each petal also has a streak near the base, a shade of pink or purple darker than the

rest of the petal, that acts as a nectar guide for visiting bees. The aggregate visual effect of the streaks on each of the five petals is that of a star in the middle of the flower.

FLOWERING: Flowering occurs from March to May.

RANGE AND HABITAT: Golden-eye Phlox is an endemic of the Edwards Plateau and nearby areas where it is common and appears in great numbers in dry, sunny locations on bare rocky outcrops and in grassy meadows on limestone soils.

COMMENTS: Golden-eye Phlox is one of the major constituents of the springtime wildflower explosion in the Texas Hill Country. In March and April, it is difficult to find a sunny spot anywhere that does not have an ample population of this little pink jewel.

Abronia ameliae
Amelia's Sand Verbena, Heart's Delight
NYCTAGINACEAE (FOUR-O'CLOCK FAMILY)

PLANT AND LEAVES: A perennial, herbaceous plant, 1 to 2 feet tall. Stems are branched, usually sprawling and often with red nodes. All parts are covered in sticky glands. Leaves are opposite, borne on ½ to 1¼ inch petioles, and are ovate to elliptical in shape and 1 to 3½ inches long. Leaf margins are smooth but wavy.

FLOWERS AND FRUIT: Inflorescences are cymes borne on long peduncles that arise from the leaf axils. Each hemispherical cyme
bears 25 to 75 pink or magenta flowers and is about 2 inches
in diameter. Flowers are salverform and five-lobed. Fruits are
dry and five winged with reticulate surfaces. The fruits are arranged in clusters (one for each flower) with each fruit bearing
one shiny dark brown achene.

FLOWERING: Flowering occurs from March to June.

RANGE AND HABITAT: This species is endemic to just a few counties
in south Texas and occurs naturally only on the Holocene Sand
Sheet there.

COMMENTS: This is one of the showiest and prettiest wildflowers
to be found in south Texas. Anyone having the pleasure of
seeing a colony of *Abronia ameliae* in flower is unlikely to ever
forget it. The species was named for Amelia Lundell, the wife
of the species' author, legendary botanist Cyrus L. Lundell.
Abronia fragrans closely resembles this plant and has a wider
distribution. It is said to cover most of west Texas on plains
and sandy hills.

Echinocereus reichenbachii

Lace Cactus, Purple Candle

CACTACEAE (CACTUS FAMILY)

PLANT AND LEAVES: Like other cylindrical cacti, Lace Cactus starts out as a sphere and gradually evolves its cylindrical form as it matures. This little plant rarely grows taller than 8 inches and is 2 to 3 inches across. It is unpredictable in its development, one plant forming a single stem, while its neighbor may branch out and form a dozen or more stems. It has 10 to 20 narrow ribs. The number of outer spines varies from 12 to 36. They are flattened against the stem. The central spines vary in number from none to six and project outward.

FLOWERS AND FRUIT: Flowers are brilliant purple or rose pink, 2 to 5 inches tall and almost as wide. There are 30 to 50 tepals with ragged edges, sometimes notched. The bases of the tepals are usually reddish brown. Stamens are cream colored to yellow, and the pistils have several dark green lobes, varying in number with each flower. Tunas are green when ripe.

FLOWERING: Flowering begins in March and continues to June.

RANGE AND HABITAT: Lace Cactus can be found on desert scrubland and prairies from the Rio Grande Valley north through central Texas and northwest throughout the Panhandle. Outside Texas, its range extends north to Kansas, west to southeastern

Colorado and eastern New Mexico, and south to northeastern Mexico.

COMMENTS: Lace Cactus' small size, brightly colored flowers, and hardiness make it a favorite for xeric gardens and rock gardens.

Hymenopappus artemisiifolius

Old Plainsman, Woollywhite

ASTERACEAE (ASTER FAMILY)

PLANT AND LEAVES: Old Plainsman is an herbaceous biennial that forms a basal rosette of simple or pinnately lobed, often woolly, hairy leaves. From the rosette, a single erect stem, 2 to 4 feet tall and branched only in the upper part, grows in early spring. Leaves on the stem are alternate and often pinnatifid or bipinnatifid.

FLOWERS AND FRUIT: Flower heads are at the end of stems, sometimes having as many as 60 florets in a cluster. The phyllaries surrounding the flower are snowy white on the outer half, giving the whole head a white appearance. Disc flowers are rose colored to dark wine, and there are no ray flowers. The flowers are funnel shaped, five lobed, and numerous.

FLOWERING: Flowering begins in March and continues into June.

RANGE AND HABITAT: Old Plainsman is native to Texas, Louisiana, and Arkansas. It grows over all of east Texas and is commonly seen along roadsides and old fields, where it often covers large areas.

COMMENTS: Old Plainsman is one of several species of *Hymenopappus* likely to be encountered in Texas, including Biennial Woollywhite (*H. biennis*), Carrizo Sands Woollywhite (*H. carrizoanus*), Fineleaf Woollywhite (*H. filifolius*), Collegeflower (*H. flavescens*), Carolina Woollywhite (*H. scabiosaeus*), and Chalk Hill Woollywhite (*H. tenuifolius*).

Oenothera speciosa
Pink Evening Primrose, Pinkladies
ONAGRACEAE (EVENING-PRIMROSE FAMILY)

PLANT AND LEAVES: Pink Evening Primrose is a mostly sprawling perennial herb growing 8 to 18 inches high. Leaves are alternate, and their shape is highly variable. However, most leaves are narrowly lance shaped, 1 to 4 inches long and about ¾ inch wide, and with toothed margins.

FLOWERS AND FRUIT: Flowers grow in a cluster at the ends of the branches. They are cup shaped, usually about 2 inches but up

to 3½ inches across, and with four broadly rounded petals usually marked with dark pink veins. The center is greenish yellow to white at the base. Flowers are pink to rose pink. Populations of white-flowered plants are common. The flower's four sepals are united into a slender tube below the petals but are pushed open and back as the petals open. The flower's eight anthers are yellow and borne in filaments that raise them above the flower. The pistil extends well beyond the stamens and is terminated by a white style having four long, narrow lobes.

FLOWERING: Flowering occurs March to June.

RANGE AND HABITAT: Grows in great masses along roadsides and in open fields in east and central Texas, rarely in west Texas. Pink Evening Primrose is a native of the Great Plains but has become naturalized from the Atlantic Coast to the Pacific. It is especially well established in the South.

COMMENTS: In certain drought years when competition is suppressed, this species puts on a floral show rivaling any in the country. In those years, some fields appear to be blanketed in drifts of pink snow.

Echinocereus chisoensis

Chisos Mountain Hedgehog Cactus, Chisos Pitaya

CACTACEAE (CACTUS FAMILY)

Synonym: *Echinocereus reichenbachii* var. *chisoensis*

PLANT AND LEAVES: Chisos Mountain Hedgehog Cactus grows 10 to 12 inches tall but seldom more than 2 inches in diameter. They are usually single stemmed but occasionally branch above the ground. The stems have 11 to 16 ribs composed of quite distinct tubercles, almost completely separated from each other by broad valleys. The surface is reddish in cool weather, fading to bluish green to deep green during warm months. There are 10 to 15 whitish spines growing from each areole, most of which lie flat on the stem.

FLOWERS AND FRUIT: The flowers are borne on spiny stalks emerging near the top of the plant, are about 2½ inches long and 1 to 2

inches across, and often do not fully open. The bases of the tepals are deep red, changing to white or pinkish white centrally and finally becoming hot pink at their terminal halves. The tepal tips are pointed. Anthers are cream colored or yellow, and the stigma has 10 dark green lobes. The tunas are covered with bristly areoles and are greenish red or red when mature about two months after flowering.

FLOWERING: Flowering may begin in March and continue until July, though most flowering takes place from March to May.

RANGE AND HABITAT: This rare cactus is known to grow only in the Chisos Mountains in Big Bend National Park in desert scrub on alluvial soils.

COMMENTS: With only a few hundred plants scattered across several locations known to exist, Chisos Mountain Hedgehog Cactus is among our most imperiled native species and deserving of all the care we can give it. It is a federal- and state-listed threatened species.

Echinocereus stramineus

Strawberry Hedgehog Cactus, Pitaya

CACTACEAE (CACTUS FAMILY)

Synonym: *Echinocereus enneacanthus* var. *stramineus*

PLANT AND LEAVES: Strawberry Hedgehog Cactus is a clump-forming species with as many as 100 to 500 stems on very old plants. These larger clumps are rounded, often 2 to 3 feet across and nearly as high. Its stems are about 10 inches tall and 3½ inches in diameter. The stems have 11 to 13 ribs with fairly deep furrows between them. This species has many long, straw-colored spines that distinguish it from *Echinocereus enneacanthus*, which often shares the same habitat.

FLOWERS AND FRUIT: The bright, red or magenta-pink to dark rose-pink flowers are sometimes dark red at the base. Flowers are borne on short stalks and are 4 to 5 inches tall and 3 to 4 inches across. The flowers' inner tepals are toothed. The tunas of this species are often spiny, about 1½ inches long, and brownish pink with green-tinted tubercles. The tunas ripen in midsummer.

FLOWERING: Flowering may begin as early as March and continue until July, but most flowering occurs during April and May.

RANGE AND HABITAT: This species occurs in the Trans-Pecos ecoregion of Texas, southern New Mexico, and northeastern Mexico. It can be found on rocky desert soils of sedimentary or volcanic origin.

COMMENTS: Strawberry Hedgehog Cactus tunas are said to be very tasty, but the fruits of wild-growing cacti should never be collected. So many of our desert plants are now imperiled owing to overcollecting.

Ungnadia speciosa

Mexican Buckeye

SAPINDACEAE (SOAPBERRY FAMILY)

PLANT AND LEAVES: Mexican Buckeye is a large, multistemmed, deciduous shrub. The plant's stiff stems usually grow to about 10 feet tall and spread about 10 feet wide, but the plant can reach 30 feet in height and nearly that broadly spread in some locations. Branching is sparse near the plant's base and increases toward the canopy. The leaves are alternate and compound with three to nine lance-shaped leaflets with toothed margins.

FLOWERS AND FRUIT: Beautiful clusters of purplish-pink, fragrant flowers adorn the upper stems of the plant. Its flowers have four petals and seven to ten stamens. The fruit is a three-valved capsule, each valve containing one shiny, brown to black seed. The seeds are poisonous.

FLOWERING: Mexican Buckeye flowers as the leaves emerge in March. It may also flower sporadically until August, depending on rainfall.

RANGE AND HABITAT: Common in scattered locales in south and south-central Texas and in the Trans-Pecos, it typically grows near streams in limestone canyons. As its common name suggests, Mexican Buckeye is also native to Mexico.

COMMENTS: *Ungnadia* is monotypic, containing this species and no other. Though not related to true buckeyes, which are in the family Hippocastanaceae, this species' fruits and seeds somewhat resemble those of true buckeye. The flowers are attractive to honeybees. Given sufficient room to spread, this species performs well in xeric landscapes in its native range. It responds well to pruning.

Acourtia wrightii

Brownfoot, Pink Perezia

ASTERACEAE (ASTER FAMILY)
Synonym: *Perezia wrightii*

PLANT AND LEAVES: Brownfoot is an herbaceous perennial. Its stems arise from a woolly, brown, woody base. That base and its early senescent lower leaves give this species its common name. It typically grows to 1 to 2 feet but may reach over 4 feet in height in some areas. Leaves are oblong with wavy, finely dentate margins. Leaves are arranged alternately along the stems.

FLOWERS AND FRUIT: The pink to purplish discoid flowers of this species are fragrant, borne in small heads, and arranged in irregular corymbs.

FLOWERING: Brownfoot's long flowering season lasts from March to November.

RANGE AND HABITAT: Brownfoot occurs in the United States from Texas to Nevada and across most of northern Mexico. In Texas,

it is found in the Trans-Pecos. It grows on sandy, gravelly, or caliche desert soils.

COMMENTS: This species is used by Native Americans of the Southwest in traditional medicine.

Oxalis drummondii

Drummond's Woodsorrel, Largeleaf Woodsorrel

OXALIDACEAE (WOODSORREL FAMILY)
Synonym: *Oxalis amplifolia*

PLANT AND LEAVES: Drummond's Woodsorrel is a perennial herb growing from a bulb. It grows as a mounding, stemless plant about 6 inches high and 12 inches across. Its leaves grow from the plant's base. The leaves have three leaflets, each about 1 inch long, 1½ inches wide, and notched slightly at the center of the outer edge. The leaves are clover-like, about 2 inches across, green above and below. They fold downward, umbrella-like, at dusk or in cloudy weather.

FLOWERS AND FRUIT: Flowers grow in clusters of 4 to 10 buds on leafless scapes, up to 10 inches tall, that grow from the base of the plant. Only one or two flowers in a cluster open at a time.

They have a shallow funnel shape, ending in five lavender-pink to purple petals. The flowers are 1 to 1½ inches in diameter and have a lime-green throat.

FLOWERING: Flowering occurs March to November, mostly May to August.

RANGE AND HABITAT: Drummond's Woodsorrel grows in open woodlands and under chaparral on limestone soils and seems to prefer disturbed sites. It is native to central, south, and west Texas. Its native range extends into Mexico.

COMMENTS: This species performs well as a garden plant, and its bulbs are easily transplanted.

Argemone chisosensis

Chisos Prickly-poppy, Pink Prickly-poppy

PAPAVERACEAE (POPPY FAMILY)

PLANT AND LEAVES: Chisos Prickly-poppy is a branching biennial or perennial herb growing 1½ to 2½ feet in height. Like other *Argemone* species, this one's stems are prickly, as are

the undersides of the leaves. The tops of the leaves are mostly unarmed, bearing only a few prickles. The leaves, especially the lower ones, are deeply and narrowly lobed with prominent white veins.

FLOWERS AND FRUIT: Flowers are borne at the ends of the branches and in the leaf axils. They are 2½ to 4 inches across, with six petals that are soft in texture and droop gracefully. The delicate flower of this species ranges in color from white to a lovely pale pink to lavender. The fruit is a prickly, elliptical capsule.

FLOWERING: Flowering begins in March and may continue to December depending on rainfall.

RANGE AND HABITAT: The Chisos Prickly-poppy name is apt for this species, which makes its Texas home in and around the Chisos Mountains in Big Bend National Park. Its native range extends from the Trans-Pecos in Texas to the Mexican states of Chihuahua and Coahuila. Like other members of its genus, it is often found on roadsides and other disturbed soils and in waste areas.

COMMENTS: The subtle pink of the flowers of some specimens of Chisos Prickly-poppy could inspire poets and artists to create masterpieces of their crafts.

Penstemon tenuis

Gulf Coast Penstemon, Brazos Beardtongue

SCROPHULARIACEAE (FIGWORT FAMILY)

PLANT AND LEAVES: Gulf Coast Penstemon is an herbaceous plant with several well-branched stems growing from a perennial crown and rootstock. It overwinters as an asymmetrical basal rosette of lance-shaped leaves with toothed margins, 4 to 6 inches long and about ¾ inch wide. In early spring, the plant's stems grow to 12 to 36 inches tall with much branching in the upper reaches, giving it a narrowly pyramidal shape. The stem leaves are up to 4 inches long and 1 inch wide, opposite, and directly attached to the stems. They are also lance shaped and toothed, but the stem leaf is more pointed than the basal leaves.

FLOWERS AND FRUIT: Flowers are copiously produced in the upper third of the plant, with clusters of flowers born on short stems emerging from each leaf axil. The flowers are lavender pink or

pink, lighter inside the flower's inflated tube, and with purple lines at the base. The flower has five rounded, petal-like lobes.

FLOWERING: Flowering occurs during April and May.

RANGE AND HABITAT: Gulf Coast Penstemon is a native of marshes and moist prairies in southeast Texas. Its range extends east through Louisiana and Arkansas to Mississippi.

COMMENTS: This is one of Texas's most stately and handsome *Penstemon* species. It is easily cultivated and performs very well in the garden.

Allium canadense var. *mobilense*

Wild Onion, Meadow Garlic, Wild Garlic

LILIACEAE (LILY FAMILY)
Synonym: *Allium mobilense*

PLANT AND LEAVES: Wild Onion is an herbaceous perennial growing from a bulb that averages about 1 inch in diameter. The plant has a hollow stem 6 to 8 inches long and bears

three or more basal leaves about as long as the stem and ⅛ to ¼ inch wide.

FLOWERS AND FRUIT: The star-shaped flowers cluster at the top of the stem, individual flowers having stems ¼ to 1 inch long. The flowers' six tepals are rose pink to white, fading with age. Each flower has six stamens.

FLOWERING: The normal flowering period is April and May. When rainfall is sufficient, it will sometimes flower again in the fall.

RANGE AND HABITAT: Wild Onion prefers open, unshaded areas and can be found in central and east Texas. Its native range extends across the South and up the Mississippi River Valley to Illinois.

COMMENTS: Wild Onion is edible and closely related to culinary onion (*Allium cepa*). It is a common sight in the spring, often appearing in large colonies. Crow Poison (*Nothoscordum bivalve*) is related and shares the same habitat, but the onion can be easily distinguished by its pungent scent.

Echinocactus texensis

Horse Crippler, Devil's Head

CACTACEAE (CACTUS FAMILY)
Synonym: *Homalocephala texensis*

PLANT AND LEAVES: The Horse Crippler cactus typically grows as a single, unjointed stem. The plant grows as a very low more or less round mound, up to 12 inches in diameter and often no more than 2 or 3 inches in height. The surface of the plant is yellowish green and deeply furrowed with ribs radiating from the center to the edge of the plant. Each rib is studded with one to several areoles that may or may not be cottony, and each areole is studded with six to eight stout, curved, pinkish-, gray- or straw-colored spines. The longest spines reach 2 to 3 inches in length.

FLOWERS AND FRUIT: The inverted bell-shaped flowers are about 2 inches across and about as tall. A flower's tepals may be orange to red at the base and range from peach colored to salmon pink at the ends. The ends of the tepals have a feathery appearance. Yellow anthers are borne on pinkish to red filaments, and the pistil is yellow to pink. The flower is somewhat fragrant.

FLOWERING: Flowering usually occurs during April and May but sometimes earlier or later depending on moisture and temperature.

RANGE AND HABITAT: This cactus is found over most of the state west of a line from Matagorda to Fort Worth and Wichita Falls and south of the Panhandle. Horse Crippler's range extends into New Mexico and southwestern Oklahoma and south into northern Mexico. It occurs mostly on grasslands and in thorn scrub.

COMMENTS: Horse Crippler's common name is well earned; many horses have been injured by stepping on it. It often grows hidden in grass and under tall forbs, making it difficult to see.

Mimosa borealis

Fragrant Mimosa

FABACEAE (PEA FAMILY)

PLANT AND LEAVES: Fragrant Mimosa is a widely branched, deciduous, woody shrub usually 2 to 6 feet and occasionally to 8 feet in height and spread. Anyone attempting to traverse through a colony of the plants quickly learns that the plant is armed with very effective short prickles, about ¼ inch long. Leaves are

small and bipinnately compound. The leaves usually branch once, but may have up to six pinnae. Each pinna bears three to six pairs of oval leaflets, up to ¼ inch in length.

FLOWERS AND FRUIT: In spring, the plant is typically heavily laden with masses of fragrant flower heads that perfume the air around the plant. Flower heads are round, baby-pink balls of flowers, ½ inch in diameter. Each flower has 10 prominent pink stamens, which account for most of the flowers' showiness, and tiny five-lobed petals. Over a few days' time, the flowers gradually fade to almost white, giving the plant a pleasing pastel hue. The fruit is a curved to crooked legume to about 2 inches long and armed with several prickles.

FLOWERING: Flowering occurs during April and May.

RANGE AND HABITAT: This species is found on dry, rocky limestone bluffs and hillsides in the Edwards Plateau, west to the Trans-Pecos and north through the Panhandle. Its range continues to southern Kansas and Colorado and eastern New Mexico. It also can be found in Mexico.

COMMENTS: Fragrant Mimosa's sprawling, irregular growth habit and its resistance to shaping by pruning make it a difficult species to find a home for in the garden. However, given ample space in a sunny, dry location, it works as an accent plant and can become a cherished member of the garden flora.

Cylindropuntia imbricata

Tree Cholla, Cane Cholla, Walking Stick Cholla

CACTACEAE (CACTUS FAMILY)

Synonym: *Opuntia imbricata*

PLANT AND LEAVES: A large cactus that earns its name, Tree Cholla frequently grows to 8 feet and can approach 15 feet in height. Its stems are cylindrical, and their surfaces are uniformly ridged with elongated tubercles, imparting an interesting,

architectural quality to the stems. An areole is situated at the distal end of each tubercle, armed with numerous glochids and 15 or fewer spines, 1 inch long or shorter.

FLOWERS AND FRUIT: Tree Cholla is an eye-catcher when in flower. The magenta-purplish-red flowers (usually appearing pink) are about 3 inches across. Filament color proceeds from green at the base to pink and then to magenta at the point of attachment of the yellow anthers. Style coloration is like the filaments, and the stigma is greenish white. The roundish yellow fruits at the end of the joints ripen in August and stay on the plant through the winter months. Since the fruit is free of spines, it is often eaten by deer and cattle.

FLOWERING: Flowering commonly occurs between April and June.

RANGE AND HABITAT: This species is a common constituent of the Chihuahuan Desert, in arid grassland and arid conifer woodlands in the Trans-Pecos in Texas, west to Utah and Arizona, and south to north-central Mexico. Ranching activities have spread its range into Oklahoma and Kansas.

COMMENTS: Tree Cholla is often found along fencerows but also forms thickets in open areas. The cylindrical joints grow in any and every direction, giving it an unpredictable and sometimes grotesque shape. The dead stems of this cactus, with holes at odd angles all along the stem, are used for lamp stands and all sorts of handicraft items, including canes and walking sticks, as its common names would indicate.

Calopogon tuberosus var. *tuberosus*

Grass Pink, Tuberous Grass Pink, Swamp Pink

ORCHIDACEAE (ORCHID FAMILY)

Synonyms: *Calopogon pulchellus*, *Limodorum tuberosum*

PLANT AND LEAVES: Grass Pink is an herbaceous, perennial orchid. It grows from a nearly spherical corm and reaches 1 to 4 feet tall. It is known as Grass Pink, in part, for its narrow, grass-like leaves to about 1 foot in length.

FLOWERS AND FRUIT: A Grass Pink's inflorescence bears 2 to 24 rose-pink, magenta, or sometimes white flowers to about

2 inches across. Flowering begins at the bottom of the inflorescence and proceeds to the apex.

FLOWERING: In Texas, flowering starts as early as April and ends as late as July. Flowering can begin as early as November in southern Florida and continue to as late as August in Canada.

RANGE AND HABITAT: Grass Pink is a plant of continuously moist areas and is most abundant on acidic soils of pineland bogs in east Texas. It can be found in similar habitat across the eastern half of North America.

COMMENTS: The genus name, *Calopogon*, comes from the Greek words meaning "beautiful beard." A round, white blotch on the lip helps to identify it. The flowers of most orchid species are resupinate; that is, their stems are twisted 180 degrees, and the flowers actually are held upside down. Though they look odd, the members of the genus *Calopogon* are among the few North American native orchids bearing flowers right side up. The native range of another botanical variety, *Calopogon t.* var. *simpsonii,* is restricted to Florida.

Centaurea americana

American Basketflower, American Star-thistle

ASTERACEAE (ASTER FAMILY)
Synonym: *Plectocephalus americanus*

PLANT AND LEAVES: American Basketflower is a coarse, herbaceous annual with large but surprisingly delicately detailed flower heads. It typically grows 2 to 5 feet tall but may reach 7 feet in ideal conditions. Leaves have no petioles, rough surfaces, and mostly entire margins that may have a few teeth. They are lance shaped, 2 to 8 inches long.

FLOWERS AND FRUIT: The flower heads of this species are especially lovely and may be 4 inches in diameter. Involucres at the base of the heads are made up of many broad bracts (phyllaries) with many fine serrations. Flowers are of two types. An outer ring of light pink to magenta, sterile florets surround a large cluster of creamy white fertile florets.

FLOWERING: In Texas, flowering occurs from April to July.

RANGE AND HABITAT: American Basketflower's native range extends from the southern Great Plains to the Chihuahua Desert in Texas, New Mexico, and Mexico. In Texas, it is common in roadside ditches and cuts throughout most of the state.

COMMENTS: This species is a bit fussy about location and is sometimes difficult to cultivate. Where it is happy, though, it tends to be very happy and will thrive there year after year. Another common name, "Shaving Brush," is immediately obvious when seeing a near fully open flower head.

Mimosa microphylla

Littleleaf Sensitive Briar, Shame Vine

FABACEAE (PEA FAMILY)

Synonyms: *Schrankia uncinata*, *Schrankia microphylla*

PLANT AND LEAVES: Littleleaf Sensitive Briar is an herbaceous perennial vine that sends several runners sprawling over the ground. The stems are usually 2 to 4 feet long and are armed with many small, curved prickles. Leaves are alternate and bipinnate, with 4 to 8 pairs of leaflets further divided into 8 to 15 pairs of tiny leaflets with prominent veins on the underside.

FLOWERS AND FRUIT: The plant's tiny fragrant flowers are clustered in spherical heads, about ½ inch in diameter, that look like pink powder puffs or pom-poms. The major portion of the flower that is visible is made up of the flower's pink stamen filaments. The fruit is a cylindrical legume, 2 to 4 inches long and less than ¼ inch in diameter, that terminates in a point or small "beak." It is often densely covered in tiny, prickly hairs.

FLOWERING: Flowering occurs from April to July.

RANGE AND HABITAT: Littleleaf Sensitive Briar can be found on sandy soils in eastern, northern, and central portions of Texas and occasionally in the Panhandle. Its native range extends across the Southeast to Virginia.

COMMENTS: The leaflets of Littleleaf Sensitive Briar are sensitive to the touch. If one brushes against them, they immediately fold up against each other, suggesting the name "sensitive briar." They also close at night and in cloudy weather.

Pogonia ophioglossoides

Rose Pogonia, Snake-mouth Orchid

ORCHIDACEAE (ORCHID FAMILY)

PLANT AND LEAVES: Rose Pogonia is a perennial herb producing a single, erect, slender stem normally 8 to 16 inches tall. Each stem bears a single, lance-shaped leaf near its middle, 4 inches long or less and about 1¼ inches wide.

FLOWERS AND FRUIT: In most cases, a single flower is borne atop the stem just above a leaf-like bract. The flower is rose or pink colored and, unlike most orchids, has a nice fragrance. The lower lip is densely bearded near the throat with white to yellow bristles.

FLOWERING: This orchid may be found flowering any time from April to July.

RANGE AND HABITAT: Rose Pogonia commonly grows in bogs and wet pinelands in southeast Texas. Its large native range covers just about the entire eastern half of the United States and Canada.

COMMENTS: One stem, plus one leaf, plus one bract, plus one flower, plus one sweet fragrance equal one very nice orchid to find in your Texas travels—the one *Pogonia* species native to North America. Another common name for this species is Snake-mouth Orchid. This odd appellation is somewhat fitting since the specific epithet of the botanical name, *ophioglossoides*, means *Ophioglossum*-like. *Ophioglossum* is a fern genus known colloquially as Adder's-tongue, with stems and leaves similar in appearance to Snake-mouth Orchid.

Sabatia campestris

Texas Star, Prairie Rose-gentian, Meadow Pink

GENTIANACEAE (GENTIAN FAMILY)

PLANT AND LEAVES: Texas Star is a multibranching herbaceous annual. The plants are low, 3 to 20 inches tall with 6 to 10 inches being the normal range for this species. Its leaves are opposite, ½ to 1¼ inches long. They are mostly egg shaped, broadest at the base, clasp the stem, and have smooth margins.

FLOWERS AND FRUIT: This species' five-lobed flowers, the lobes joined only at the base, are about 1 inch across. They are usually deep pink but occasionally purplish pink to white. There are star-shaped yellow markings at the base of the petals. The single, short-stemmed flowers grow from the axils of the upper leaves. The pistil in this flower lies flat in the early stages but becomes erect and prominent as the flower matures.

FLOWERING: Flowering occurs between April and July.

RANGE AND HABITAT: Texas Star can be found in prairies, in fields, and along roadsides throughout the eastern half of Texas. Its native range extends north and east through the southern Great Plains and the Mississippi River Valley.

COMMENTS: When flowering, this species is covered with pretty pink and yellow flowers, looking much like a ready-made bouquet. Like many other members of its family, Texas Star performs well as a garden plant.

Lygodesmia texana

Texas Skeletonplant

ASTERACEAE (ASTER FAMILY)

Synonym: *Lygodesmia aphylla* var. *texana*

PLANT AND LEAVES: Texas Skeletonplant is an herbaceous perennial that grows 12 to 15 inches tall with smooth, almost leafless, stems. Its few leaves are at the base of the plant and have very narrow, gray-green lobes.

FLOWERS AND FRUIT: Flower heads are rose to lavender (rarely white) and 2 inches across; they grow singly at the end of flower stems. Only one flower head flowers at a time on each slender, forked stem. The flower head's involucre forms a tube about 1 inch long, with the ligulate florets extending from it opening out almost flat. It has 8 to 12 ligulate flowers with five minute teeth at the tip and orchid-colored bifurcate stigmas that curl toward the center of the head.

FLOWERING: Texas Skeletonplant usually flowers heavily in April and May and sporadically through September.

RANGE AND HABITAT: Found on prairies throughout the western three-quarters of Texas, this species also occurs in eastern New Mexico, southern Oklahoma, and northern Mexico.

COMMENTS: Texas Skeletonplant's bare stems, growing at odd angles, suggest its common name. When the stems are broken, they exude sap that coagulates into a gum. In the Trans-Pecos ecoregion, it hybridizes with its close relative, Pecos River Skeletonplant (*Lygodesmia ramossisima*).

Allionia incarnata var. *incarnata*

Trailing Four-o'clock, Pink Windmills, Trailing Allionia

NYCTAGINACEAE (FOUR-O'CLOCK FAMILY)

PLANT AND LEAVES: Trailing Four-o'clock is an herbaceous, vine-like perennial (occasionally annual) that may spread on the ground up to 10 feet across. The stems, leaves, and buds are covered with soft white hair.

FLOWERS AND FRUIT: The stems and flowers are sticky, and one rarely finds a flower without grains of sand stuck on the upper surface. Flower color is magenta to dark pink. Technically, what appears to be one flower is a cluster of three, but no one but a trained botanist would ever guess it.

FLOWERING: Trailing Four-o'clock may flower any time from April to October.

RANGE AND HABITAT: This taxon is native to dry, sandy regions of the US Southwest, Mexico, Central America, West Indies, and South America. In Texas, it is most often found in the Trans-Pecos but occasionally appears in other arid areas to the north and southeast.

COMMENTS: *Allionia choisyi* also grows in west Texas and is very similar. However, it has smooth stems, and the leaves are whitish on the underside.

Chilopsis linearis
Desert Willow, Flowering Willow
BIGNONIACEAE (TRUMPET-CREEPER FAMILY)

PLANT AND LEAVES: Desert Willow is a deciduous tree or large shrub growing 10 to 15 feet tall as a rule but occasionally higher. The plant's branches are rough barked and quite flexible. Its leaves are both opposite and alternate, 4 to 12 inches long—usually in the 5-inch range—and average about ½ inch wide.

FLOWERS AND FRUIT: The flowers are bell shaped, 1 to 1½ inches long, and spread at the opening into five ruffled, petal-like

lobes, about 2 inches across. Flower color varies from pink to deep purple, often with white or yellow and purple streaks within the throat. By early autumn the violet-scented flowers, which appear after summer rains, are replaced by numerous slender capsules, 6 to 10 inches long and containing many winged seeds with fringes of long white hairs. The fruits remain dangling from the branches through the winter and serve to identify the tree after its flowers and its leaves are gone. Its seeds are an important wildlife food.

FLOWERING: This species flowers from April to October—mostly during May and June.

RANGE AND HABITAT: Desert Willow thrives in sandy or gravelly soils in arroyos and is common in the Trans-Pecos below 4,000 feet; abundant at higher elevations in the Chisos and Davis Mountains. It is native from west Texas to southern California and to north-central Mexico.

COMMENTS: Though "willow" is a part of most of this species' many common names, that term refers to the shape of its leaves. Desert Willow is not related to the true willows (*Salix* spp.) but is closely related to Crossvine (*Bignonia capreolata*), Trumpet Creeper (*Campsis radicans*), and Yellow Bells (*Tecoma stans*).

Oenothera lindheimeriana

Lindheimer's Gaura, Lindheimer's Beeblossom, White Gaura

ONAGRACEAE (EVENING-PRIMROSE FAMILY)
Synonym: *Gaura lindheimeri*

PLANT AND LEAVES: Lindheimer's Gaura is a widely branched herb, growing 2 to 5 feet tall from a woody perennial root. The stems, especially in the upper reaches of the plant, are covered in long, soft hairs. The leaves are very narrowly lance shaped, 1 to 3½ inches long and ⅛ to ½ inches wide, and with a strong central vein and coarse, marginal teeth.

FLOWERS AND FRUIT: The flowers of Lindheimer's Gaura are pink or white with four narrowly diamond-shaped petals that are not evenly spaced but gathered toward the top of the flower. The flower is about 1 inch across. Eight longish stamens and

one pistil curve down from the center of the flower and then back up, vaguely giving the flower the appearance of a flying insect.

FLOWERING: Flowering begins in April and may continue until November.

RANGE AND HABITAT: Lindheimer's Gaura is a native of the coastal prairies of southeast Texas and Louisiana.

COMMENTS: This is one of our showier gauras, and so it is a favorite for native plant gardens in Texas. Cultivars with dark pink flowers and reddish foliage have been selected and are quite common in horticulture.

Pavonia lasiopetala

Rose Pavonia, Texas Rock Rose, Wright's Pavonia

MALVACEAE (MALLOW FAMILY)
Synonym: *Pavonia wrightii*

PLANT AND LEAVES: Rose Pavonia is a short-lived, widely branched perennial shrub growing 18 inches to 4 feet in height and spread. Its branches are not especially woody and are almost herb like. The foliage is arranged alternately but produced in clusters of five to seven velvety, dark green leaves. The leaves are heart shaped, gently toothed, and 1 to 2½ inches long and almost as broad.

FLOWERS AND FRUIT: Rose Pavonia has a rose-pink flower that looks like a miniature hibiscus flower. The flower has five petals, is veined in deeper pink, and is about 1½ inches across. The sepals and petals open out almost flat. The staminal column

bears numerous yellow stamens and a pistil with a 10-lobed pink stigma. The fruit has segments that dry and split open when mature, each containing a single seed.

FLOWERING: Flowering begins in April and continues until November.

RANGE AND HABITAT: Rose Pavonia is native to thin, dry, rocky soils from south-central Texas to the Rio Grande. It is also native to northern Mexico.

COMMENTS: Rose Pavonia's ability to thrive and flower in hot, dry weather is remarkable. This species is easy to cultivate and should find a place in almost any native plant garden within its native range. Owing to its exuberant seed production, though, it should not be cultivated in other regions because of the possibility of it becoming yet another invasive species there.

Echinacea sanguinea

Sanguine Purple Coneflower

ASTERACEAE (ASTER FAMILY)

Synonym: *Echinacea pallida* var. *sanguinea*

PLANT AND LEAVES: Sanguine Purple Coneflower is an herbaceous perennial that grows as a single, unbranched stem reaching about 3 feet in height. The stems are usually hairy and sometimes have a purple hue. Leaves are alternate, mostly clustered near the base. They are 4 to 10 inches long and ¼ to 1 inch wide with untoothed but hairy margins.

FLOWERS AND FRUIT: There is one flower head to each stem, with 10 to 20 ray flowers, often conspicuously drooping, very pale pink, rose pink, to pale purple, as much as 2 inches long and ⅛ to ¼ inch wide. The center is cone shaped, 1 inch in diameter, and ¼ to ¾ inch high, often purplish brown on the outside ring of disc flowers and greenish in the center.

FLOWERING: Sanguine Purple Coneflower flowers during May and June.

RANGE AND HABITAT: The native range of this species is situated along the Texas–Louisiana state line and just reaches across their respective northern borders into southeastern Oklahoma and southwestern Arkansas. *Echinacea sanguinea* is most

likely to be found in Texas on sandy roadsides and open, pine woodlands in the Pineywoods ecoregion.

COMMENTS: This species requires well-drained acidic soils. Its long taproot helps it thrive in times of drought.

Rosa setigera

Climbing Prairie Rose, Pink Prairie Rose

ROSACEAE (ROSE FAMILY)

PLANT AND LEAVES: The beautiful Climbing Prairie Rose is a deciduous, perennial shrub with semiwoody arching or scrambling canes reaching 6 to 15 feet long, usually with scattered prickles along their length. Leaves are borne one per node, up

to 5 inches long and divided into three to five sharp-pointed leaflets, with many small teeth along their margins.

FLOWERS AND FRUIT: The flowers grow in clusters at the end of stems but often open one or two at a time. The five-petaled flowers are 2 inches across, with many yellow stamens. When newly opened, the flowers are bright pink in color; as days go by the pink progressively fades through pastel shades until the flowers are finally white before the petals are shed. During the two or three peak weeks of flowering, the plant often presents a stunning "Joseph's coat" display of multiple colors festooning the arching branches of the plant. After flowering, the plant produces abundant clusters of bright red fruits (hips).

FLOWERING: In Texas, flowering occurs in May or June, elsewhere as late as August.

RANGE AND HABITAT: Climbing Prairie Rose is native to ancient prairies in northeast Texas. Its range extends through most of the eastern half of the United States, excluding New England.

COMMENTS: This species is functionally unisexual. That is, each plant will be of only one sex even though its flowers have both male and female parts. Though it has no fragrance, this species makes a fine landscape plant where it has some support to scramble upon and room to spread. Especially welcome to gardeners is a cultivar, *Rosa setigera* "Serena," which has no prickles. Flowering on the previous year's growth, it should be pruned shortly after flowering in the spring.

Monarda fistulosa

Wild Bergamot, Mintleaf Beebalm

LAMIACEAE (MINT FAMILY)

PLANT AND LEAVES: Wild Bergamot is an attractive member of the horsemint group. It is an herbaceous plant with several stems growing 2 to 4 feet tall from a perennial crown. Its slender square stems are branched near the top. The leaves are opposite, directly attached to the stem, narrowly lance shaped, up to 4 inches long, and with a few short teeth on the margins.

FLOWERS AND FRUIT: Each stem ends in a flower cluster about 2 inches across, with flowers surrounding the stem. The leaf-like bracts that surround the flower heads are often streaked with pink. The lavender-pink flowers are two-lipped and 1 to 1½ inches long.

FLOWERING: Flowering occurs from May to August.

RANGE AND HABITAT: Wild Bergamot can be found in old fields and on prairies in east Texas. It has one of the largest native ranges of any wildflower, occurring across nearly all of the United States and Canada.

COMMENTS: Like other members of its genus, Wild Bergamot makes a wonderful and easy-to-grow garden plant for sunny locations. It spreads by rhizomes and also can be propagated by seeds. This species reputedly has a number of medicinal uses and is a key ingredient in several herbal remedies.

Callicarpa americana

American Beautyberry, French Mulberry

VERBENACEAE (VERBENA FAMILY)

PLANT AND LEAVES: American Beautyberry is a much-branched, rounded, deciduous shrub, usually having multiple stems arising from the roots. The stems are thin, flexible, and often arching, giving the plant a fountain-like appearance. The

shrub usually grows 3 to 8 feet tall with about equal spread. Leaves are opposite, light green, more or less oval and tapering to a point at each end, 3 to 6 inches long and 2 to 4 inches wide, and with finely toothed margins.

FLOWERS AND FRUIT: The inflorescences and, later, the berries are in the axil of the leaves, surrounding the stem in a firm, tight cluster. Flowers are ⅛ to ¼ inch across, pale pink or white. The stems, lined with clusters of flowers, are lovely. However, it is not so much the flowers as the berries of the American Beautyberry that grab your attention. The plant's magenta-colored berries, about 3/16 inch in diameter, are borne in tight clusters in the leaf axils just as the flowers had been earlier in the season.

FLOWERING: Flowering occurs from May to September. Fruits mature in September and October.

RANGE AND HABITAT: American Beautyberry is a common under-story shrub, especially under pines, in east and east-central Texas. Its native range reaches across the South and as far up the Atlantic Coast as the Eastern Shore of Maryland.

COMMENTS: This species' berries hold their shape and color for weeks. For that reason, they are excellent in flower arrange-ments. The plant is suitable for partially shaded gardens and is widely cultivated. When its leaves drop in the fall, left behind are attractive, somewhat formally arranged stalks of berries up to 2½ feet long. The berries remain until frost or much later, if birds do not find and eat them.

Rhexia virginica

Virginia Meadowbeauty, Handsome Harry

MELASTOMATACEAE (MELASTOME FAMILY)

PLANT AND LEAVES: Virginia Meadowbeauty is a perennial herb, usually under 2 feet high but occasionally up to 3 feet. The stems are four sided, with narrow wings along the corners. The leaves are opposite and, having no petioles, are attached directly to the stems. They are oval to lance shaped and up to

4 inches long and 1 inch wide, though usually smaller. The leaf margins are lined with shallow toothed serrations.

FLOWERS AND FRUIT: Flowers are rose pink to pale pink, with four oval or nearly circular petals that tend to fold backward. The yellow anthers on the eight stamens are sickle shaped and conspicuous. A long, curving pistil is situated beneath the stamens. The fruit is an urn-shaped capsule that splits open when mature, releasing the seeds within.

FLOWERING: Flowering occurs from May to September.

RANGE AND HABITAT: Virginian Meadowbeauty grows in low, damp ground in east Texas, from Wills Point to the Louisiana state line and southward. It is common in wet meadows, marshes, glades, and other mostly sunny, consistently moist soils across the South and coastal areas of the Mid-Atlantic states.

COMMENTS: Bumblebees easily access the pollen hidden in Virginia Meadowbeauty's curved, narrow stamens. The bee sidles up to the stamens and begins buzzing. The vibrations shake the pollen grains within out through a pore in the end of the stamen and onto the waiting bee. Honeybees do not have the ability to use this buzz technique for gathering pollen.

Mimosa dysocarpa

Velvetpod Mimosa

FABACEAE (PEA FAMILY)

PLANT AND LEAVES: Velvetpod Mimosa grows 2 to 3½ feet tall—sometimes to 6 feet—with many branches spreading widely from the base. Its stems are generally thin and pliant, often three sided, and well armed with numerous stout prickles. Its bipinnate leaves are alternate, with 10 to 24 pinnae, each having 12 to 30 tiny, elongate leaflets. When touched, the leaflets of this species quickly fold up like those of the Littleleaf Sensitive Briar (*Mimosa microphylla*) and other related species.

FLOWERS AND FRUIT: Large numbers of the small flowers grow along a short stem forming a cylindrical head about 2 inches long and consisting of 20 to 30 buds that open at the same time. They are slightly fragrant. Most of the color seen in the inflorescence is provided by the 10 long stamens protruding from each tiny flower. Stamen color ranges from baby pink to purple. The fruit is a prickly legume with a velvety, brown- or rust-colored surface when mature.

FLOWERING: Flowering occurs between May and October.

RANGE AND HABITAT: Velvet Mimosa can be found on slopes with other brushy plant species in the Davis and Chisos Mountains in the Trans-Pecos ecoregion. Its native range extends through southern New Mexico and southern Arizona and south into Mexico.

COMMENTS: When in flower, Velvet Mimosa's usual "ugly duckling" appearance transforms into a pink "beautiful swan" visage rivaling any other species in its area for sublime loveliness. The seeds of this species are an important food for ground-feeding birds.

Polygala cruciata

Drumheads

POLYGALACEAE (MILKWORT FAMILY)

PLANT AND LEAVES: Drumheads is an annual herb, usually with sparsely branched, squarish stems growing 3 to 16 inches tall. The narrow leaves, to 1½ inches long and about ¼ inch wide, are arranged in whorls of four in a cross-shaped orientation.

FLOWERS AND FRUIT: Flowers are tiny, usually pink, occasionally white, and grow in a compact cylindrical cluster, 1½ inches tall and ¾ inches in diameter, at the tops of the stems.

FLOWERING: Most flowering takes place in summer but begins as early as May and can continue to as late as October.

RANGE AND HABITAT: Drumheads requires wet soil and is found primarily on the coastal plains in areas with consistently moist earth. In Texas, it is found in the southeast on the coastal plains. Despite its rather limiting soil-moisture needs, its native range is very large and encompasses most of the eastern United States.

COMMENTS: Drumheads is one of those uncommon species that you stumble upon when you are out looking at something else—a happy bit of lagniappe during a good day on the coastal prairie.

If examined with a botanist's loupe or a magnifying lens, Drumheads and other members of *Polygala* reveal extraordinary floral details that are frankly too lovely to describe but well worth the effort to see.

Boerhavia linearifolia

Narrowleaf Spiderling

NYCTAGINACEAE (FOUR-O'CLOCK FAMILY)
Synonyms: *Boerhavia lindheimeri*, *Boerhavia tenuifolia*

PLANT AND LEAVES: The linear to narrowly lance-shaped leaves on the many slender branches of the Narrowleaf Spiderling suggest its name. Its pale green stems are erect or decumbent and grow to 1 to 3 feet tall. The stems are brittle at the joints. There are one or more spots between the joints, maroon colored and very sticky. Leaves are narrow and slightly thickened, about 1¼ to 2½ inches long.

FLOWERS AND FRUIT: Showy, small, pink, red, or usually magenta five-lobed flowers are held above the plant in loose, airy cymes. Each corolla lobe is notched, the lobes curling back with age, leaving the exserted cream-white stamens extending beyond the flower for some time.

FLOWERING: Narrowleaf Spiderling's flowering season occurs from June to September.

RANGE AND HABITAT: This species is native to northern Mexico and New Mexico as well as dry, rocky areas in west Texas.

COMMENTS: Narrowleaf Spiderling's delicate, dainty flowers, widely spread in airy inflorescences, give it something of an oriental feel. Notable, closely related species you are likely to encounter in Texas include Scarlet Spiderling (*Boerhavia* *coccinea*), with small clusters of purple-red flowers and sprawling habit, and Erect Spiderling (*Boerhavia erecta*), with open clusters of tiny white flowers.

Proboscidea louisianica ssp. *louisianica*

Devil's Claw, Unicorn Plant, Ram's Horn

PEDALIACEAE (SESAME FAMILY)

Synonym: *Martynia louisianica*

PLANT AND LEAVES: Devil's Claw is a widely branched annual herb with a mounding habit, 1 to 3 feet tall and broad overall. The plant's stems and leaves are covered with stinking, glandular hairs that make them clammy to the touch. The plant has large heart-shaped leaves on long petioles, which are up to 5 inches across and 1 foot long.

FLOWERS AND FRUIT: Flowers are 1 to 2 inches long and have five pink, pale pink, white, or purplish petal-like lobes. All flowers have yellow or orange mottling or streaks inside the lower part of the flower's throat, with reddish spots surrounding that. The fruit is a large capsule that partially splits at maturity and bears two long, curving "horns" or "claws" that are used in the dispersal of the plant's seeds.

FLOWERING: Flowering occurs June to September.

RANGE AND HABITAT: Occurs on disturbed soils in scattered localities over much of the state; most common in south, central, and west Texas. The center of this species' native range is western Kansas, and its range extends into surrounding states and south into Texas. Widely cultivated, it has naturalized over much of the United States.

COMMENTS: The closely related *Proboscidea louisianica* ssp. *fragrans* always has purple flowers and is found in Texas only in the Trans-Pecos. The two tough claws of this species' fruit grab and hold the feet of grazing animals. As the animal walks about with the fruit attached to their foot or hoof, the fruits' seeds are scattered in new locations. Animals have been known to be made lame by the sharp points of tightly clinging fruit's claws.

Kosteletzkya virginica

Virginia Saltmarsh Mallow

MALVACEAE (MALLOW FAMILY)

Synonym: *Hibiscus althaeifolia*

PLANT AND LEAVES: Virginia Saltmarsh Mallow is a short-lived, shrub-like, widely branching, perennial herb that can reach 6

feet in height and 4 feet or more in breadth. It has thin but stiff dark green stems. The stems and leaves are densely coated in coarse hairs. The hairs on the leaves give them a grayish cast. Its leaves are more or less triangular or narrowly heart shaped, 2½ to 6 inches long. The leaves on the upper parts of the plant are smaller and narrower and are lance shaped.

FLOWERS AND FRUIT: The flowers are borne on long peduncles emerging from the leaf axils in the upper part of the plant. They have five slightly overlapping, oval-shaped, pink petals. A long staminal column with bright yellow stamens and a five-lobed dark pink style emerges from the flower's center and noticeably droops downward. The plant's flowers close at night. The fruit is a five-parted, squatty capsule covered inside and out with glassy hairs. Each section of the fruit contains several small, round seeds.

FLOWERING: Flowering occurs from June to October.

RANGE AND HABITAT: Virginia Saltmarsh Mallow, as its common name implies, is a coastal species. It can be found near the Texas Gulf Coast along brackish marshes and along freshwater estuaries. Its native range includes areas with the same habitat along the US Gulf and Atlantic Coasts as far north as New York.

COMMENTS: Virginia Saltmarsh Mallow is a lovely and heavily flowering plant, closely related to and resembling the *Hibiscus* species. It is an excellent choice where a large, fast-growing marginal plant is needed for a water garden.

Palafoxia hookeriana

Sand Palafox, Hooker's Palafox

ASTERACEAE (ASTER FAMILY)

PLANT AND LEAVES: Sand Palafox normally grows to 16 to 40 inches tall on a single stem that branches near the top of the plant. It is lightly covered with somewhat sticky glandular hairs. Leaves are lance shaped, 2 to 4 inches long and about ¾ inch wide.

FLOWERS AND FRUIT: The showy flower heads are 1½ to 2 inches in diameter and bear 6 to 12 rose-colored ray flowers, deeply three toothed and about ½ inch in length. There are 75 or more rose-colored disc flowers in the central disc.

FLOWERING: Sand Palafox's flowering season lasts from June to October with most flowering in September and October.

RANGE AND HABITAT: Sand Palafox is endemic to Texas, where it grows on sandy soils from the Post Oak Savannah ecoregion in east Texas through the coastal plain to south Texas.

COMMENTS: The flower is quite attractive and very effective when used in mass plantings in gardens with sandy soils. We found Sand Palafox on the banks of Village Creek on the east side of the Big Thicket in October.

Phytolacca americana var. *americana*

Pokeweed, Pokeberry

PHYTOLACCACEAE (POKEWEED FAMILY)

PLANT AND LEAVES: Pokeweed is a large perennial herb that grows from a stout, tuberous root. Where winter freezes occur, it dies to the ground each year and resprouts in the spring, quickly growing to 6 to 10 feet tall and sometimes to as much as 20 feet in extreme circumstances. The plant is widely branching with a red main stem and red or green branches. Its leaves are lance shaped to oval and large, up to 12 inches long and 6 inches wide.

FLOWERS AND FRUIT: The flowers of Pokeweed are borne on mostly pendulous racemes at the ends of the branches. Each raceme is 3 to 12 inches long and bears from 10 to more than 100 white to greenish-white to pink five-sepaled flowers about ¼ inch across. The fruit is a squatty, black or purple berry that matures in late summer or fall.

FLOWERING: This species has an unusually long flowering season beginning in spring and continuing until fall.

RANGE AND HABITAT: Grows at the edge of cultivated ground and in fencerows or recent clearings in east Texas and across most of North America, excluding the Rocky Mountain states.

COMMENTS: The mature shoots, roots, fruits, and leaves of Pokeweed are poisonous, though an edible and delicious pot herb, known as poke salat, can be made from its young leaves when properly and carefully prepared. Pokeweed's seeds pass through the guts of birds, which relish its berries, and so it tends to pop up unexpectedly in home gardens. It is a robust species in every sense and is one that demands attention. The Lady Bird Johnson Wildflower Center receives more, "What's this plant?" identification requests for Pokeweed each year—by far—than any other species.

Pluchea odorata var. *odorata*

Southern Marsh Fleabane, Sweetscent

ASTERACEAE (ASTER FAMILY)
Synonym: *Pluchea purpurascens*

PLANT AND LEAVES: Southern Marsh Fleabane grows to as much as 6 feet tall as an annual or usually perennial herb or sub-shrub in marshes or other areas that are always moist. It has several leafy branches on the upper part, none below. Leaves vary, some long and narrow and some broad at the base, 2 to 4 inches long, pointed at the tip, and irregularly toothed on the margins.

FLOWERS AND FRUIT: The fragrant, bright rose- or magenta-colored flowers grow in small disk-shaped heads in a flat-topped cluster at the end of the stems.

FLOWERING: Southern Marsh Fleabane typically flowers between June and October.

RANGE AND HABITAT: Native on salt marshes and in saline or fresh-water habitats from northern South America to the US maritime and southern border states from Maryland to California

and to Arkansas, Oklahoma, Kansas, Utah, and Nevada. In Texas, it is especially common along the Gulf Coast but regularly appears in east-central Texas in moist environments and in moist, saline habitats in west Texas.

COMMENTS: On warm days, this plant emits a faint camphor fragrance. However, descriptions of the aroma emanating from its crushed leaves usually recall body odor, which better fits with another name common in many locales, Stinkweed.

Hibiscus laevis

Halberd-leaved Rose-mallow

MALVACEAE (MALLOW FAMILY)
Synonym: *Hibiscus militaris*

PLANT AND LEAVES: Halberd-leaved Rose-mallow is a widely branched, shrub-like herbaceous perennial growing to 6 feet or more in height and spread. The interestingly shaped leaves are alternate and prominently lobed at the base, the lobes wide spreading and sharp toothed.

FLOWERS AND FRUIT: Flowers are produced from the axils of the leaves and from the bottom to the top of the stem. The large cup-shaped flowers, about 5 inches in diameter, are pink,

sometimes white, with maroon or purple throats. Their five overlapping petals open by day and close tightly at night. The fruit is a five-parted capsule, each section containing a number of small, hard, hairy, brown seeds.

FLOWERING: Flowering occurs for the most part in July and August but may begin as early as May end as late as November.

RANGE AND HABITAT: Halberd-leaved Rose-mallow is encountered in swamps and damp areas in the eastern third of the state. Its native range covers nearly the entirety of the eastern half of the United States.

COMMENTS: Halberd-leaved Rose-mallow makes a very nice garden plant where sufficient soil moisture is available. It is especially desirable for use in water gardens where a large, colorful, marginal plant is needed.

Mirabilis longiflora

Sweet Four-o'clock, Long-flowered Four-o'clock

NYCTAGINACEAE (FOUR-O'CLOCK FAMILY)

PLANT AND LEAVES: Sweet Four-o'clock is an herbaceous perennial normally growing to around 3 feet but may reach 5 feet in height. Its stems are heavy, brittle, and sticky, with several branches near the base. The leaves are opposite. The lower leaf petioles are 1½ inches long; the leaves themselves are 3 to 4 inches long. The upper leaves have short petioles or are sessile.

FLOWERS AND FRUIT: Stems bear many buds but usually only two flowers are open at one time on a stem. The slender tubes of the salverform flowers are 4 to 6 inches long and greenish white to pinkish and pubescent outside. The corolla limb has five white lobes flaring to about ¾ inch in diameter from the tube, which is magenta red or green inside. Six magenta filaments bearing orange anthers extend up to 2 inches beyond the corolla. The flowers are borne near the top of the plant.

FLOWERING: Sweet Four-o'clock flowers from July to September.

RANGE AND HABITAT: This species is native to Texas, New Mexico, and Arizona in the United States and to Mexico. In Texas, it can be found in the Big Bend area in brushy canyons and banks.

COMMENTS: Flowers open late in the day, are sweetly fragrant in the evening, and close in the morning. Though attractive to hawk moths, Sweet Four-o'clock may be mostly self-pollinated.

Cosmos parviflorus

Southwestern Cosmos

ASTERACEAE (ASTER FAMILY)
Synonym: *Coreopsis parviflora*

PLANT AND LEAVES: Southwestern Cosmos, an herbaceous annual native, grows 2 to 3 feet tall and is branched several times in the upper half with a single flower head, about 1¼ inch across, at the end of each slender, bare stem. Leaves are threadlike, divided two or three times.

FLOWERS AND FRUIT: Flower color may vary, but most heads bear eight ray flowers that are usually a lovely, delicate orchid pink and, at the end of flowering, fade to whitish basally. The lamina of each ray flower has three lobes, with the center lobe longer than the other two. The small cluster of disc flowers in the center of the head is yellow to orange yellow.

FLOWERING: This species flowers from August to October.

RANGE AND HABITAT: Southwestern Cosmos is native to western Texas, central and southern New Mexico, southeastern Arizona, and much of Mexico. In Texas's Big Bend it grows in gravelly soil up to 7,500 feet in elevation. It is often found in open conifer woodlands on hills and mountain slopes and on roadsides.

COMMENTS: This species is not as abundant as it was in the past, as it is readily grazed by livestock. The fruit of this species, a cypsela, is barbed, which facilitates dispersal on the fur of passing animals.

Blue
Flowers

Lupinus havardii

Big Bend Bluebonnet, Chisos Bluebonnet

FABACEAE (PEA FAMILY)

PLANT AND LEAVES: Big Bend Bluebonnet is a multistemmed herbaceous annual growing from a winter rosette. Reaching a stately 3 or even 4 feet in height, it is the tallest of Texas's Bluebonnet species. Like other lupines, its leaves are palmately compound, each usually having seven leaflets.

FLOWERS AND FRUIT: Inflorescences may extend a foot or more above the foliage. The flowers are very showy, deep bluish purple, with white blotches that turn lemon yellow and then red as they age. An occasional lavender- or white-flowered specimen is seen.

FLOWERING: Flowering begins in early February and may continue into April. The floral display usually peaks in March. Big Bend Bluebonnet flowers earlier than the other Texas bluebonnet species.

RANGE AND HABITAT: This species has a limited range, occurring only in west Texas and there, naturally, only in the Big Bend and in nearby areas. Its native range extends south across the Rio Grande River into Chihuahua, Mexico.

COMMENTS: Big Bend Bluebonnet is very common in the Big Bend area, where we have seen it blooming continuously from Shafter to Boquillas Canyon, over 100 road miles. It was mixed with Desert Marigold (*Baileya multiradiata*), making both more appealing than either would be alone. In favorable years it covers the slopes and hillsides, presenting a magnificent picture against the desert background. Like the other native Texas bluebonnet species, for garden use its seeds should be sown between early summer and early fall.

Nemophila phacelioides

Texas Baby Blue Eyes, Flannel Breeches

HYDROPHYLLACEAE (WATERLEAF FAMILY)

PLANT AND LEAVES: Texas Baby Blue Eyes is an annual herb growing 3 to 24 inches tall, often in large, mounding colonies. Leaves are simple but deeply cut, divided into five to nine lobes and irregularly toothed.

FLOWERS AND FRUIT: The flowers are showy, ranging from baby blue to purple, always with a pale center. They are borne singly or in few-flowered cymes from opposite the leaf axils and at the end of stems in the upper parts of the plant, each flower on a slender, hairy pedicel. The flowers are about ½ to 1 inch across, with five petals, five stamens, and one pistil.

FLOWERING: This is an early spring-flowering species, sometimes beginning in late February and usually finished by April.

RANGE AND HABITAT: Texas Baby Blue Eyes can be found in moist open woodlands in east-central and south-central Texas. It is also native to western Arkansas.

COMMENTS: This species is easily grown from seed and can be cultivated in gardens with partial or filtered shade and reasonably moist soil. Texas Baby Blue Eyes is one of our loveliest woodland plants. When encountered in nature, it is easy to imagine that you must have just stumbled upon a fairy's private garden. It is difficult to think any but sweet thoughts when admiring this plant in flower.

Androstephium coeruleum

Blue Funnel-lily, Prairie Lily, Fragrant Lily

LILIACEAE (LILY FAMILY)

PLANT AND LEAVES: Blue Funnel-lily is an herbaceous perennial growing from a corm. This attractive little plant is unusual in that the leaves are much longer than the plant is tall. The flowering scape grows to about 1 foot or less, but the smooth, gray-green leaves, which tend to spread outward around the plant, are often 12 to 18 inches long.

FLOWERS AND FRUIT: Topping a scape, the plant produces an umbel with about six flowers, each having six fleshy tepals that may

be white, baby blue, or lavender. The tepals are partly joined to form a funnel-like tube. The flower has a pleasant, spicy fragrance. Though fruits (capsules) are rarely produced, those that are mature in April, and seeds are dispersed by the wind.

FLOWERING: This is an early spring-flowering species, sometimes appearing as early as February, though March to April is the more common flowering period.

RANGE AND HABITAT: An uncommon native of the Great Plains, the southern extremity of Blue Funnel-lily's range is located around San Antonio. The plant can be found on undisturbed grassy plains and rocky soils in the middle third of Texas, Oklahoma, and Kansas.

COMMENTS: The Blue Funnel-lily flower, also known as Fragrant Lily, has a sweet, chocolate scent, making it one of two native wildflowers (along with Chocolate Daisy, *Berlandiera lyrata*) that emits a chocolate fragrance and which you are likely to encounter in your Texas travels. The rarity of this species is likely to make finding it in flower a very happy and memorable occasion. Owing to that rarity, when found, Blue Funnel-lily should be left undisturbed. Some botanists now place *Androstephium* and other related genera arising from corms in the family Themidaceae.

Amsonia ciliata
Fringed Blue Star
APOCYNACEAE (DOGBANE FAMILY)

PLANT AND LEAVES: Fringed Blue Star is an herbaceous, perennial, multistemmed plant arising in clumps from woody stolons. The stems are usually about 2 feet in height but may exceed 5 feet in ideal conditions. Leaves are borne singly but very close together all the way up the stem to the inflorescence. They are sessile (attached directly to the stem), ½ inch wide and 2 inches long, with one vein running lengthwise down the center. Leaves toward the top of the stems are smooth, soft, and slightly smaller than those below.

FLOWERS AND FRUIT: The narrow tube of the pale blue flower, ½ inch long, opens into five petal-like lobes in a star shape, ½ inch

across, with a ring of white at the center. Numerous flowers are produced in a loose cluster at the tips of the stems.

FLOWERING: The early flowering season of Fringed Blue Star begins in March and ends in May.

RANGE AND HABITAT: This species occurs from Texas to Missouri and in the Deep South. In Texas, it can be found on the Edwards Plateau and in the Cross Timbers and Rolling Plains ecoregions of north Texas.

COMMENTS: The specific epithet, *ciliata*, references the long, loose hairs often found on the margins of this species' leaves, bracts, and calyces.

Lupinus texensis

Texas Bluebonnet

FABACEAE (PEA FAMILY)

PLANT AND LEAVES: Texas Bluebonnet is a taprooted winter annual herb. Its seeds germinate in the fall and the plant grows as a basal rosette until late winter when several stems begin to grow upward from 8 to 20 inches tall. Its leaves are palmately compound with four to seven (usually five) lance-shaped

leaflets. Like other *Lupinus* species, tiny hairs and water-repellant wax on the leaflet surfaces and the bowl-like shape of the leaves help each leaf capture a large drop of water, giving the plant a shimmering diamond-like effect after a rain.

FLOWERS AND FRUIT: A raceme of usually deep blue flowers terminate each stem. Occasionally, white-, pink- or lavender-flowered individuals can be found. Each flower's upper petal has a white center that usually turns wine red or purplish as it ages. The fruit is a legume. When mature in June, the fruit pops open and propels its small, rock-hard seeds as much as 20 feet away.

FLOWERING: Flowering begins as early as the beginning of March and continues until early May.

RANGE AND HABITAT: East, central, and south Texas.

COMMENTS: In 1901, the Texas legislature designated the Sandyland Bluebonnet, *Lupinus subcarnosus*, the official state flower of Texas. Seventy years later, the same legislative body acceded to the demands of those who supported Texas Bluebonnet for state flower, but being politicians and not wanting to alienate any constituency, they compromised and declared all native bluebonnet species to be the new official state flower. And so it is to this day. Texas Bluebonnet is an iconic symbol of Texas. Each spring for generations, Texas parents have been plopping their babies down amongst drifts of roadside bluebonnets for photos that have become as much a state tradition as barbecued brisket and Friday night football.

Phacelia congesta

Blue Curls, Fiddleneck

HYDROPHYLLACEAE (WATERLEAF FAMILY)

PLANT AND LEAVES: Blue Curls is an herbaceous annual growing to about 30 inches tall and is mostly unbranched except at the flower heads. It often forms extensive colonies. The leaves are alternate, 2 to 4 inches long, with two to seven blunt lobes, and covered in fine hairs.

FLOWERS AND FRUIT: The flowers are very showy, blue to lavender, and borne at the top of the plant on interesting inflorescences known in botanical parlance as scorpioid cymes. In everyday terms, they look a bit like curled caterpillars or the heads of elephants adorned for an Indian festival. The flowers begin opening at the base of the tightly curled inflorescence, which gradually unfurls as the numerous buds come into flower. Each flower has five petals and five stamens. The stamens' purple filaments, capped by yellow anthers, spread widely as they extend beyond the flower's petals and contribute to the flowers' festive, effervescent appearance.

FLOWERING: Flowering occurs from March to May.

RANGE AND HABITAT: Blue Curls is native to central and southwest Texas, where it grows predominantly as an understory plant. However, it is not unusual to find it in fencelines, on roadsides, and sometime even blanketing sunny meadows in lavender loveliness. It is occasionally found in Oklahoma and New Mexico.

COMMENTS: There are many *Phacelia* species in Texas. Some have larger flowers and differently shaped leaves, but all have the tightly curled inflorescence. It is a good clue to their identity, though some of the heliotropes and borages have curled flower heads also. Like its relative Texas Baby Blue Eyes (*Nemophila phacelioides*), Blue Curls is an excellent candidate for the home garden. Easily grown from seed, it has the added benefit of being more forgiving of full-sun situations than its shade-loving cousin.

Delphinium carolinianum

Carolina Larkspur, Plains Larkspur, Gulf Coast Larkspur

RANUNCULACEAE (BUTTERCUP FAMILY)

PLANT AND LEAVES: Carolina Larkspur is a perennial herb growing 8 to 32 inches tall. Two subspecies commonly occur in Texas: Plains Larkspur (*Delphinium carolinianum* ssp. *virescens*) and Gulf Coast Larkspur (*Delphinium carolinianum* ssp. *vimineum*). Where their ranges overlap, they hybridize, and intergrading individuals are common. The leaves of the former subspecies have five or more major lobes, while those of the latter have three major lobes. The lobes of all are long and narrow.

FLOWERS AND FRUIT: The spike-like terminal inflorescences of Carolina Larkspur are 6 to 20 inches tall, bearing 5 to 25 flowers. The flowers vary in color from deep blue or purple to lavender to white. The "showy" part of the flower is the sepals; the actual petals are less conspicuous. The upper two petals have spurs that extend backward within the spur of the sepal. The other two are bearded and deeply lobed.

FLOWERING: Flowering occurs between March and July.

RANGE AND HABITAT: Gulf Coast Larkspur, as its name suggests, is most commonly found on Texas's coastal plain and the Pineywoods in Texas. Its range extends eastward to Louisiana and Arkansas and southward into Mexico. Plains Larkspur is a true plains' native, its range spreading north from north-central Texas throughout the Great Plains to Manitoba, Canada. Both subspecies prefer sandy or loamy soils.

COMMENTS: The larkspurs are easily distinguished by the hollow tube that extends back from the uppermost sepal in the shape of a spur.

Alophia drummondii
Prairie Iris, Propeller Flower
IRIDACEAE (IRIS FAMILY)
Synonyms: *Eustylis purpurea*, *Cypella drummondii*, *Herbertia drummondii*

PLANT AND LEAVES: A bulb-forming perennial, Prairie Iris is usually unbranched and grows 1 to 1½ feet tall. Its three to six leaves are as much as 1½ feet long and about 1 inch wide. Two or three leaves grow from the base and are conspicuously veined, clasp the stem directly at the base, and are folded (pleated) for most of their length.

FLOWERS AND FRUIT: Each stem bears an inflorescence with two to four flowers at the end of the stem that open one at a time for several days in succession. The flowers are cup shaped to flat. The three outer tepals are spreading, about 1½ inches wide, and light to deep purplish blue; the three inner tepals are dwarfed, cupped or crimped, marked yellow centrally, and usually a deeper shade of purple. The lower portion of each tepal is creamy yellow, spangled with reddish-brown spots.

FLOWERING: Prairie Iris may begin flowering as early as April. Flowering usually peaks in May but can continue sporadically until September.

RANGE AND HABITAT: Abundant in the Pineywoods of east and southeast Texas and along the coastal plain to the Rio Grande Valley. Its range extends east to Mississippi and north to Oklahoma and Arkansas and south through Central America to northern South America.

COMMENTS: A springtime population of Propeller Flowers cheerfully decorating an east Texas meadow really does resemble a squadron of purple, three-bladed propellers soaring skyward.

Sisyrinchium sagittiferum

Spearbract Blue-eyed Grass

IRIDACEAE (IRIS FAMILY)

PLANT AND LEAVES: Spearbract Blue-eyed Grass is a clump-forming perennial herb with thin stems. It usually tops out in the 8- to 12-inch range but sometimes grows to 18 inches. Tufts of erect fibrous strands surround the base of the stem. Leaves are narrow, 4 to 6 inches long.

FLOWERS AND FRUIT: The two spathes that enclose the inflorescence are often reddish brown, brown, and sometimes tinged lavender. The flowers have six blue to purple tepals (occasionally white) with a bright yellow center, ½ to ¾ inch across.

FLOWERING: Flowering occurs primarily in April and May, but some plants may flower again in fall.

RANGE AND HABITAT: Spearbract Blue-eyed Grass likes moist soils in grassy meadows and along roadsides in southeast Texas. Its native range also includes most of Louisiana and southern Arkansas.

COMMENTS: Thirty-seven *Sisyrinchium* species are native to North America; 13 of those are included in Texas's flora. Most species are difficult to distinguish from one another; some are exceedingly difficult. Blue-eyed grass is a lovely but somewhat unfortunate common name. Though the tepals of most species are blue or near blue, the "eye," or center of the plant's flower, is almost always yellow. Also, a member of the iris family, *Sisyrinchium* is unrelated to the grasses. Of course, we're probably fortunate the common name is not taken from the genus name as is the case with so many plants—*Sisyrinchium* is derived from the Greek words for pig and snout.

Salvia lyrata

Lyre-leaf Sage, Cancer Weed

LAMIACEAE (MINT FAMILY)

PLANT AND LEAVES: Lyre-leaf Sage is a perennial herb with one to a few stems growing 1 to 2 feet tall. The plant grows from a basal rosette of leaves. The flowering stems are naked or have

one or two pairs of small leaves near the base. The basal leaves are large with long petioles, together up to 1 foot in length. The larger leaves, especially, are deeply three lobed; the margins of smaller leaves may be simply scalloped. Leaves, especially older ones, are often tinged on the margins or on the main veins with purple.

FLOWERS AND FRUIT: The flowers are borne in whorls at nodes along the stem. The flower is blue or violet, often in a shade so pale as to appear white, and about 1 inch long. The two-lobed lower lip is much longer than the upper, which has three lobes, the middle one forming a sort of hood. The sepals are purplish brown.

FLOWERING: Flowering occurs primarily from April to June, but occasionally flowering may be seen at other times.

RANGE AND HABITAT: Lyre-leaf Sage is common in moist woods, meadows, and roadsides of east Texas. Its native range extends across most of the eastern United States.

COMMENTS: This species has the typical square stem and two-lipped flowers common among the mints. This species was given the unusual common name Cancer Weed because a preparation made from it was once used as a topical treatment for cancer.

Salvia farinacea

Mealy Blue Sage, Mealy Sage, Mealy-cup Sage

LAMIACEAE (MINT FAMILY)

PLANT AND LEAVES: Mealy Blue Sage is an upright to somewhat sprawling perennial herb. It averages about 2 feet tall but can

range in height from 1 to 3 feet. The size of its leaves varies but may reach 4 inches long and up to 1 inch wide. Leaves are lance shaped, and each leaf has a petiole averaging about half the length of the leaf blade. The leaves grow in clusters and may or may not have toothed margins. The lower leaves are typically larger and coarsely toothed, and the upper leaves are smaller and often have smooth edges.

FLOWERS AND FRUIT: Spikes of clustered flowers terminate the plants' stems. The flowers are five lobed and two lipped, ⅔ to ¾ inch long, and with two stamens and one pistil. They have an aromatic fragrance typical of sages. Flower color is almost always blue, the shade varying somewhat between plants and populations of plants, but often violet blue. White-flowered plants are occasionally seen.

FLOWERING: Flowering begins in April and may continue until July.

RANGE AND HABITAT: Mealy Blue Sage is common in meadows and on roadsides on alkaline soils from north-central through central Texas and west through much of the Trans-Pecos. Its range also extends into New Mexico.

COMMENTS: In botanical terminology, the word farinaceous is defined as having a mealy or powdery surface or texture. Both the botanical name and the common names of Mealy Blue Sage are derived from the very notable mealy-white (sometimes purple) appearance of the sepals, which are covered with felted hairs.

Commelina erecta

Widow's Tears, Slender Dayflower

COMMELINACEAE (SPIDERWORT FAMILY)

PLANT AND LEAVES: Widow's Tears is a perennial, herbaceous monocot with multiple, more or less erect stems making a clump to about 12 inches in height and spreading 3 feet or more in diameter. The leaves are alternately arranged with sheaths that surround the plant's stem and have "ears" where the laminae begin. The leaves' laminae may be lance shaped or linear to about 6 inches long.

FLOWERS AND FRUIT: Like other members of its family, Widow's Tears flowers have three petals. The flowers emerge from a closed spathe. The two upper petals, which resemble Mickey Mouse ears, are large, rounded, and true blue, sometimes lavender, or occasionally white in color. The lower petal is white, notched, and much reduced, making it barely noticeable.

FLOWERING: Flowering occurs when conditions are suitable between May and October.

RANGE AND HABITAT: Widow's Tears can be found throughout Texas on well-drained soil, preferring partial shade. It is also native to all of the United States east of the Rocky Mountains except New England and to Central America and northern South America.

COMMENTS: This species and other members of its genus are known as dayflowers because of the single-day duration of their flowers. Although it does not produce nectar, a "teardrop" of mucilaginous fluid can be produced by squeezing the spathe, thus the name Widow's Tears.

Eustoma exaltatum ssp. *russellianum*

Texas Bluebells, Prairie Gentian

GENTIANACEAE (GENTIAN FAMILY)

Synonyms: *Eustoma grandflorum*, *Eustoma russellianum*

PLANT AND LEAVES: Texas Bluebells is an herbaceous perennial growing 1 to 2 feet tall with glaucous, erect stems. The plant's opposite, blue-green leaves are long and oval with pointed tips, 1 to 2½ inches long.

FLOWERS AND FRUIT: The large, bell-shaped flowers, 2 to 3 inches across, have five to seven bluish-purple petals, about 1 inch long, that are constricted into a small tube at the base and have prominent purple markings in the throat. Forms with white, pink, and lavender flowers are sometimes found.

FLOWERING: Flowering occurs June to September.

RANGE AND HABITAT: Texas Bluebells is found nearly statewide on moist prairies and along ponds and streams. Its native range extends through the Great Plains as far north as Wyoming and South Dakota.

COMMENTS: *Eustoma* means "open mouth," referring to the large throat of the flower. There are several species in Texas. The one shown here grows in nearly all parts of the state except the pine forests in the east and the mountains in the west. It prefers damp areas and seems to reach peak condition on moist prairies, where it sometimes grows in profusion. An excellent if not somewhat persnickety garden plant in its own right, plant breeders have used this species as a parent in developing a number of hybrid garden cultivars known in horticulture as Lisianthus. Texas Bluebells was famously one of Lady Bird Johnson's favorite wildflowers.

Pontederia cordata

Pickerelweed

PONTEDERIACEAE (PICKERELWEED FAMILY)

PLANT AND LEAVES: Pickerelweed is an aquatic, emergent perennial that forms thick mats of roots from which spreading rhizomes grow and produce stems that can rise above the water's surface to nearly 4 feet. Pickerelweed often forms large colonies that can cover many acres. The plant dies back to the roots during winter, and new growth emerges each spring. The leaves are waxy and smooth to about 10 inches in length with a petiole that can reach 24 inches. Leaf shape is variable and can be broadly heart shaped, narrowly heart shaped, lance shaped, or oval.

FLOWERS AND FRUIT: This species' showy inflorescence is a spike rising above or nearly above the foliage. Each spike, 3 to 6

inches tall, may have as many as 50 to 100 lavender-blue or lilac-colored flowers, each with a pair of bright yellow spots on its upper tepal. The flowers open in succession from the bottom of the spike to the top. White-flowered plants are occasionally seen. The flowers are open for just one day. Once it has finished flowering, the stem bends to submerge and protect the developing fruit.

FLOWERING: In Texas, flowering occurs from June to September.

RANGE AND HABITAT: Pickerelweed grows in mud in shallow water along the shores of ponds, lakes, marshes, and other bodies of still water in southeast Texas and across the eastern half of the United States and Canada.

COMMENTS: *Pontederia cordata* is the only member of its genus in the New World. It is immune to most diseases and pests, but its seeds are a favorite of waterfowl.

Hydrolea ovata

Blue Waterleaf, Hairy Hydrolea

HYDROPHYLLACEAE (WATERLEAF FAMILY)

PLANT AND LEAVES: Blue Waterleaf is a perennial herb spreading over large areas by rhizomes. The sprawling, sturdy plant grows to about 2 feet tall, with spiny and rough-hairy stems. Several branching stems grow from each plant's base. There is a prominent spine on the stem just below the leaf. The leaves are alternate, more or less egg shaped, 1 to 2½ inches long, and 1 inch wide.

FLOWERS AND FRUIT: Many flowers and buds grow in clusters at the ends of the stems. Flowers are deep blue or purplish, about 1 inch across, and funnel shaped; they open into five broad, petal-like lobes. The conspicuous purple stamens extend beyond the petals.

FLOWERING: Flowering may commence as early as June and continue as to as late as October, with August and September being the best months to see this species in flower.

RANGE AND HABITAT: This species is native to the eastern third of Texas. Its native range extends east to Georgia and Florida and north to Arkansas and Oklahoma.

COMMENTS: Blue Waterleaf tends to form large colonies around the edge of lakes, ponds, and streams and may stand in water for weeks without apparent damage. There are two circumstances in which you are likely to notice Blue Waterleaf. If you're wading in shallow water and attempting to pass through a patch of them and their spiny stems, you unhappily will notice them. Or if you happen upon a colony of this species bespangled in its arresting blue flowers, then you very happily will notice them. Most flowers described as blue are actually some shade of violet or purple. The stunning Blue Waterleaf presents what are among the few "true blue" flowers to be found in nature.

Conoclinium coelestinum

Blue Mistflower, Wild Ageratum

ASTERACEAE (ASTER FAMILY)
Synonym: *Eupatorium coelestinum*

PLANT AND LEAVES: Blue Mistflower is an herbaceous perennial sometimes reaching 3 feet in height but often less. Its leaves are opposite, somewhat triangular in shape, and bluntly toothed. At the top of the plant the branches, with their short-stemmed clusters of flowers, form an almost flat top.

FLOWERS AND FRUIT: Species in the genus *Conoclinium* have no ray flowers. Flower heads have only disc flowers, which are bright blue or violet, about ¼ inch long.

FLOWERING: Blue Mistflower has a rather long flowering season stretching from June to November.

RANGE AND HABITAT: Blue Mistflower can be found in just about any moist soils from New York to Florida and west to the central and southern Great Plains. In Texas, it is commonly found along woodland streams, ponds and on wet roadsides in the eastern third of the state.

COMMENTS: The flowers of this species are a favorite of butterflies, helping to make it a popular garden plant. However, in some gardens its rampant spreading habit makes it a bit of a garden thug that requires regular roguing to keep in check. A closely related species, Gregg's Mistflower (*Conoclinium greggii*), a native of west Texas, southern New Mexico and Arizona, and northern Mexico, is like candy to Queens and other butterfly species. Gregg's Mistflower is nearly always awash in a cloud of butterflies any time it is in flower.

Eryngium heterophyllum

Wright's Eryngo, Mexican Thistle

APIACEAE (CARROT FAMILY)

PLANT AND LEAVES: Wright's Eryngo is a widely branching perennial herb growing from a thick taproot. Though the stems are mostly green, the entire plant has the appearance of a silvery

thistle. It grows 1½ to 3 feet tall, with a heavy, stout stem densely branched on the upper half. The stems are smooth, but the leaves are divided into sharp lobes on each side of a midrib. The leaves, as well as the bracts just beneath the flower heads, are bristle toothed.

FLOWERS AND FRUIT: The flowers are clustered on a more or less egg-shaped head, up to ¾ inch long and about ½ inch across. They are surrounded by a showy collar of silvery, three-lobed bracts. When the tiny flowers mature, they turn a sky-blue color uncommon in nature.

FLOWERING: Wright's Eryngo begins flowering in July and continues until September in Texas and until October in the US Southwest and Mexico.

RANGE AND HABITAT: In Texas, the native populations of this species are limited to sandy soils in the Davis Mountains. However, the species' range extends west to southern Arizona and south into northern Mexico.

COMMENTS: Wright's Eryngo is an arresting plant when seen flowering in nature. In those circumstances, its blue flower heads and surrounding silvery collar of bracts make the plant look like a miniature living fireworks show or a bouquet of twinkling stars. It is well suited for use in flower arrangements, as the flowers hold their form and color for an extended period and, though quite prickly, can be handled easily enough if one is careful in cutting them.

Symphyotrichum drummondii

Drummond's Aster

ASTERACEAE (ASTER FAMILY)
Synonyms: *Aster sagittifolius*, *Aster drummondii*

PLANT AND LEAVES: Drummond's Aster is an herbaceous perennial that grows 1 to 4 feet tall, often with many branches. Leaves are simple, cordate, and alternate.

FLOWERS AND FRUIT: Each flower head bears 10 to 20 ray flowers, deep purplish blue to lavender or rarely white, with a center of yellow disc flowers turning to purple with age.

FLOWERING: Drummond's Aster flowers in August to November.

Individual specimens are sometimes seen flowering out of season in April and May.

RANGE AND HABITAT: In Texas, Drummond's Aster occurs in south-central and east Texas. Outside Texas, its range extends east to Alabama and as far north as Minnesota and Pennsylvania. A disjunct population has been noted in Coahuila, Mexico. It prefers open, deciduous woodland on rich, dry to mesic soils, though it occasionally occurs on roadsides.

COMMENTS: Two botanical varieties of Drummond's Aster occur in Texas and intergrade where their ranges overlap. *Symphyotrichum drummondii* var. *drummondii* is, in general, the more robust of the two taxa and usually bears more colorful flowers. *Symphyotrichum d.* var. *texanum* is typically more diminutive, not as brightly colored, and a bit later-flowering than *S. d.* var. *drummondii*.

Ecoregions of Texas

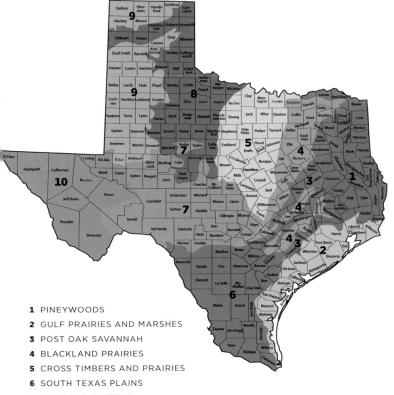

1. PINEYWOODS
2. GULF PRAIRIES AND MARSHES
3. POST OAK SAVANNAH
4. BLACKLAND PRAIRIES
5. CROSS TIMBERS AND PRAIRIES
6. SOUTH TEXAS PLAINS
7. EDWARDS PLATEAU
8. ROLLING PLAINS
9. HIGH PLAINS
10. TRANS-PECOS, MOUNTAINS AND BASINS

Modified from *Checklist of the Vascular Plants of Texas* (Hatch et al. 1990). Nearly identical maps have been used in numerous works on Texas including Gould (1962) and Correll and Johnston (1970).

Glossary

Note: *See illustrated glossary for figure references.*

Acaulescent Having no aboveground stem.

Achene A dry, one-seeded fruit that does not split open when mature.

Allelopathic Having plant-produced biochemicals that inhibit the growth of nearby plants.

Alluvial Of soils deposited by running water.

Alternate (adv. Alternately) Placed singly at different heights on the stem; not opposite or whorled. (fig. 7a)

Annual Growing from seed to maturity and dying in one year or growing season.

Anther The pollenbearing part of the flower. (fig. 1)

Apical Located at, or related to, the growing tip of a stem or other plant part.

Appressed Of leaves that are held against the surface of a stem but not united or fused with it.

Arborescent Of plants that are trees or have a tree-like growth or appearance.

Areole A spot in the form of a pit or a raised area on the surface of a cactus through which spines or other structures grow. (fig. 13)

Auriculate Of a plant part shaped like an ear.

Auriculate-clasping Of a leaf with ear-like appendages that encircle the stem at its point of attachment.

Axil The upper angle between any two structures or organs, as where a leaf or branch joins the stem. (fig. 6a)

Basal leaves The leaves that are concentrated near the base of the main stem.

Basal rosette A cluster of leaves at ground level borne in a whorl or whorl-like arrangement. (fig. 7b)

Baygall In the southern United States, a bog-like or swampy area with spongy soil, lying between areas of higher ground, and dominated by Sweetbay (*Magnolia virginiana*), Gallberry (*Ilex coriacea*), sometimes Swamp Bay (*Persea palustris*), and other broadleaf evergreens.

Beard A tuft or line of hairs, as on certain petals. (fig. 4d)

Biennial A plant that takes two years to complete the flowering cycle. Typically, the plant grows leaves (often a basal rosette) and fleshy roots the first year and produces flowers and fruits the second.

Bifurcate Of plant parts that are forked or split into two like parts.

Bipinnate Twice pinnate. Of compound leaves with primary leaflets that are again divided into secondary leaflets.

Bipinnatifid Of simple (not compound) leaves that are deeply divided into leaflet-like lobes.

Blade The expanded portion of a leaf. (fig. 6a)

Bloom A loosely adhered, white or bluish, waxy covering of fruits, leaves, or stems. Also, a colloquial term for a flower.

Bract A reduced or modified leaf occurring at the base of a flower or group of flowers. (fig. 5)

Bristly Having stiff, rigid, rather thick hairs on the surface of stems or leaves.

Bulbel A bulblet formed at the base of another bulb or on a belowground stem.

Bulbil A bulblet formed in an inflorescence or on an aboveground stem.

Bulblet A small bulb—including both bulbels and bulbils.

Bur (also, Burr) The prickly covering of a seed or fruit.

Calcareous A soil type that is rich in calcium carbonate and has a high pH. A rock type that is largely composed of calcium carbonate.

Calyx (pl. Calyces) The sepals taken collectively. These may be distinct or joined to form a cup or tube; they may be of any color but are usually green. When the calyx is present, it encloses the other parts of the flower in bud. (fig. 1)

Capitulum (pl. Capitula) The flower head of a species in Asteraceae, composed of densely crowded florets. (fig. 3a)

Carpel A single unit of a flower's female reproductive structure.

Caudex (pl. Caudices) The thickened, sometimes woody, base of a plant.

Compound leaf A leaf that is divided into two or more distinct leaflets. (fig. 10)

Cordate Heart shaped. Descriptive of leaves and occasionally other plant parts with the shape of a Valentine's heart. (fig. 12a)

Corm A short, fleshy underground stem, broader than high, producing stems from the base and leaves and flower stems from the top.

Corolla The petals collectively; usually colored or showy. These may be distinct or united to form a cup, trumpet, tube, or two-lipped body. (fig. 1)

Corymb (adj. Corymbose) A flat-topped or convex inflorescence, with the lower or outer stems longer; the flowers on these stems open first. (fig. 5f)

Cultivar A portmanteau of the words "cultivated" and "variety" or "cultigen" and variety. A special name given to a horticultural selection of a species. A cultivar name is capitalized and set in single quotes and is not the same as a trade name.

Cyme (adj. Cymose) A usually flattish inflorescence in which the central or terminal flower matures first. (fig. 5i)

Cypsela (pl. Cypselae) A dry, indehiscent, single-seeded fruit formed from an inferior ovary and typical of plants in Asteraceae.

Deciduous Having leaves that are shed at the end of the growing season.

Decumbent Having stems that grow horizontally along the ground before turning and growing vertically.

Dentate Descriptive of leaf margins with tooth-like serrations. (fig. 9b)

Dioecious Of plant species with separate male and female plants.

Disc flower (Disc floret) The tubular flowers located centrally on the capitulum of a plant in Asteraceae. (fig. 3a, c)

Discoid Descriptive of the capitula of some species in Asteraceae bearing only disc florets.

Dissected Deeply divided, as a leaf with long, narrow lobes.

Distal Descriptive of a plant part, or area, that is relatively remote compared with the base or point of origin. Farther away.

Dorsal Descriptive of a plant part that is above or behind the plant's axis or the part's supporting structure.

Dropper A stem emerging from corm or a bulb that produces a new plant away from the original plant.

Drupe A fleshy fruit enclosing a single seed with a hard, inner layer.

Endemic Descriptive of a taxon having a natural distribution restricted to a specified geographic area.

Entire Of leaf margins without teeth or lobes. (fig. 9a)

Even-pinnate (Paripinnate) Of a pinnate leaf with an even number of leaflets.

Evergreen A plant that has green leaves year-round.

Filament The stalk that bears the stamen's anther. (fig. 1)

Floret A small flower, especially one in a dense cluster such as on a capitulum. (fig. 3b, c)

Floriferous Descriptive of a plant or species that bears noticeably large numbers of flowers.

Flower head A dense arrangement of flowers arising from a common point, as in the Apiaceae, or as in the Asteraceae, where many ray flowers and/or disc flowers make up one flower head. (figs. 3a, 5f, g)

Follicetum (pl. Folliceta) An aggregate fruit made up of clusters of follicles.

Follicle A dry fruit formed from one carpel, splitting along a single suture.

Genus (pl. Genera) The taxonomic rank below family and above species. A group of closely related species. The genus name is the first element in the binomial species name.

Glaucous Having a whitish or bluish-white, waxy bloom.

Glochid (pl. Glochids) A small, barbed, hair-like bristle emergent from the areoles of some cacti.

Gypseous Descriptive of soil consisting, in large part, of gypsum.

Herbaceous Descriptive of plants lacking lignified tissues. Not woody. Plants with stems that are usually green and soft in texture.

Hip (pl. Hips) The fruit of a rose.

Holdfast A pad-shaped area at the end of a tendril that exudes a glue-like substance allowing attachment to a supporting plant or other structure.

Hybridize To produce offspring through the sexual union of gametes from individuals of two different taxa.

Inflorescence An organized group or cluster of flowers and its constituent parts. (fig. 5c–i)

Infructescence An organized group or cluster of fruits and its constituent parts.

Insectivorous Descriptive of plants that catch and extract nutrients from insects.

Intergrade The gradual shift of expression of plant characteristics between two related and cross-breeding populations of plants.

Involucre A whorl of distinct or united bracts beneath a flower or cluster of flowers. (fig. 5g–i)

Labellum (pl. Labella) The large, usually lower, petal of an orchid flower.

Lamina (pl. Laminae) The blade of a leaf or the expanded upper part of a petal, sepal, or bract. (fig. 6a)

Leaflet A leaf-like segment of a compound leaf.

Legume The fruit of a plant species in Fabaceae.

Ligulate Descriptive of florets of plants in Asteraceae with strap-shaped laminae or of capitula bearing only that type of floret.

Linear Descriptive of leaves that are long and narrow with parallel or nearly parallel sides.

Lobe A part of a leaf or petal, its shape formed by one or more indentations in the margin.

Lobed flower A tubular or funnel-shaped flower that opens into petal-like lobes. (fig. 4)

Lobed leaf A leaf with indentations not more than halfway to the midrib, with the tips of the segments rounded. (fig. 9c, d)

Mesic Descriptive of soil that is normally moderately moist.

Midrib The main or central rib or vein of a leaf. (fig. 8c)

Monocot (Shorthand for monocotyledonous plant.) A flowering plant with its embryos each having only one cotyledon (seed leaf).

Monoecious Of plant species that normally bear separate male and female flowers on the same plant.

Monotypic A taxon at any level having only one taxon at the next lower rank.

Mycorrhiza (pl. Mycorrhizae) A group of soil-borne fungi that form symbiotic relationships with vascular plant roots.

Nerve A colloquial term for a leaf vein.

Nodding An erect stem, peduncle, or pedicel that bends over at the end.

Node The place on a stem where leaves or branches normally originate; a swollen or knoblike structure. (fig. 6a)

Oblanceolate Descriptive of a leaf shape that is generally lance shaped but broadest close to the apex.

Odd-pinnate (Imparipinnate) Of a compound leaf having an odd number of leaflets, usually with pairs of leaflets and a single terminal leaflet.

Opposite Of leaves originating in pairs at a node, with the members of each pair opposite each other on the stem. (fig. 7b)

Ovary The basal part of the pistil that bears the ovules and often becomes the fruit. (fig. 1)

Ovate Egg shaped. Usually used in describing the shape of a leaf. (fig. 12e)

Palmate Divided or radiating from one point, resembling a hand with the fingers spread. Leaves may be *palmately compound* and/or *palmately lobed*; they may also have *palmate venation*. (figs. 8d, 9d, 10b)

Panicle A branched raceme; a raceme of racemes. (fig. 5e)

Pappus (pl. Pappi) A tuft of usually whitish hairs or bristles found around the base of the florets of some species in Asteraceae and often retained at the apex of the fruits that develop below them. (fig. 3)

Parallel venation Main veins running from base to apex of leaf. (fig. 8b)

Pedicel The stalk of a single flower in an inflorescence or in a cluster of flowers. (fig. 5b, d–i)

Peduncle The stalk of a solitary flower or the main stalk of an inflorescence or of a cluster of flowers. (fig. 5b–f)

Pepo A berry-like fruit with a hard rind, fleshy interior, and many seeds. The fruit of plants in Cucurbitaceae.

Perennial Any plant with a normal lifespan of more than two years.

Perfoliate Of leaves and bracts with blades that surround and appear to be pierced by the stem. (fig. 11a)

Petal A unit of the corolla, the whorl of often colorful and showy plant parts between a flower's calyx and the stamens. (fig. 1)

Petiole A leaf stem. (figs. 6a, 7a, 10a)

Phyllary (pl. Phyllaries) One of the bracts that surround the capitula of plants in Asteraceae and collectively form the involucre. (fig. 3a)

Pinna (pl. Pinnae) The primary segment of a compound leaf.

Pinnate Arranged along an axis. Leaves may be *pinnately compound* (see entry below) and/or *pinnately lobed*; they may also have *pinnate venation*, with veins extending from the midrib. (figs. 8c, 9c, 10a)

Pinnately compound Of leaves with leaflets opposite each other on each side of the midrib, like a bird's feather. They may be *odd-pinnate*, ending with a single leaflet at the tip, or *even-pinnate*, with no leaflet at the end. These leaflets may be twice compound, like the leaves on the sensitive briar (*Mimosa* spp.). (fig. 10a)

Pinnatifid Pinnately lobed.

Pistil A flower's seed-producing or female organ, consisting of ovary, style, and stigma; usually located in the center of the flower. (fig. 1)

Pistillate flower A female flower. A flower with pistils but no stamens.

Pith The spongy, central core of some stems and roots.

Pocosin A marshy wetland with acidic peat soils and often with shrubby vegetation.

Pubescent Of stems or leaves with soft hairs.

Raceme An inflorescence on which each flower is attached to the main stalk by a short stem (pedicel). The youngest flowers, at the tip, may continue to develop while those below are forming fruit. (fig. 5d)

Rachis (pl. Rachides, Rachises) The axis of an inflorescence above the peduncle or of a pinnate leaf.

Ray flower (Ray floret) An outer, irregular flower on the capitulum of a plant in *Asteraceae*. Each usually has a single, tongue-shaped corolla. (fig. 3a, b)

Receptacle The terminal end of a flower stem to which the various flower parts are attached. (fig. 1)

Reflex (Reflexed) Of plant parts that bend sharply back or down.

Resupinate Of leaves or flowers that are in an inverted position because the petiole or pedicel is twisted 180 degrees.

Reticulate Of veins that form a netted pattern.

Rhizome A perennial underground stem, usually growing horizontally.

Rib (of cactus) A ridge; a raised surface running vertically, or sometimes spiraling, and bearing areoles in a row along its summit. Often thought of as being composed of more or less united tubercles, which may be evident as bulging masses along it. (fig. 13c)

Rootstock The combined underground parts of a plant.

Rosette An arrangement of leaves radiating from the stem at a nearly common level, frequently at or just above the ground line. (fig. 7b)

Salverform Trumpet shaped; with a long, slender tube that abruptly flares to an expanded, flattened end. (fig. 4a)

Scape A naked (leafless) flower stem rising from the ground. (fig. 5a)

Scorpioid Of plant parts (usually inflorescences) that are curled, like the tail of a scorpion.

Senescent Of a plant or plant part that is aging or dying.

Sepals Flower parts that surround the petals, stamens, and pistil; often green and leaf-like. Sometimes they are the same size, shape, and color as the petals, as in *Cooperia pedunculata* (Rain Lily), in which case both sepals and petals are collectively called *tepals*. (fig. 1)

Serrate Of leaf margins with regular, acute teeth pointing forward; like the cutting edge of a saw.

Serrulate Of leaves with finely serrate margins.

Sessile Lacking a stalk of any kind: a flower without a pedicel or a leaf without a petiole. (figs. 5c, 6b, 7b, c)

Silicle A short silique, less than three times as long as wide. The fruit of some species in Brassicaceae.

Silique A dry, dehiscent fruit (more than three times as long as wide) formed from a superior ovary of two carpels, with two parietal placentas and divided into two loculi by a "false" septum. The fruit of some species in Brassicaceae.

Solitary Borne singly or occurring alone. (fig. 5a, b)

Sp. The abbreviation for a single species. Written in lower case and not italicized (sp.).

Spadix A spicate (spike-like) inflorescence with a stout, often succulent axis and an enclosing bract (spathe). The inflorescence type of Araceae and some other monocot families.

Spathe A large bract enclosing or partially enclosing an inflorescence.

Spatulate Of a leaf, petal, or any other plant part shaped like a spoon.

Specific epithet The second component (along with the genus name) in a scientific binomial. For example, the botanical name *Lupinus texensis* is formed by combining the genus name, *Lupinus*, with the specific epithet, *texensis*.

Spike An inflorescence with its flowers attached directly to the main stem; no pedicels are present. The youngest flowers or buds are at the top. (fig. 5c)

Spp. The abbreviation for multiple species. Written in lower case and not italicized (spp.).

Spur A tubular or saclike extension of a sepal, petal, or corolla, usually containing nectar. (fig. 5j)

Ssp. (or subsp.) The abbreviation for a subspecies and part of the botanical name of a subspecific taxon. Written in lower case and not italicized (ssp. or subsp.).

Stamen One of the male organs of the flower, it produces the plant's pollen. The stamens are located between the petal and the pistil, if present. Their constituent parts are filaments and anthers. (fig. 1)

Staminate flower A male flower. A flower with stamens but no pistil.

Staminode A sterile stamen that is often rudimentary and sometimes petal-like and showy.

Stellate Of a star-shaped plant part. Often used in describing plant hairs with multiple spreading branches.

Stigma The tip of the pistil, which receives the pollen; may be rounded, lobed, or branched. (fig. 1)

Stipule A basal appendage of the petiole; usually in pairs. Varies in shape and may be minute and hair-like or stiff and sharp, or like segments of the leaf blade. (fig. 6a)

Stolon A slender, prostrate stem that produces roots and sometimes erect shoots at its nodes.

Style The stalk-like part of the pistil, connecting the ovary and the stigma. (fig. 1)

Subopposite Of a leaf arrangement with leaves that are held very close to, but not quite, opposite or with mostly opposite leaves but some a bit offset.

Taproot A central, vertically descending root of a plant with a single dominant root axis.

Taxon (pl. Taxa) A name of a plant or group of plants at any level of classification.

Tepals The collective term for the sepals and petals of a flower when the sepals are very petal-like, as in *Cooperia pedunculata*.

Tooth (pl. Teeth) The marginal appendages of sepals, petals, or leaves that are more or less sharply indented. (fig. 9b)

Trifoliate Of a plant with compound leaves having three leaflets. (fig. 10c)

Trilobate Of a plant part, such as a leaf, with three main lobes.

Tripinnately dissected Pinnately dissected leaves in which the dissected lobes are also pinnately dissected.

Tuber (adj. tuberous) An underground storage organ formed by the thickening of a stem or a rhizome.

Tubercle A more or less pyramidal knob rising from the stem surface of a cactus and having an areole on or near its summit. (fig. 13b)

Tuna The fleshy, often red, purple, or yellow berry-like fruit of a cactus.

Two-lipped flower (also, Bilabiate flower) A flower that has an upper and a lower division, as in Lamiaceae (mint family). (fig. 4d)

Umbel (adj. Umbellate) A rounded or flat-topped inflorescence on stems that radiate from the tip of the main stem. A **compound umbel** has smaller umbels at the ends of the radiating stems. (fig. 5g, h)

Undulate Wavy. As the margin of a leaf.

Unisexual Of one sex; bearing only male or only female

reproductive organs. Plants that are functionally unisexual bear flowers with both male and female organs, but the organs of one sex or the other will be nonfunctional.

Var. The abbreviation for a botanical variety. Part of the botanical name of a subspecific taxon. Written in lower case and not italicized (var.).

Whorled leaves or flowers Three or more leaves or flowers arranged in a circle around a stem. (fig. 7c)

Winter annual A plant from autumn-germinating seeds that flowers and fruits the following spring.

Illustrated Glossary

Note: *Terms are defined in the alphabetical glossary.*

FIG. 1. Flower Parts

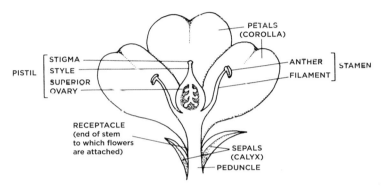

COMPLETE FLOWER

FIG. 2. Flower Symmetry

a. Radial Symmetry

b. Bilateral Symmetry

FIG. 3. Section through a Composite Flower Head

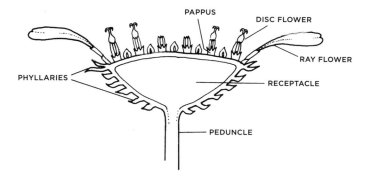

PAPPUS

DISC FLOWER

RAY FLOWER

PHYLLARIES

RECEPTACLE

PEDUNCLE

a

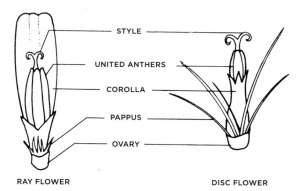

STYLE

UNITED ANTHERS

COROLLA

PAPPUS

OVARY

RAY FLOWER

DISC FLOWER

b

c

FIG. 4. Flower Shapes

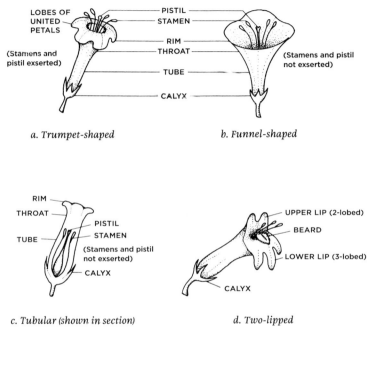

LOBES OF UNITED PETALS

(Stamens and pistil exserted)

PISTIL
STAMEN
RIM
THROAT
TUBE
CALYX

(Stamens and pistil not exserted)

a. Trumpet-shaped

b. Funnel-shaped

RIM
THROAT
PISTIL
STAMEN
TUBE

(Stamens and pistil not exserted)

CALYX

c. Tubular (shown in section)

UPPER LIP (2-lobed)
BEARD
LOWER LIP (3-lobed)
CALYX

d. Two-lipped

THROAT
RIM
PETAL-LIKE LOBES
CALYX

e. Urn-shaped

f. Bell-shaped

FIG. 5. Arrangement of Flowers on Stem

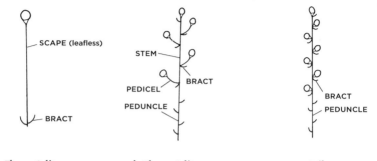

a. Flower Solitary,
Terminal

b. Flower Solitary,
Axillary, 1 Terminal

c. Spike
(Flowers Sessile)

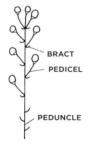

d. Raceme
(Flowers Pediceled)

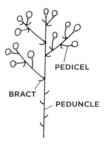

e. Panicle
(Branched Raceme)

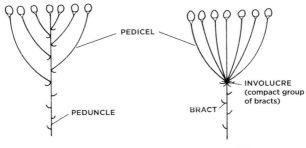

f. Corymb

g. Umbel

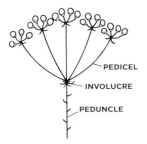

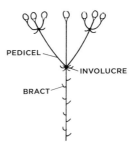

h. Compound Umbel

i. Cyme

SEPAL SPURRED

COROLLA SPURRED

j. Spur

FIG. 6. Leaf Parts

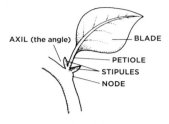

AXIL (the angle)

BLADE

PETIOLE

STIPULES

NODE

a. Leaf with Petiole

b. Sessile Leaf (with no Petiole)

FIG. 7. Leaf Arrangement

PETIOLE

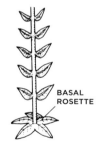

BASAL
ROSETTE

a. Alternate, Petioled

b. Opposite, Sessile

*c. Whorled, Sessile
(3 or more at node)*

FIG. 8. Venation (Vein Pattern)

MIDRIB

a. Forking

b. Parallel
(Main veins run
from base to apex)

c. Pinnate
(Main veins extend
from midrib)

d. Palmate
(Main veins radiate
from base)

FIG. 9. Simple Leaves

a. Entire

b. Toothed

c. Pinnately Lobed

d. Palmately Lobed

FIG. 10. Once Compound Leaves

PETIOLE

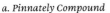 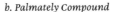

a. Pinnately Compound

b. Palmately Compound

c. Trifoliate

FIG. 11. Leaf Types

a. Encircling

b. Clasping

c. Sheathing

FIG. 12. Leaf Shapes

a. Heart-shaped   *b. Arrow-shaped*   *c. Linear*   *d. Lanceolate*

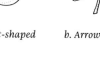

e. Ovate   *f. Oblong*   *g. Awl-shaped*   *h. Spatulate*   *i. Elliptic*

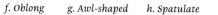

(A combination of two terms indicates a shape between them.)

FIG. 13. Cactus Parts

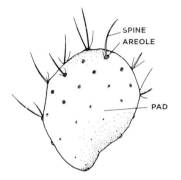

SPINE
AREOLE

PAD

a

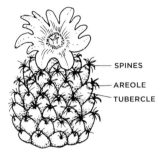

SPINES
AREOLE
TUBERCLE

b

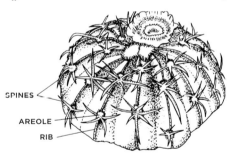

SPINES

AREOLE

RIB

c

Bibliography

Ajilvsgi, Geyata. 1979. *Wildflowers of the Big Thicket, East Texas, and Western Louisiana*. College Station: Texas A&M University Press.

Brown, Clair A. 1972. *Wildflowers of Louisiana and Adjoining States*. Baton Rouge: Louisiana State University Press.

Correll, Donovan S., and Marshall C. Johnston. 1970. *Manual of the Vascular Plants of Texas*. Renner: Texas Research Foundation.

Cray, Asa. 1899. *Manual of Botany*. 6th ed. Edited by Watson Sereno. New York: American Book Company.

Dirr, Michael A. 1975. *Manual of Woody Landscape Plants: Their Identification, Ornamental Characteristics, Culture, Propagation and Uses*. 4th ed. Champaign, Illinois: Stipes Publishing Company.

Dodge, Natt N. 1963. *100 Desert Wildflowers in Natural Color*. Globe, Arizona: Southwestern Monuments Association.

Epple, Anne Orth. 1995. *A Field Guide to the Plants of Arizona*. Guilford, Conneticut: Globe Pequot Press.

Gould, Frank W., G. O. Hoffman, and C. A. Rechenthin. 1960. *Vegetational Areas of Texas*. Texas Agricultural Experiment Station Leaflet 492. College Station: Texas A&M University Press.

Harrington, Harold D., and Lawrence W. Durrell. 1957. *How to Identify Plants*. Chicago: Swallow Press.

Hatch, Stephan L., Kancheepuram N. Gandhi, and Larry E. Brown. 1990. *Checklist of the Vascular Plants of Texas*. Texas Agricultural

Experiment Station MP 1655. College Station: Texas A&M University Press.

Jaeger, Edmund C. 1940. *Desert Wild Flowers*. Stanford, California: Stanford University Press.

Linux, Ricky J. 2014. *Range Plants of North Central Texas – A Land User's Guide to Their Identification, Value and Management*. Weatherford, Texas: US Department of Agriculture Natural Resources Conservation Service.

McDougall, Walter B., and Omer E. Sperry. 1957. *Plants of the Big Bend National Park*. Washington, DC: US Government Printing Office.

Porter, Cedric L. 1967. *Taxonomy of Flowering Plants*. 2nd ed. San Francisco: Freernan and Company.

Reeves, Robert G. 1972. *Flora of Central Texas*. Fort Worth: Prestige Press.

Richardson, Alfred. 1995. *Plants of the Rio Grande Delta*. Rev. ed. Austin: University of Texas Press. Original title: *Plants of Southernmost Texas* (1990).

———. 2002. *Wildflowers and Other Plants of Texas Beaches and Islands*. Austin: University of Texas Press.

Richardson, Alfred, and Ken King. 2011. *Plants of Deep South Texas: A Field Guide to the Woody and Flowering Species*. College Station: Texas A&M University Press.

Rickett, Harold William. 1969. *Wildflowers of the United States*. Vol. 3, *Texas*. New York: McGraw-Hill.

Rose, Francis L., and Russell W. Strandtmann. 1986. *Wildflowers of the Llano Estacado*. Dallas: Taylor Publishing Company.

Shinners, Lloyd A. 1972. *Spring Flora of the Dallas–Ft. Worth Area*. 2nd ed. Edited by William F. Mahler. Fort Worth: Prestige Press.

Stefferud, Alfred. 1950–1953. *How to Know the Wild Flowers*. New York: New American Library of World Literature.

Tveten, John L., and Gloria A. Tveten. 1997. *Wildflowers of Houston and Southeast Texas*. Austin: University of Texas Press.

Vines, Robert A. 1960. *Trees, Shrubs, and Woody Vines of the Southwest*. Austin: University of Texas Press.

Warnock, Barton H. 1970. *Wildflowers of the Big Bend Country, Texas*. Alpine, Texas: Sul Ross State University.

———. 1974. *Wildflowers of the Guadalupe Mountains and the Sand Dune Country, Texas*. Alpine, Texas: Sul Ross State University.

———. 1977. *Wildflowers of the Davis Mountains and Marathon Basin, Texas*. Alpine, Texas: Sul Ross State University.

Weniger, Del. 1970. *Cacti of the Southwest: Texas, New Mexico, Oklahoma, Arkansas, and Louisiana*. Austin: University of Texas Press.

West, Steve. 2000. *Chihuahuan Desert Wildflowers: A Field Guide to Common Wildflowers, Shrubs and Trees*. Helena, Montana: Falcon Publishing.

Wharton, Mary E., and Roger W. Barbour. 1971. *A Guide to the Wildflowers and Ferns of Kentucky*. Lexington: University Press of Kentucky.

Whitehouse, Eula. 1936. *Texas Flowers in Natural Colors*. Austin: Privately published.

———. 1962. *Common Fall Flowers of the Coastal Big Bend of Texas*. Sinton, Texas: Bob and Bessie Welder Wildlife Foundation.

Wills, Mary Motz, and Howard S. Irwin. 1961. *Roadside Flowers of Texas*. Austin: University of Texas Press.

Photography Credits

155 Carolyn Fannon
156 Joe Marcus
157 Melody Lytle
158 Joe Marcus
159 Pam Williams
161 Campbell & Lynn
    Loughmiller
162 Norman G. Flaigg
163 Gene Sturla
164 Melody Lytle
165 Melody Lytle
166 Maggie Livings
168 Alan Cressler
169 R. W. Smith
170 Bruce Leander
172 Campbell & Lynn
    Loughmiller
173 Kimberly Kline
174 Melody Lytle
175 Andy & Sally Wasowski
176 Pam Williams
177 Joe Marcus
179 R. W. Smith
180 Norman G. Flaigg
182 Andy & Sally Wasowski
183 W. D. & Dolphia Bransford
184 W. D. & Dolphia Bransford
186 Carolyn Fannon
187 R. W. Smith
189 Campbell & Lynn
    Loughmiller
190 R. W. Smith
192 Peggy Romfh
193 Joe Marcus
194 Bruce Leander
196 R. W. Smith
197 W. D. & Dolphia Bransford
198 Thomas L. Muller
200 Bruce Leander
201 Carl Fabre
203 Campbell & Lynn
    Loughmiller
204 Ray Mathews

205 Andy & Sally Wasowski
206 Alan Cressler
208 Andy & Sally Wasowski
209 R. W. Smith
210 Gene Sturla
211 Andy & Sally Wasowski
212 Andy & Sally Wasowski
214 Brenda K. Loveless
215 W. D. & Dolphia Bransford
216 Lee Page
217 Sandy Smith
219 Joe Marcus
220 Campbell & Lynn
    Loughmiller
222 Ray Mathews
224 Gene Sturla
225 Norman G. Flaigg
227 Joe Marcus
228 Campbell & Lynn
    Loughmiller
229 Alan Cressler
231 Andy & Sally Wasowski
233 Andy & Sally Wasowski
235 Alan Cressler
236 Andy & Sally Wasowski
238 Ray Mathews
240 Andy & Sally Wasowski
241 W. D. & Dolphia Bransford
243 Campbell & Lynn
    Loughmiller
244 Campbell & Lynn
    Loughmiller
245 Carolyn Fannon
246 Dwight Platt
248 Lee Page
249 Ray Mathews
251 Steven Faucette
252 Sean Watson
253 Melody Lytle
255 W. D. & Dolphia Bransford
257 Randy Heish
258 Carolyn Fannon
259 Andy & Sally Wasowski

Family Index

The family index is arranged by botanical family and then by botanical name.

Index

Accepted botanical names and common names of plants treated in this volume and their page numbers are highlighted in bold type. Botanical synonyms and their page numbers are in roman. Botanical names and common names of other native species mentioned in the text are followed by an asterisk. These names and page numbers are in roman. Botanical names and common names of species not native to North America are followed by two asterisks. These names and page numbers are in roman. Where more than one page number is referenced, the number in bold is the primary page for that species.

Journal